THE LAST DAYS OF ELISHA

F.W. KRUMMACHER

BAKER BOOK HOUSE

Grand Rapids, Michigan 49506

Reprinted 1981 by
Baker Book House Company
from the 1854 edition published by
Robert Carter & Brothers

ISBN: 0-8010-5434-6

PHOTOLITHOPRINTED BY CUSHING - MALLOY, INC.
ANN ARBOR, MICHIGAN, UNITED STATES OF AMERICA

CONTENTS

LAST DAYS OF ELISHA

I.—JEHU

ONE of the most profound and important parables which the New Testament contains, is that which we meet with in Matt. xiii. 24—30. A large and extensive field is there brought before us, and "This field," says our Lord, "is the world." It is a consolatory fact that the world is here represented to us, not as a desert, or desolate wilderness, or as an abandoned solitude, but as a field, which is cultivated and attended to. Who are the husbandmen of this wide locality? You are aware that they consist of the men of this world, the poets, the artists, the self-constituted enlighteners of mankind, who believe themselves especially called to this work, and of which they conceive they have a monopoly. But, God be thanked, they are not the only ones who plant and sow in this field, else what would become of the harvest? The field would exhibit ornamental shrubs of every kind, but no trees capable of bearing fruit for eternity. The agriculturists above mentioned are only able to rear, train, and cultivate; but what we require is one who can

regenerate and form anew.   And such a one has
been walking for centuries, with unwearied fidelity,
over the wide field of humanity, ever active in rendering it productive, and protecting the tender
plant.   All that is truly beautiful, that ever flourished under heaven, was of his planting.   The
seed sown by the Son of man was all divine, pure,
and holy.

"The kingdom of heaven is likened unto a man
which sowed good seed in his field."   Mark, "in
his field."   The world is, therefore, Christ's property.   He has bought it, at a costly price, to be the
scene of his glorification ; and, although other powers may for the present occupy it, yet they will be
obliged, in due time, to quit it.   Inundate it, as ye
may, with your anti-christian writings; cover it with
your memorials of human adoration; build upon it
your lofty towers of Babel; stuff it full with your
lying doctrinal systems ; inscribe upon your cre-
ations and edifices, "More durable than iron or
marble!"   Truly, the prince of darkness sees deeper
than ye all ; for he knows that the world is not his,
and "that he hath but a short time."   The cross is
the achievement that ought to hang over the gate
of the world, and will eventually expel every other.
Nothing will remain, but that which proceeds from
Christ and his Spirit.   Every thing else awaits the
coming of Him, who shall "throughly purge his
floor," and has its own set time.

"The kingdom of heaven is likened unto a man
which sowed *good seed* in his field."   "*Good seed.*"
Oh, how these words elevate the heart !   It is, there-

fore, no longer the seed of the serpent and the progeny of Cain, who are the sole possessors of the
earth ; something better, something noble and holy
has likewise its share of it. "The good seed,"
says our Lord, "are the children of the kingdom."
Mark, not the wise, according to the flesh, nor the
noble of the world, of whom we hear it said, "Of
what consequence is it, that they are of another persuasion? They have *works;* what need have they
of faith?" But "the good seed," according to our
Lord's own interpretation, "are the children of the
kingdom ;" that is, such as gather under Zion's banner, and lie at Jesus' feet. Yes, it is those who,
despairing of themselves, know only one source of
comfort, namely, that a Mediator came ; one hope,
which is, that free grace reigns ; need only one
thing—to be washed in Jesus' blood ; and have but
one desire—that of being united with him.

They are called *good* seed ; for the righteous
ness of the Lamb is theirs ; their intentions are
good ; "the spirit is willing ;" the good Spirit is
operative within them ; and there is something in
them that supremely loves the Lord of lords, and
incessantly strives after "that which is good."

They are called "seed," or, in the Lord's own
words "wheat," therefore, a valuable production;
and this with good reason. The plant may appear
poor, from a long want of rain, or it may grow lux-
uriantly ; it may be still young and tender, or be
already strong and vigorous ; it may creep on the
ground, or have again elevated itself; it may wave
and tremble beneath the storm, or, invigorated, bid

defiance to the blast. It may still contain the ear within it, or have already unfolded it to the light of day. In every case, they are noble germs, sown, not *in* the field, but, more correctly speaking, *on* the field. The field, the world, is only the locality, where the Lord prepares his spiritual plantation; but by no means the soil in which the plants take root. It is in Christ himself that they are by faith implanted; and it is a supermundane element to which they cleave with the tenderest ramifications of their hope and longing, their wishes and desires. Their conversation and citizenship is in heaven, and they are certainly the seed of Jesus, and the flower-garden of God. Their entire conversion, from the first slight inclination of the will, to the vigorous completion, is a work of grace. 'We are his workmanship,' saith the apostle, "created in Christ Jesus unto good works."

But the good seed does not stand alone in the world. A different kind grows near it, and shoots up in, and about it. "But while men slept, his enemy came and sowed tares among the wheat, and went his way." What are these tares? Not merely error, as some might suppose; but those who are in error; not deceit, but the deceitful and unbelieving, or the children of the "wicked one," as the Lord himself says. The "wicked one," or the enemy, who with inextinguishable fury opposes the kingdom of heaven, is, according to Christ's own interpretation, no other than "the devil." Now let any one still doubt, whether Jesus taught the existence of a prince of darkness! Even presupposing that the impious sentiment of the Neologians, that the Saviour had occasionally accommodated himself to the erroneous ideas of his contemporaries, was not entirely unfounded ; I would ask, what could have here induced him to think of the devil, if he had not been most deeply convinced of the identity of such a being, and that he plants and nourishes the tares ? The "wicked one" came. When ? "While men slept." At night-time, therefore ; that is, insidiously, unseen, unexpected, unawares ; and, perhaps, it was under the guise of an angel of light, pretending that he would teach "true and pure religion," that he accomplished the delusion of the sinners asleep in carnal security, and fettered them with the bonds of delusion and lies.

And after he had finished his work, continues the parable, he " went his way ;" that is, the poor deceived people thenceforth affirmed that they followed the suggestions of a good spirit ; and that their cause was the cause of reason, of truth, nay, even of God himself; and we are laughed to scorn as often as we give them to understand that the "wicked one" has moved them away, and blinded and bewitched them.

The "wicked one" came in the dark, and in disguise ; he stole away again in the dark ; and his seed manifest themselves ignorant of their origin ; a people whose hearts have never been softened, and who refuse to hear of Jesus and his blood. Our Lord calls them, " Zizania," worthless wild flowers, corncockle, darnel. Certainly, they may, like the former, present a pretty appearance, and glitter in a variety of glowing and friendly colors, the result of a good education ; but still they remain nothing but " tares," tended by an appalling hand.

" But when the blade was sprung up, and brought forth fruit, then appeared the tares also." And such is wont to be the case still. The tares cannot prevent the Lord's seed from springing up ; but before it shoots up, the true character of the former is not apparent. It remains quiet, and appears in the garb of the greatest innocence until the blade springs up. But scarcely does the divine seed unfold itself, or begin to bring forth the fruit of a bold confession of the name of Jesus, of a decided renunciation of the dead and blinded world, and of a newness of life in the Lord, than the difference is very perceptible, the opposition manifests itself strong in blasphemy, ridicule, and scorn, and the more so, the more the Lord's seed flourishes, and the further it developes and extends itself.

Now listen to the conclusion of this deeply significant parable. Our Lord goes on as follows : " So the servants of the householder came, and said unto him, Sir, didst not thou sow good seed in thy field ; from whence then hath it tares ?" Such is also usually the first inquiry made with pain and surprise by new converts. With what large expectations do they enter the church, supposing that all the world must do homage at the feet of the Lamb, and then find an innumerable multitude, who feel no need of Christ, and refuse to hear of his salvation. They cannot comprehend the reason of it, since the Lord from heaven is the Husbandman of the mighty field, and since no greater blessedness can be imagined than that of resting on his bosom, and in his arms. Hence, they are greatly amazed; and quite at a loss to account for it, they exclaim, " Sir, didst not thou sow good seed in thy field ? from whence then hath it tares ?" And on receiving the reply, " An enemy hath done this," their astonishment not unfrequently breaks out into a fiery zeal; and they eagerly exclaim, with the servants in the parable, " Wilt thou, then, that we go and gather them up ?"

The Lord does not censure this zeal for his sacred cause ; on the contrary, he would unhesitatingly have granted the request of his servants, had it solely had reference to the rooting up of deceit, irreligiousness, and sin. But individuals are implicated here, with reference to whom, excommunication, extirpation, expatriation, and the like, must not immediately be had recourse to. The Christian's watchword, here, is not, " Send down fire from heaven;" on the contrary, the patience of hope, and charitable tolerance are requisite here.

" But he said, Nay; lest while ye gather up the tares, ye root up also the wheat with them." How consolatory is this ! It might be the case, that under the idea of weeding out the tares, the wheat itself might be rooted up. So strongly may the latter occasionally resemble the former ; and who can with reason prevent us from cherishing the hope, that even amongst those whom we have deeply lamented as being of the number of those that are without, many a plant of Divine planting may be found, although it may not yet have developed its perfect form. On such, hands must not yet be laid ; and with respect to them, all anathemas must be avoided. Before the full and final development has taken place, who would with certainty affirm which are tares, and which the Lord's seed ?

"Let both," saith Jesus, " grow together until the harvest." How great and dignified does the Lord appear in these words ! How majestically elevated is the position from whence he so calmly contemplates every thing that exalts itself against him ! He knows that nothing, that no one can hinder his work. He fears none of the schemes of cunning or of wickedness. Let the kingdom of the evil one reach its utmost maturity ; the Mighty One of Israel, by quiet conquests, accomplishes his object, despite all opposition ; and his banners will indubitably be the last, which, planted on the ruins of Satan's kingdom, shall float over the whole earth.

But till then, the conflict will continue. The powers of darkness shall first try all their schemes against him, employ their stratagems, and shoot their arrows. The time is then arrived, when he shall dash them in pieces, and make their mighty ones his footstool. " In the time of harvest," saith the householder, " I will say to the reapers, Gather ye together first the tares, and bind them in bundles to burn them : but gather the wheat into my barn."

The meaning of this part of the parable is obvious. " The harvest is the end of the world ; and the reapers are the angels. As therefore the tares are gathered and burned in the fire; so shall it be in the end of this world. The Son of man shall send forth his angels, and they shall gather out of his kingdom all things that offend, and them which do iniquity; and shall cast them into a furnace of fire: there shall be wailing and gnashing of teeth.' Such is the language of Him who uttered the parable.

Many an awful prelude of this great judgment-day has been already experienced in the world, and the sequel of Elisha's history invites us thoughtfully to contemplate at least the preparations for such an act of Divine retribution. May the terrors of the Lord, now about to be unveiled before us, salutarily affect our souls, and give a more powerful sound, and a more impressive solemnity to the words, "Work out your own salvation with fear and trembling!"

2 KINGS IX. 1—8

" And Elisha the prophet called one of the children of the prophets, and said unto him, Gird up thy loins, and take this box of oil in thine hand, and go to Ramoth-Gilead: and when thou comest thither, look out there Jehu the son of Jehoshaphat the son of Nimshi, and go in, and make him arise up from among his brethren, and carry him to an inner chamber; then take the box of oil, and pour it on his head, and say, Thus saith the Lord, I have anointed thee king over Israel. Then open the door, and flee, and tarry not. So the young man, even the young man the prophet, went to Ramoth-Gilead: And when he came, behold, the captains of the host were sitting, and he said, I have an errand to thee, O captain. And he arose, and went into the house: and he poured the oil on his head, and said unto him, Thus saith the Lord God of Israel, I have anointed thee king over the people of the Lord, even over Israel. And thou shalt smite the house of Ahab thy master, that I may avenge the blood of my servants the prophets, and the blood of all the servants of the Lord at the hand of Jezebel. For the whole house of Ahab shall perish."

THESE words present to us a new transaction in which Elisha is called to engage. Scarcely is he permitted to take breath. One ominous event rapidly succeeds another. Would that it had reference only to the wearing of garlands, instead of the binding of rods and scourges, and that the redness which appears above Samaria's horizon were any other than that of blood! I. The approaching retribution; II. The Divine commission to Elisha; III. The sending of the young man; IV. The anointing of Jehu: and, V. Its object; are the historical events, around which, as a framework, the ideas which may at this time occur to us, shall entwine themselves.

I. The atmosphere in Israel is sultry. Dreadful thunder-storms are hastening on. On every side, black and threatening clouds rise above the horizon of the land; and he that has an ear for it, already hears in the distance the roaring of the storm, and the rolling of the thunder. Long enough has the sceptre of patience been swayed over the wicked. The Divine mercy flies with rapid pinions, whilst the justice of God walks slowly on foot. A Joram has been suffered to sit twelve years upon his throne, and equally long has space for reflection been given to Jezebel, and to Joram's whole house. They have not come to reflection. The long-suffering they experienced, rendered these worthless individuals the more secure. The miracles they saw exhibited, passed before them only like the shadows of a magic-lantern, as subjects of the day's conversation. The sound of the awakening voices of the prophets was quickly banished by the riot and uproar of their sinful lives, and the visitations of Divine wrath operated only to harden them, even as the emanations of his kindness lulled them to slumber, and confirmed them in their frivolity. The wickedness of the Amorites was filled up; the temples of Baal elevated as before their proud cupolas in the land. The abominable priestly caste of the Sidonian goddess, seems to have risen up again, in greater numbers and increased depravity, from the slaughter at the brook Kishon. The children of God wear, as before, the thorny crown of public shame and contempt; and the spectacle presented by a court life, is by no means more pure than it was in the times of Ahab.

Oh, if Joram and his house had known what was silently impending over them, how would their mirth have ceased! But they have no presentiment of the coming storm. They have long since committed to the tomb of oblivion, the curse which Elijah uttered in Jehovah's name, upon Ahab and his offspring. From the fact of the sword over their heads reposing so long in its sheath, they think themselves at liberty to draw favorable inferences for their future scandalous and sinful life. But Divine anathemas can be wholly interred only in the blood of atonement; every other grave retains them but for a while. Unexpectedly they break through locks and bolts, and prison walls ; and the longer they retain their burden, the more awful, as it seems, becomes its fury. Such was the case with the curse upon Ahab and his house. Though forgotten, yet it continued like a deceitful thunder-cloud, to brood in silence. For a time it lay bound, like a secret mine, beneath Joram's throne ; but the dreadful moment was now approaching, when it would explode, project its contents, and shatter to pieces and destroy every thing around it.

What a heart-rending spectacle, to see a person thinking no harm, and pursuing his way, dreaming only of happiness and joy ; whilst at the same time, we know that he has already in his pocket, the letter, though sealed, which informs him that his house is burned down, and his wife and children devoured by the plague ; so that when he returns home, he will find a heap of ruins and a scene of desolation, where previously a charming Eden had flourished.

These, however, are only the terrors of the present time. But to be able to say of a careless individual of that description, " To morrow, at this time, thou shalt no longer be numbered amongst the living, but shalt be the victim of an impenitent death, and be agonizing amongst the lost !"—O my God, what can be more heart-rending than this ? It is with feelings of such a nature, that we look at present into the festive palace of Jezreel ; for it is there the royal family are now residing, and luxuriously entertaining a dignified guest, in the person of Ahaziah king of Judah. Oh that no one amongst us may be found in a similar position to those who are thinking themselves so secure! But who knows, if the veil were this moment removed from our real position what would present itself to our view, even amongst ourselves! Certainly it would then be found that not a few, who now walk mournfully and dejected, have been long pursuing their gloomy path, only from a foolish mistake respecting themselves, and not from the want of a well-founded title to exult and rejoice. But a Belshazzar, immersed in worldly pleasures, likewise emerges from behind the veil, and the " Mene, Tekel" is already flaming on his walls. Haman also, intoxicated with the fumes of sensuality and ambition; but what is erecting behind his back, and for whom is the rope thus twisted in secret? Thou, too, who art satiated with the husks of this world, and on whose lips is the exclamation of security, " Peace, peace, there is nothing to fear!" although, only by a silken thread, hangs the glittering sword above thy head, threateningly, and thirsting for thy blood. —Oh may God open your eyes! yes, yours most of all, ye unhappy mortals, that ye may be seized with a salutary amazement; and to you also, who rest unconsciously in the arms of eternal compassion, may he disclose your true position, that your groundless complaints may be changed into rejoicing, to the praise and glory of his name!

Divine vengeance approaches. " I will avenge," saith the Lord, " the blood of my servants, the prophets, and the blood of all the servants of the

Lord at the hand of Jezebel." Hear! hear! **He**
has permitted her to lay her hand on those that
were his ; but he has not overlooked or forgotten it.
Oh how kindly does he feel towards his elect ! **He**
forgets no one who gives the least of them even "a
cup of cold water." He rewards and blesses him
for it.   But woe unto him who dares to touch and
trouble one of those, who are dear to him as " the
apple of his eye !" With horror he will find that
he has been assailing one of God's children ; one
of his, who can manifest his wrath and anger in
equal measure with his kindness and his love.
Nothing rises up from earth and penetrates the
clouds more powerfully than the voice of the blood
of persecuted saints.   Nothing is better fitted to
pour oil into the fire of Divine wrath against the
wicked, than the groans extorted by their scourges
from a child of God.   Act cautiously, therefore,
towards these people, for your own sakes, more
than theirs.   But ye Christians, pray the more
for your enemies, instead of sighing against them,
since your complaints may so easily bring upon
them swift destruction.   If God loves you sufficiently to draw the sword for you against your
foes, the same love will also incline him to remember them with blessing, whom ye bless, and in whose
behalf you lift up holy hands.   Therefore seek advantage for your neighbor from the special favor, which
God designs to manifest towards you.   Tell him
how much it would increase your happiness, if he
would, by his Spirit, awaken and sanctify this and
that particular soul ; and it seems to me, he will

the less suffer this addition to your happiness to fail, the more definite are his promises to hear, which he has given to those who supplicate the increase of his kingdom.

"The blood of my servants!" Oh, this blood has often cried aloud from earth to heaven; and what answers has it received, what judgments has it called down! Stand forward, ye slayers of the saints in every age, and bear your historical testimony to it! Let Nebuchadnezzar, the horribly smitten king, who was banished among the beasts, take the lead. Let Belshazzar, the oppressor of Israel, and the profaner of its holy things, stand next, and show himself, trembling, as of old, before the mysterious and maledictory writing upon the wall, and, as shortly after, trodden down in the street, and weltering in his blood. Come hither, Herod Antipas, the Baptist's murderer, and ever after a fugitive ghost-seer, cast out at length into barren and desert lands, all because of that blood, which thy hand has spilt. And thou, Herod Agrippa, ravening wolf amongst Christ's flock, but, for that very cause, smitten by the angel of the Lord, and eaten up of worms whilst still alive. Appear, thou Roman bloodhound, Nero, and confess that in the terrific visions, which armed thy own hand against thee, the spirits of those just persons appeared to thee, with whose burning bodies thou didst once illumine thy festive orgies! Stand forth, ye other crowned executioners of God's favorites in the Roman empire, and testify by your end, how dangerous it is to lay destructive hands on those whom

Christ has purchased by his blood. Join yourselves
to them, as accessories in the same cause, ye blood-
thirsty inquisitors of Spain, who have drawn
down a curse upon your country, which still burns
and glows in the points of those swords with which
its wretched population destroys itself. Rank thyself with them, Louis of France, thou purple-clothed
adulterer, armed with the fatal knife against the
members of Christ, but on that very account forever branded with the curse of God. And thou,
Charles the Ninth, who didst toll the bell to thy
bloody nuptials, relate with what measure God re-
paid thee, when on the rack of despair, drops of
blood exuded from thy veins instead of deathly
perspiration, and who whilst thy body became a
mass of corruption, didst depart this life, a horrible
example to all the world. Yes, all of you, who
from your numbers, may well be called legion,
come forward, ye flaming brands of hell, bound in
chains of darkness, and testify how dangerous it is
to touch the saints of the Most High !

But when the wrath of God is thus inflamed
against those who shed the blood of his elect, and
prepares to avenge this blood, why does he not
rather protect his people against the injustice of
their enemies, and hurl the latter to the ground
before they accomplish their misdeeds ? The all-
unfolding key to the depths of this inquiry, eternity
only can furnish. Till then, the words are in force,
" Here is the patience of the saints ;" and faith con-
fesses that this Divine procedure is good and holy.
" But the pitiable victims !" Oh, call not by such

a name those, who, although by a bloody path, enter into glory, with which " the sufferings of this present time are not worthy to be compared." Neither call those objects of pity, who, under temporal oppression ripen for heaven, and must pass through fire and through water to meet Him there, who said, " the flood shall not overflow thee, nor the flames kindle upon thee." The sufferings of the children of God are like the vernal breezes which agitate the soil, and assist in developing the slumbering germs of the future plants. Like the latter, in the season of adversity, the buds of the new nature expand themselves in the regenerate heart in fervent aspirations, earnest prayers, longings after heaven, and hopes that cheer the rugged path of the pilgrim. The trials of believers are like the whirling of the storm, which, whilst it elevates and divides the billows, discovers to the seaman's view the pearl banks which lie below. It is thus that sufferings unfold to the Lord's saints those everlasting treasures which the God of grace hath hidden in their vital principle, and make the heart, which is athirst for comfort, acquainted with the method in which the sheep of Christ are kept by the power of God, with their hidden life in him who is their head, and with the impossibility that one of them should perish, by reason of their mysterious union with the second Adam, who hath overcome on their behalf. " If ye endure chastening, God dealeth with you as with sons."

II. At the impending judgments over Israel, Elisha had to resume his functions. He was staying at Gilgal, in the social circle of the sons of the prophets, and how unspeakably happy did he feel whilst reposing in that peaceful haven! It was long since his days had passed so delightfully as they then did. Divided between the calm investigation of the Holy Scriptures, and cordial, harmonious, and instructive converse with the enlightened and truth-seeking disciples, his life wore almost the reflection of a superior state of being; and if the lively wish was excited within him, that it might still be some time before he should be obliged to weigh anchor and take his departure from this pleasing shore, nothing could be more natural or more pardonable. Scarcely, however, had he entered this sweet retreat, and rejoiced in its loveliness, than he descried the portentous signal, which destined him again to be the harbinger of approaching storms, and called him to act as an officer of justice, in preparing the scourge, with which the Avenger of blood on high had resolved to smite the persecutors of his saints. In all probability the words of his master, the Tishbite, " Lord, it is enough !" were at least excited in the heart of the seer of Abel-Meholah ; and thus, from other motives than to observe the state of the wind, with a sacred tear in his eye, he gazed upon the sailing clouds, and contemplated the stars above, those silent lamps, those pleasing and alluring tapers of the eternal home. And with respect to ourselves, my brethren, when occasionally we feel as if dwelling in Mesech, pent up, and apprehensive, we ought to reflect how happily we are situated, compared with others, as respects our spiritual privileges. Oh that we better knew how to appreciate what God has so graciously given us, and abounded more in gratitude and thankfulness! But the habit of enjoyment, even of the most valuable of Heaven's bestowments, is wont to gradually draw them down into the sphere of every-day life, nay, even of those things which we overlook; and it is only through the repeated endangerment of our possession, that the consciousness of it continues fresh, and the flames upon the altar of our gratitude are fanned.

Elisha must again go forth. The Divine and portentous commission, to anoint Jehu to be king over Israel, was transferred from his predecessor to himself. The forbearance of God had for a time deposited this command, as it were, in the archives of heaven. Divine justice now brings it forth, and urges the prophet to its fulfilment. Elisha well knew the effects of this mission. He perceived in Jehu, the dreadful scourge, which an angry God was about to employ against his adversaries in Israel. The man of God had already called forth such an implement of wrath for the desolation of Israel, in the person of Hazael the Syrian; and he was now to let loose a more terrible one than Hazael, for the spoliation of his beloved country. You may easily imagine, how difficult and painful this must have been to him. Nothing could have been more opposed to his kind and charitable feelings, than this commission. But it came from the

Lord himself, and Elisha knew what was due to such a message.

The spiritual greatness of the Old Testament saints consists chiefly in that unconditional submission, with which they blindly gave themselves up to the Divine disposal, even when the Lord's will was like a lofty barrier to their most rational reflections, and their tenderest feelings; and it is just in this particular, that the saints appear in their most exalted character, when they bid their charity be mute on being commissioned to execute Divine judgments, when they yield up their natural compassion to the judicial commands of God, and submit their patriotism, their consanguinity, their human pity, as an offering to his decisions, and cast their penetration, wisdom, and opinion, in honor of the mysterious arrangements of his government, as incense on the coals of his altar. The power of God then manifests itself in the most striking manner, as mighty in human weakness; the Lord's name is then praised in a loftier strain, and the poverty of the creature glorifies the Creator.

In like manner was Elisha prepared to present his feeling heart to the Lord as a paschal lamb, and to yield obedience to the Divine command. Very often the Lord requires nothing more than this willing offering, and accepts the self-denying inclination for the deed; sparing his friends the rest. In Elisha's case, likewise, he exempts him from personally placing the sword of vengeance in Jehu's hands, whilst permitting him to send one of the sons of the prophets in his stead, and thus accomplishing the mission through the medium of another. This, of itself, was a desirable relief to the seer. Oh the parental tenderness of God, who knows the inmost recesses of his children's hearts, and ordains, with affectionate solicitude, what is required from each of them! He is a kind master, and regards even the purely human organization of every individual heart as worthy of the tenderest consideration; and very frequently chooses the harmonies they are called to utter, according to the nature of the strings with which the mind is furnished; and does not impose upon trembling Æolian harps, the utterance of the storm and the curse, but commits the song of the tempest to stouter strings, and to the weaker, the music of the promises. Oh incomparable condescension, kindness, and love!

III. Elisha avails himself of the Divine permission, and selects, as his herald, from the schools of the prophets, a young man, who had probably often served as his companion and assistant in his sublime missions. This young man felt less painfully the burden of his commission. Even the youthful gratification of being thought worthy of so high an office may have, in a measure, counterbalanced the pain at the object, and the obvious consequences of his embassy. " Gird up thy loins," says the prophet to him, " take this box of oil in thine hand, and go to Ramoth-Gilead. And when thou comest thither, look out there Jehu, the son of Jehoshaphat, the son of Nimshi, and go in, and make him arise up from among his brethren, and carry him to an inner chamber; then take the box of oil, and pour it on his head, and say, Thus saith the Lord, I have anointed thee king over Israel.—And thou shalt smite the house of Ahab thy master, that I may avenge the blood of my servants the prophets, and the blood of all the servants of the Lord, at the hand of Jezebel. For the whole house of Ahab shall perish.—And the dogs shall eat Jezebel in the portion of Jezreel, and there shall be none to bury her." The young man was also directed, when he had accomplished his mission, to "open the door and flee, and tarry not!"

Thus spake Elisha. Had he uttered these words in his own name, he would have been worthy of death as a traitor and a rebel; but he spoke them as the messenger of him who setteth up kings, and casteth them down. This was not the first time that God had lifted the destroying axe against a radically decayed dynasty. It is true that, for a time, he frequently makes use of such degenerate royal races for the chastisement of his people; but he never fails, eventually, to pronounce sentence of rejection upon them, and to bring upon the reprobates swift destruction. The experience of thousands of years confirms the fact, that it is only by the fear of the Lord that the throne is established.

But what must have been the feelings of the young man at these words of the prophet? He had probably never so much as dreamed of being selected for such a mission. He holds in his hands the crown of Israel. Though one of the meanest in Samaria, he sees himself authorized to tear away at length, the sceptre and the purple from the house of Joram, because it had never ceased to trample under foot the Lord's people, and to bestow them upon another. Poor and inconsiderable as he is, yet he bears a kingdom to Ramoth! How great does the Lord appear in this feature of the narrative! and at the same time, how he mocks by it, all the boundless self-exaltation of God-forgetting earthly potentates!

The young man sets forth, concealing a new era for Israel beneath the seal of his mission. What must have been his feelings on this momentous occasion! He must have been aware, that he was sent to open the flood-gates of Divine vengeance against Samaria, and to prepare the way for a horrible desolation. He is not anxious with regard to himself. He knows that he is the Lord's property, and therefore that he is safe. Never was he more inwardly happy in God, than now in prospect of the approaching storm. The consciousness of the most blissful connection in which it is possible to enter, may often slumber long in the breasts of believers, till it awakes, and becomes reanimated by something of a diametrically opposite nature. The Christian, at times, premeditatedly encamps on the verge of the pit, that, in the face of its terrors, he may taste the more fully the blessedness of that security, to which he has attained; and intentionally calls to mind the terrors and horrors of the judgment day, in order to lead his spirit up this flaming path, to the full and joyful feeling of its incomparable security in Christ, the Rock of Ages. And oh

what pleasure it affords him, to call up around him
every thing that is dangerous and dreadful, every
accuser and judge, nay, even death and hell, and to
be able in a firm tone to exclaim, in the face of them
all, "Who is he that condemneth? It is Christ that
died."

But where did we leave our herald? See him
yonder, proceeding on his way, unheeded, and in
his simple garb. He rapidly hastens past Samaria,
as well as Jezreel's glittering palace and its sumptuous gardens. Had he been inclined to break his
silence, how might he have caused the land to
tremble with his news. He might have cried aloud
in the royal apartments, "Take your fill of pleasure
to-day; to-morrow ye will howl in the eternal des-
erts;" and amongst the priests, "Your hour is
come!" and in the pagodas of Baal, "Woe, for the
fire is in the roof, the worm in the beam!" and in
the saloons of the magnates and the mighty, "Death
is gone up into your chambers!" But the young
man is silent, and mutely carries his secret along
with him, and the land continues in its deadly slumber.

But let us ask, my friends, whether, if such a
messenger as this young man hastened past us, as
was formerly the case at Jezreel, aware of what
was about to befall us, and ready to unseal his secret—what would he have to say to us? That
which Balaam once uttered, whilst looking upon Israel, "How goodly are thy tents, O Jacob, and thy
tabernacles, O Israel! As the valleys are they
spread forth, as gardens by the river's side, as the

trees of lign aloes which the Lord hath planted, and as cedar trees beside the waters.—He hath not beheld iniquity in Jacob, nor perverseness in Israel: the Lord his God is with him, and the shout of a king is among them!" Would this portray our future state? God grant that it might! But I apprehend the message would sound differently. Have not, even amongst us, the barriers of that holy opposition begun to give way, against which the antichristian spirit of the times has so long and vainly employed his destroying powers? Has not that frivolity already gained ground amongst us, which, detached from the basis of eternal truth, beholds, in carnal enjoyments, the end and aim of life, and in the most positive infidelity, the summit of polite education? Has not, at least partially, that horrible perversion of ideas broken in upon us, in which genius takes the place of the Holy Spirit, material worship that of religion, in which the sentiment, "Help thyself, and God will help thee," is exalted in the room of faith ; and human wit, art, sentimentality, and wisdom, in the place of God? But wherever the cancer of this blasphemous spirit of the times has eaten itself in, there is the mark of the beast from the bottomless pit ; and where this branded mark is found, there the arena is prepared, on which, sooner or later, the anger of God, and the fire of his wrath, will celebrate their triumphs.

IV. The young man has finished his journey, and reached Ramoth-Gilead, his destination. At that time, the king's host lay there to observe the Syr-

ian army, which, under Hazael, had already made
victorious inroads into the country.   Joram no longer headed his legions in person.   He had received
a slight wound in the first collision with the Syrians,
and had retired to his palace at Jezreel, there to
await his convalescence.   The army, meanwhile,
continued under the command of his generals, and
Jehu was one of the boldest, most ardent, and determined amongst them.

Elisha's messenger, on his arrival at the camp,
immediately inquired for the man he sought; and,
on entering the house pointed out to him, found the
whole staff assembled there.   In dependence on
God, in whose name he appeared, the young man
boldly stepped forward, and fixing his eyes on Jehu,
whom he either previously knew, or whom God
pointed out to him in some way or other at that moment, he said to him, "I have an errand to thee, O
captain!" and beckoned him on one side.   After
they had entered an adjoining apartment, the young
man took the vial, and pouring the anointing oil
upon the warrior's head, exclaimed, "Thus saith
the Lord God of Israel, I have anointed thee king
over the people of the Lord, even over Israel!"
and then disclosed to him, in God's name, the reason why the crown was taken from Joram, and
for what purpose it was committed to him.   After
having thus executed his commission, he pushed
open the door, and returned home without delay,
even as Elisha, Divinely commissioned, had commanded him.

Jehu, clothed with his new dignity, appeared to

himself as in a dream, and scarcely able to credit
his senses. As an Israelite, he well knew that Jehovah, as unlimited Lord and Master over his people, sets up kings and dethrones them at pleasure
in Israel ; but in the present case it seemed to him
hazardous to regard the matter so implicitly as correct, even though the fact of one of the sons of the
prophets having performed the ceremony of anointing him with oil, scarcely permitted him to suspect
that his brethren in arms had been attempting to deceive him. On returning to the circle of his companions, struggling to appear composed, he was received on all sides with the bantering inquiry, "Is all
well ?   Wherefore came this mad fellow to thee?"
They soon recognized the man and the colors he
wore. Their calling him a madman, a fanatic, or a
fool, as their most recent kindred spirits in the present day are wont to do with respect to us, only reminds us of the saying of the wise man, "There is
nothing new under the sun."

To the question of his companions, "Wherefore
came this mad fellow to thee ?" Jehu replied with
prudence and consideration, "Ye know the man,
and his communication." By which he means, "Ye
are yourselves the authors of this deception." He
was so well acquainted with his brethren in arms,
that he could charge them with such an artifice,
even at the expense of that which is most holy.   His
friends were this time not conscious of any thing of
the kind, and replied with no small degree of excitement, ".Jehu, thou art mistaken. Tell us now
what the man said to thee." Then Jehu replied

with more firmness and confidence, "Thus and thus spake he to me, saying, Thus saith the Lord, I have anointed thee king over Israel." The generals, on hearing this, believe the communication made to Jehu, and do so the more willingly, the more brilliant the prospects which connect themselves with the idea of seeing, henceforth, their social companion on the throne of Israel. "Then they hasted, and took every man his garment, and, in the absence of a throne, spread them upon the top of the steps, and cried out, whilst the trumpets resounded, Jehu is king!"

V. A heavy storm was, therefore, now gathering over Israel. The Lord made use of Jehu as the medium of his avenging and destroying indignation against his adversaries. Their destruction was the object of the calling and elevation of that zealot in the Lord's cause, who is therefore properly exhibited to us as a scourge in the hand of God.

Truly, "our God is a consuming fire!" Let no deceitful inferences be drawn from the forbearance and long-suffering which he exercises, frequently for years together, towards "the vessels of wrath." Though it may *rest* for a time, his sword does not *rust* in its scabbard. Oh, whatever may be your pursuits, my friends, do not think yourselves happy, so long as you have not concluded a lasting peace with God! But this peace is not made merely by your showing the white flag; he must unfurl it also; and this he only does when the individual surrenders at discretion, and calls out for mercy.

The " Remember me" of the dying thief, as well as the exclamation of the overthrown disciple of the Pharisees, on his way to Damascus, " Lord, what wilt thou have me to do ?" show you the way. Both these sinners not only laid down, before God, those arms which they had previously borne against him and his ways ; but they also surrendered the fortress of self-righteousness, in which they expected to be able to force from the Almighty the prize of his good-pleasure ; and renouncing all self-justifica- tion, despairing of all self-redemption, and not know- ing what to do, they appealed to free mercy in Christ, and committed their fate, in a self-condemnation as sincere as their surrender was unconditional, whilst confessing, weeping, and supplicating, into the hands of eternal love. The Lord then inclined the sceptre of his grace, and the words, " Ye are forgiven !" descended into their wounded hearts like harp notes from on high. Heaven celebrated the happy peace with loud acclamations ; hell murmured ; and two new names were added to the list of the citizens of God's kingdom.

There is only one refuge from the terrors of judgment—Christ, sought as the last resource un- der the pressure of inward distress, and found and clung to as the only tenable point. In him, who presents us to the Judge, divested of our sins, we only hear the soft and gentle music of peace. The heavens are azure over us ; light and free the air we breathe. The thunders aloft terrify us no longer ; nor does the blood cease to flow in our veins, when a passing funeral reminds us of the nearness of our own exit from this world. That which so often lay, like a heavy and oppressive incubus, on our souls, even in our happiest hours, entirely leaves us; for it was nothing else but the spectral consciousness of our misunderstanding with God, and the horrible dangers to which it exposed us.

Whoever, therefore, wishes to save his soul, let him flee to Christ. Our Zoar, our Pella, lies where the cross is exhibited. Embrace the horns of the altar on Calvary, and ye are safe. Around this city of refuge the Divine command, "Hitherto shalt thou come, but no further," sets bounds to every hostile power. "One thing is needful." Long for, and entreat, till you obtain it; and what is that? "He that hath ears, let him hear;" it resounds in the following lines:—

> Sprinkle the threshold of my heart,
>   Thou Prince of Peace, with thy dear blood;
> And bid each stain of sin depart,
>   Wash'd out by that all-cleansing flood.
>
> Whatever else may dark remain,
>   Let me thy cross in glory see,
> And teach me what those words contain:
>   'Tis finished, Christ hath died for me!
>
> Then boldly I pursue my way;
>   My soul the curse no longer heeds;
> I seek no other guiding ray,
>   Than that which from thy cross proceeds.
>
> 'Tis there that wrath was turn'd to grace,
>   There mercy gain'd the victory;
> Redemption for our fallen race,
>   Was purchased on Mount Calvary.

II.—THE TERRORS OF GOD

"JUDGE me, O God!" exclaims the royal psalm-ist, Psa. xliii. 1. A short but most weighty expres-sion. The greatest antitheses present themselves in it, in the most marvellous connection. The words unfold to our view one of the most awful events that can befall us, one of the most indispensable transactions in which we must engage, and the most blissful state in which we can be placed.

"Judge me, O God!" The first impression pro-duced by this prayer, can only be that of surprise and astonishment. Had the words been uttered by an angel, we should have been terrified on his account. And yet they are uttered by a sinner, to that God, who is the source of light, in whom is no darkness, and who would be compelled to deny his own nature, in order to unite himself with any thing unclean. How awful, therefore, when this Judge rises up to judgment! Behold the fugitive Cain, shuddering at his own shadow; and this shuddering is only an anticipation of judgment. Look at Bel-shazzar, petrified with awe, and trembling before the handwriting on the wall, which only summoned him before the dread tribunal. See Judas in de-

spair, committing suicide; but know, that this is
only the beginning of judgment. Do you wish to
look into the terrors of the judgment itself? Think
of the rich man in torments; of the impassable gulf,
which separates him from the abodes of blessedness; of the inextinguishable flame, which envelopes without consuming him; of the drop of water,
which he in vain implores; of the closing of the
eternal gates upon him—think of these things, and
you will begin to have an idea how God judges.
Much that is painful may meet us in this life; when
the foundations of our domestic happiness give way
beneath us; when poverty surrounds us with its
privations; when the cares of this life expel sleep
from our couches; when the world refuses to acknowledge us; when peace removes from our
threshold; when appalling disease paralyzes our
limbs; and when the grave hides from our view
those who were the most dear to us. How events of
this kind are able to prostrate us, becloud our days,
and make life a burden to us! Look at aged Jacob,
robbed of his son Joseph; at Job on the smoking
ashes of his happiness; at Jeremiah on Jerusalem's
ruins; at Hezekiah on his couch, mourning like a
crane! But what is all this, compared with the misery of those, who fall as criminals into the hands of
Divine justice? "Be not a terror unto me!" exclaims
the prophet: "thou art my hope in the day of evil!"
Jer. xvii. 17. Whatever may befall me, only let
not this one thing happen to me. "Be not a terror
unto me!" The apostle, in writing to the Hebrews,
chap. x. 31, responds to these words, and exclaims,

"It is a fearful thing to fall into the hands of the living God."

But you inquire, appalled, How shall we escape these terrors? Listen,—be judged here, lest ye be destroyed hereafter. Say with David, "Judge me, O God!" Utter the words to-day, whilst still a merciful judgment may be expected, and before the cause is finally decided. This must of necessity be experienced. Do not let your first aspiration be, "Sanctify me!" but begin with, "Judge me, O God!" for God makes no one holy, whom he has not previously judged. And when he thus enters into judgment with us for our salvation, he first of all presents before us, the mirror of his holy law, in which we see unfolded to our view, what? Alas, a lost life! And yet we hesitate with our surrender! we grasp at fig-leaves, subterfuges, and evasions! But the eye of the Omniscient and the Judge is upon us, penetrating into the deepest recesses of our being, and discovering everywhere nothing but death and corruption, by which we are rendered mute as the grave. He requires holiness, and we daily find ourselves only the more guilty, powerless, and heavy laden. At length the moment arrives, when we give up the idea of appeasing him, and the cry of despair arises from the depth of our wretchedness: "It is in vain; I have no righteousness of my own; I find none; I am under the curse!" We long and languish for one thing alone; we cry for mercy; and, God be praised! mercy is to be found. A bloody cross presents itself to our view, and a voice exclaims,

"Comfort ye, comfort ye my people;—speak ye comfortably to Jerusalem, and cry unto her that her warfare is accomplished, that her iniquity is pardoned." Through the horrors of judgment, we press to Jesus; and through Jesus into the kingdom of life and love. Hence how necessary is the prayer, "Judge me, O God!"

"He that believeth on me," saith Jesus, "shall not be condemned." But when once we are one with Jesus, how willing are we then to be judged of God! The prayer to be so, then, points out a state of the greatest blessedness to which we can attain in this world; for we then appear before God, clothed with the spotless robe of Christ's righteousness, and his judgment respecting us can then be only mild and favorable—a judgment such as that pronounced upon Abraham, Daniel, Paul, or John.

Formerly we might have said, "Oh let not God enter into judgment with us!" but now we rejoice that the final decision rests with him: and when our conscience condemns us, we take refuge with him, consoled by the consciousness, that he "is greater than our heart, and knoweth all things." It causes us pleasure to perceive, that he continues to reprove us inwardly, and ceases not to judge us, by his Spirit, respecting our faults, until we again stand humbled before him. We are then happy in observing that he is really our Father, and know that renewed forgivenesses go hand in hand with the renewed consciousness of judgment and feelings of humiliation; whilst on the contrary, there is nothing more painful than when we are left unnoticed to proceed on our way, and when we are no longer conscious of his eye being fixed upon us, and no longer feel the hand of his correcting love. In this sense, therefore, it continues one of our most essential petitions, as long as we live, "Judge me, O God,"—yea, judge me daily, but in mercy!

2 KINGS X. 10

" Know now that there shall fall unto the earth nothing of the word of the Lord, which the Lord spake concerning the house of Ahab ; for the Lord hath done that which he spake by his servant Elijah."

SUCH are the words of Jehu, addressed from smoking ruins and the blood-stained soil, to the assembled populace. He praises the faithfulness of Jehovah, although it elevates its glorious throne upon the ruins of cities and the corpses of kings. God is not less glorious in the flaming robe of his justice, than in the starry crown of his mercy. Let us then cause the bloody events, of which Jehu reminds us, to pass once more in transient imagery before us. Their signification, as respects ourselves, will naturally be unfolded as we proceed.

I. Come then, and observe how "God is a consuming fire," when, laying aside his patience and compassion, he presents himself to us in the dark array of his retributive holiness. Jehu is the living sword of his vengeance, which he draws ; the destructive thunderbolt, which he hurls. But the sinners against whom he turns his hand, are such as may be found by thousands amongst us, on whom the overflowing riches of his forbearance, patience, and alluring mercy have exhausted themselves in vain; who harden their hearts, and will not that God should reign over them.

Scarcely had Jehu been anointed king, and received the enthusiastic homage of the whole army, when he unfurls his banner, and calls the host to arms against his former lord, the king of Israel. "If it be your minds," said he, addressing the assembled legions, "then let none go forth nor escape out of the city to go to tell it in Jezreel." "We ourselves will be the first," he means to say, "by whom the prince shall learn what is impending over him." The legions unanimously applaud his plan, smite their shields, and prepare their swords for immediate battle. Jehu, without delay, ascends his chariot, and hastens, at the head of the thousands who are devoted to him, to the little town of Jezreel, where, as you already know, Joram was residing in his summer palace, in which, besides Jezebel, the queen-mother, he was entertaining another royal guest, Ahaziah, the despicable ruler of the kingdom of Judah.

Joram, recovered of the wound he had received in the battle with the Syrians, was sitting carelessly and jovially at his table, when the watchman, who stood on the tower of Jezreel, perceiving, in the distance, an armed force approaching, and immediately rushing into the banqueting hall, informed his master of the fact. But the king, still suspecting no evil, imagined, on hearing the intelligence, that

a division of his army was on the way to bring him
news of some victory, and under this idea, he dis-
patched a horseman to meet the troop, and inquire,
saying, " Is it peace ?" that is, were they bringing
good news ?

The horseman galloped off, and on approaching
the squadron, was convinced that it was a division
of the royal army, which, under the command of
Jehu, was marching upon Jezreel. Having reached
the point of the cohorts, the herald greets the com-
mander-in-chief with the words, " Thus saith the
king : Is it peace ?" But what must have been
his feelings, on receiving the harsh reply, " What
hast thou to do with peace ? turn thee behind me ;"
and when he saw himself the same moment surrounded by men, who, on being informed that he
was their prisoner, disarmed him, and then conducted him to the rear of the host !

The watchman on the tower of Jezreel, on observing that the horseman did not return, antici-
pates nothing good. He hastens a second time
into the king's chamber, and, with fear in his countenance, exclaims, " The messenger came to them,
but he cometh not again." Neither is this news
capable of awaking Joram out of the deep sleep of
his security. Destruction hastens towards him in
full sail, but Joram dreams he is in a secure port.
The curse that hangs over him, is already brooding,
but the king forces himself to think the best of the
matter, and merely sends a second horseman with
the same message to the approaching host. The
latter also approaches the vanguard of the army

with the white flag, and says, " Thus saith the king. Is it peace?" but experiences the same reception. "What hast thou to do with peace?" exclaims Jehu in a voice of thunder, "turn thee behind me."

The watchman appears the third time before the careless prince, and in the greatest consternation says, "My lord, the second messenger came even unto them, and cometh not again: and the driving is like the driving of Jehu, the son of Nimshi; for he driveth furiously;" yet Joram still entertains no suspicion. His feeling of security, under these circumstances, is incomprehensible, and might almost induce the idea of judicial delusion. Joram's fate is sealed. Divine justice requires him as its victim. He still cherishes the hope that Jehu may have something important to disclose to him. He orders his chariots, and two are made ready, just as if it were merely a drive for pleasure; the one for Joram, the other for Ahaziah, who wishes to accompany him. After they have taken their seats, they hasten out of the palace-gates to meet the host. But they may soon pull up the horses, for the troops have already entered the town of Jezreel, and the advance-guard, led on by Jehu, has penetrated into the palace gardens. On the very piece of ground, which was formerly Naboth's vineyard, and torn from him in such an impious manner, the two monarchs meet the general. Alas! we remember that a Divine curse broods over the very spot. " On this field, I will requite thee the blood of Naboth and his sons," said the Lord, by the mouth of the Tishbite, to king Ahab. The entire import of these words had not yet been fulfilled. But mark! the whole of its terrors are now about to be poured forth and realized.

After Joram had welcomed Jehu with the question "Is it peace?" the latter replied in a cold and firm tone, "What peace, so long as the whoredoms of thy mother Jezebel and her witchcrafts are so many." The king's eyes were then opened to perceive the real state of the case. Trembling and pale with terror, he gives his charioteer the sign to return; but scarcely had he turned his back, exclaiming, "There is treachery, O Ahaziah!" when Jehu seized his bow, drew it with all his might, and smote Joram between his arms, so that the arrow went out at his heart. The mortally wounded man sinks down bleeding in his chariot. "Then said Jehu, to Bidkar his captain, Take up, and cast him in the portion of the field of Naboth the Jezreelite." And the captain cast thither the corpse, even as carrion is cast out into the open field. But Jehu pronounced his epitaph, whilst saying to Bidkar, "Remember how that, when I and thou rode together after Ahab his father, the Lord laid this burden upon him: Surely I have seen yesterday the blood of Naboth, and the blood of his sons, saith the Lord; and I will requite thee in this plat, saith the Lord."

Thus the storms of God's threatenings often hang motionless for a long time, and restraining their destructive power, over the heads of his enemies. The Divine forbearance casts itself in their way, and restrains, for a time, the forked lightnings.

Happy they who, recognizing the value of this temporary suspension, hastily lay hold of the horns of the only altar, which can afford them safety and protection against the arrows of the Almighty! But on the contrary, woe to those who, drawing false inferences from the momentary calm, walk the broad road only the more securely, rocking themselves to rest by the delusive idea of a blind love, which rules in heaven, and of a God, who neither sees nor hears, though he created the eye and the ear. Ere they are aware, the hour of the most terrific unveiling arrives. The thunders of God begin to roll over them on high; the fiery flames burst the bounds which patience had hitherto prescribed them; and the doom of the unhappy mortals must serve as a foil and a candle to the solemn and appalling truth, that the Lord is a faithful God, both as regards his promises and his curses. Blessed is he who knows that the heavens above him are unclouded and serene! But who does so? Only he who is in Christ. "The just shall live by faith."

When Ahaziah perceived the fate of his royal host, he drove his horses at still greater speed, and hoped to escape a similar doom by fleeing to the royal summer-house. But Jehu's eagle eye had already discovered the fugitive, and he pursued him with equal rapidity. The same Divine judgment, however, impended over the head of the idolatrous Ahaziah, as over that of the execrable ruler of Israel. The trembling fugitive succeeded indeed in reaching Samaria, before his pursuers, but

only to be there overtaken, overpowered, and cut
down. And it was probably owing only to the respect and veneration, in which the memory of his
father, the excellent Jehoshaphat, was still cherished in Israel, that his corpse was not left a prey
to the dogs in the street, but given up to his servants to take to Jerusalem, and there be interred
in the family sepulchre.

After Ahaziah had met his fate, the judgment
followed on the queen-mother, that horrible woman,
who had been the chief and primary cause of all
the corruption which abounded in the land. Jehu
had taken the royal palace by storm; and just as
he was riding through the gate into the inner court,
Jezebel, decked out in all her finery, and surrounded by her courtly attendants, presented herself at
one of the upper windows of the palace, in order
to disarm Jehu by her meretricious arts; but, in
spite of the danger by which she saw herself menaced, she was unable to restrain the rage which
filled her heart, and called out to Jehu in cutting
irony, " Had Zimri peace, who slew his master?"
Zimri, it was well known, was the rebel who as-
sassinated the Israelitish sovereign, Elah, whilst
the latter was sitting drinking at a feast; and ascended the throne of his murdered sovereign in order, only seven days after, to succumb, in a dreadful manner, to Divine vengeance. Jezebel intended, therefore, in sarcastic language, to say, " Thou
regicide—thou second Zimri, what art thou doing?
Remember Zimri's fate!"

But Jehu took a welcome of this nature much

amiss. He lifted up his eyes, and perceiving the courtiers about the queen, said in a tone, which announced nothing good to the disaffected, "Who is on my side?" Two or three of the chamberlains, who had never stood in any other connection with their tyrannical mistress than that of self-interest, then gave him obvious signs that they were ready to join him and fulfil his command. "Well then," exclaimed Jehu, "throw her out of the window."

No sooner said than done. They laid hands on the accursed woman, and, notwithstanding her struggles and cries for mercy, cast her, unrelentingly, from the lofty window, into the court below. She was dashed upon the pavement; her blood was sprinkled on the wall, stained the horses' flanks, and the corpse was trodden under their feet; the brute beasts becoming the instruments of Divine vengeance.

After this horrible affair, Jehu repaired with his companions in arms to the castle, in order to rest from their bloody work, and partake of a jovial feast. Towards the close of the banquet, the victor addressing his servants, said to them, "Go, see now this cursed woman, and bury her, for she is a king's daughter." On going out, however, they found nothing but her skull, feet, and the palms of her hands. The rest of the carcass had been devoured by dogs. The servants returned with horror to Jehu, and informed him of the fact. The latter again lifted up his voice, as for a lamentation for the dead; but hear how his requiem over Jezebel sounds : " This is the word of the Lord, which he spake by his servant Elijah the Tishbite, saying. In the portion of Jezreel shall dogs eat the flesh of Jezebel: and the carcass of Jezebel shall be as dung upon the face of the field in the portion of Jezreel ; so that they shall not be able to say, This is Jezebel."

Such was the end of the proud Sidonian, who, immersed in the lusts and vanities of the world, made her body her idol, and found her paradise in the adoring homage and flattery of a slavishly devoted swarm of attendants. Here we learn to understand what is meant, when it is said, " He that sitteth in the heavens shall laugh ; the Lord shall have them in derision." And observe how remarkable ! She, who, whilst her ungodly heart still beat, was the bitterest enemy and persecutor of Elijah the Tishbite, after perishing thus horribly under the sword of the Divine wrath. is compelled, by her death, to make the most striking reparation to him whom she had trodden under foot : she who, during her lifetime, covered that friend of God with obloquy, must now be content to add increased lustre to his prophetic testimony. Oh, how holy is God in all his ways ! How faithfully he keeps his word ; and how fully and completely are his purposes eventually accomplished !

His vengeance proceeds further. Ahab had seventy male descendants, children and grandchildren, in Samaria. To the rulers, elders, and preceptors of these princes, Jehu wrote the following letter : " As soon as this letter cometh to you, seeing your master's sons are with you, and there are with you chariots and horses, a fenced city also, and armor; look even out the best and meetest of your master's sons, and set him on his father's throne, and fight for your master's house."

This is proudly spoken. "I do not intend," is his meaning, " to put you and your noble pupils clandestinely away. I challenge you to an open combat. Measure yourselves with me, and let battle decide the possession of the crown." The parties receive the bold and brief epistle, but terror and amazement overpower them at its perusal. "No," say they, "two kings stood not before him: how then shall we stand?" and they immediately sit down and reply in the most obedient and submissive manner, "We are thy servants, and will do all that thou shalt bid us; we will not make any king: do thou that which is good in thine eyes."

A second missive from the victor, to the following effect, is then sent them: "If ye be mine, and if ye will hearken to my voice, take ye the heads of the men, your master's sons, and come to me to Jezreel by to-morrow at this time." A horrible proposal; but still it is accepted. During the night, the rulers, with a troop of hired assassins, fall upon their pupils unawares, slay them one after another, then separate the heads of the murdered princes from their bodies, and send them off to the appointed place, according to orders. Oh, how worthless the friendship, favor, and fidelity of the world! Is it not like a tree planted in a loose and light soil: as long as it is held and supported, it seems kindly to extend its shade over thee; but when the storm howls through its topmost boughs, and it inclines to fall, it no longer regards thee, but crushes thee in its descent, that it may at least come to the ground more gently upon thy corpse.

Very soon after the order had been issued, the horrible and bloody objects, packed in baskets, arrive at Jehu's head-quarters. "And there came a messenger and told him, saying, They have brought the heads of the king's sons." Jehu shuddered at hearing the news; but, recovering himself, he says, "Lay ye them in two heaps at the entering in of the gate until the morning." His orders were silently obeyed, in the obscurity of the night. The next morning Jehu went out, approached the two horrible and bleeding pyramids, and said to the astonished multitude, "Ye be righteous;" that is, you are able to form a correct judgment; "behold, I conspired against my master, and slew him: but who slew all these?" "You must be aware," he intends to say, "that it was not I, who was the primary cause of this bloody overthrow, but that it is the result of a Divine procedure. For by whose hands did these seventy fall? Not by mine, but by those of their own rulers and preceptors." "Know now that there shall fall unto the earth nothing of the word of the Lord, which the Lord spake concerning the house of Ahab: for the Lord hath done that which he spake by his servant Elijah."

Such were the words of Jehu over the slain of the royal family of Israel; but the sword of the Lord was not yet satiated. The friends and great men of Ahab and Joram are numbered with the slain. There shall not a root or a twig remain of the royal house. Just as Jehu was marching towards Samaria, he was met, near the shearing-house, by a train of splendid equipages. On riding up to them, and inquiring of the strangers their names, rank, and the object of their journey, he was told that they are relations of Ahaziah, king of Judah, and that they were going to pay a visit to the children of Jezebel and Joram. "The Judge of Israel is therefore sending you also to the slaughter," thought Jehu, and commanded his people to take them alive. But on their attempting to execute his orders, a show of defence was made. This served as a signal for an immediate execution. Compassion and mercy were compelled to give way to the severity of the laws of war. Jehu's armor-bearers drag the princes from their chariots, slay them, one after the other, at the pit of the shearing-house, and cast their bodies into it. Of these princely victims, there were no less than forty-two.

The atmosphere in Israel is become increasingly oppressive. The arrows of God are hurled more and more fiercely and numerously at his enemies. Entire races are crushed beneath the weight of his avenging arm, even to the very root. The iniquities of the fathers are visited upon the children unto the third and fourth generation of them that hate him. Lord, when thou art wroth, who can withstand? When thou pourest forth thy fury, it consumes the adversaries like chaff. Woe unto those

to whom thou givèst to drink of the cup of thy vengeance !   They reel, totter, fall ; and who is there
that can raise them up again ?

Another massacre in Samaria succeeded the one
at the shearing-house.   Arrived in that city, Jehu
immediately assembled the people, and said unto
them, certainly with deceitful words, " Ahab served
Baal a little, but Jehu shall serve him much.   Now,
therefore, call unto me all the prophets of Baal, all
his servants, and all his priests : let none be wanting ; for I have a great sacrifice to do to Baal ;
whosoever shall be wanting, he shall not live."
Obedience is rendered to his command.   The
priests of Baal, from all parts of the country, assemble in the metropolis, and the immense temple
of Baal can scarcely contain the multitude.   And
Jehu sent for vestments for the idolaters, and said
unto them, " Search and look that there be here
with you none of the servants of the Lord, but the
worshippers of Baal only."   And the priests of
Baal obey his orders, and after assembling in the
court of sacrifice, they there begin to prepare their
idolatrous burnt-offerings.

Meanwhile, Jehu appointed fourscore men without, and issued the order of the day, saying, " If
any of the men whom I have brought into your
hands escape, he that letteth him go, his life shall
be for the life of him."   Those within now proceed
unsuspectingly to work, and begin to display the
follies and abominations of their Sidonian worship.
On this, Jehu gives the previously appointed signal
to his warriors, who rush in, draw their weapons,

and whilst Jehu exclaims, "Go in and slay them; let none come forth," penetrate into the temple, fall upon the idolatrous priests, and before the latter can cry for mercy, slay them with the edge of the sword, and leave them lying in their blood.

After the slaughter of the lying prophets was completed, and not one of them left, they fell upon the temple itself. The pillars are dragged out and burned, the statue of the idol Baal is dashed into a thousand pieces, the pagoda itself demolished, and its halls and courts turned into a receptacle for all the filth of the city. Thus was Baal rooted out of Israel, and the Divine sentence, pronounced years before on the house of Ahab, and the servants of Baal, fully executed. Truly, "not one word of all that the Lord had spoken" by the mouth of his prophets had fallen to the ground. Every syllable of the predicted curse had been like the cloud as big as a man's hand, from whence proceeded an awful thunder-storm; every word had been a destructive mine, and Jehu the firebrand cast into it by the hand of an offended God.

II. The appalling events, which have just been unfolded before you, speak to us in a language so extremely loud and intelligible, that it seems scarcely necessary to add to them a personal application. I feel, however, impelled to direct your attention expressly to their general contents, and more fully to expose the sting they carry with them, which it would perhaps be impossible to render more acute, and to turn it against ourselves.

Behold the Lord standing over the bleeding corpses of the malefactors, who have fallen beneath the sword of his vengeance! What an idea does it convey to us of the living God and his character! Where are now the mawkish sentiments of his nature and attributes, of which the world so gladly dreams! Where do we find, in this representation, the modern " Universal Father," devoid of power and consistency, and that universal love, with which, in the end, every worthless individual consoles himself? A consuming fire is here unveiled to us. Here is a God of wrath and of vengeance, who hath no pleasure in iniquity, and who is " angry with the wicked every day." Let every one, therefore, take good heed on what footing he stands with such a Master. He that has no other ground of consolation than the idea of God's universal goodness, or than that which he derives from his own store of virtue, grossly miscalculates. The man may, from that which is his own, carry fuel to the fire which is to consume him, but no flower to the garland of his salvation, no water to extinguish the flames which his sins have kindled. " Other foundation can no man lay, than that is laid, which is Jesus Christ."

Listen! Ezekiel the prophet, as you will read in the eighth chapter of his book, was one day sitting in his house, when the hand of the Lord came upon him, and a variety of Divine visions were afforded to the man thus gifted with the spirit of prophecy. They were visions of an awful and terrible kind. The Lord himself appeared to him, not in the mild radiance of his benignity, but in the fiery splendor of his judicial majesty. He took him by the hair of his head, as the prophet relates, and carried him to Jerusalem, to the door of the inner gate, where was the image of jealousy, which provoketh the Lord to jealousy. And God said to the seer, "Seest thou what they do? even the great abominations that the house of Israel committeth here, that I should go far off from my sanctuary; but turn thee yet again, and thou shalt see greater abominations." And the Lord brought him to the door of the court, where was a hole in the wall, and the Lord said unto him, "Dig now in the wall;" and when he had dug through the wall, what a horrible spectacle presented itself to his view! There was nothing but wicked abominations, "every form of creeping things, and abominable beasts, and all the idols of the house of Israel." Before them stood the elders offering incense; for they said, "The Lord seeth us not; the Lord hath forsaken the earth." There were "women weeping for Tammuz;" priests turning their backs to the temple, and worshipping the sun; and various other abominations which were seen by the prophet. Then said the Lord to the seer, "Therefore will I also deal in fury; mine eye shall not spare, neither will I have pity; and though they cry in mine ears with a loud voice, yet will I not hear them."

"Son of man, dig now in the wall!" Such is the message this day unto us. And this is not to be done in Jerusalem, or in Israel, but in our own Christian country, and especially in our own city, our own congregation, and our own hearts. Our native land has a good character, and presents a specious appearance. This is the wall through which we are to dig. For this land forms one of the brightest spots in the whole earth. For where do we meet with a better regulated government, and wiser rulers? Where is public tranquillity better preserved, or industry, in every department, more abundant? Where does science flourish more, or is greater encouragement given to the arts? Where do civilization, intellectuality, loyalty, and patriotism more abound than in our native land? a land and nation distinguished above all others by flourishing schools, benevolent institutions, liberality towards laudable objects, and a cosmopolite susceptibility for all that is good and beautiful even in foreign countries,—a land and nation, which recognizes moral worth, and appreciates man according to education, and a righteous standard; a people, who leave it to other nations to wear themselves away by intestine divisions, and to brand themselves by treason,—a quiet, faithful people, on whom reliance may be placed, and who are inclined to move when the common weal demands. Such a people are we, and viewed from a distance, it might be said that a national fast, such as we are in a few days to celebrate, is perfectly unnecessary with regard to us, and may be very proper in this place or that, but least of all in Germany and in Prussia.

"Son of man, dig now in the wall: and when I had digged in the wall, behold a door. And he

said unto me, Go in, and behold the wicked abominations that they do here." And as I went in and
looked, oh how much of that specious appearance vanished away, and a heavy black cloud
ascended before me, which was the sins of my
people. I broke through into the dwellings of the
noble and the great ; and lo, there they stood in an
extended circle all kinds of images, and a dense
cloud of incense enveloped them. One was doing
idolatrous service to Mammon ; another burned incense before a golden chain, which he wore round
his neck ; another bent his knee before an airy
deity, which he called " Title ;" a fourth before a
similar one, termed by him " Grace and Favor,"
but not the favor for which David prayed. And
many other images glared around ; but thou, O
God, wast forgotten by all !

And I dug through the wall, behind which the
priests and Levites sat, and listened to them "between the porch and the altar," and behold, the majority, at least many of them, turned their backs to
the true temple and altar, and worshipped towards
the rising of the sun, and were blind leaders of the
blind, crying, " Peace, peace !" when there was no
peace, daubing with untempered mortar, and de-
ceiving the people every way ; selling self-made
glass corals for genuine pearls, and adulterating the
word of God ; counting the blood of the lamb an
unholy thing ; exterminating the Lord Christ, and
tearing from him the priestly and kingly crown,
in order to place it upon their own heads. Then
remembered I the word of the Lord, saying, " Be-

hold, I will turn upon the shepherds, and require my flock at their hands ! Woe unto you shepherds, that destroy and scatter the sheep of my pasture ! Howl and lament ; sit in ashes, ye rulers of the flock."

And I digged again, and I was in the universities, amongst the masters in Israel, the learned in the Scriptures, and behold, there was the seat of the image of jealousy ; pride upon his forehead, impudence in his look, and many blasphemous speeches in his mouth. "Philosophy" was his haughty name, and vile seduction his work and object. And the image spoke in lofty language ; at one time, that there was no God ; at another, that all things were God ; and then again, that God was only an idea, the produce of the human mind ; —and he called Jesus, "the sage of Nazareth," but himself, Wisdom ; the Scriptures, "a useful book," his own doctrine, "the sure and universal truth." Many lay prostrate at the feet of the image ; hosts of students with their teachers, whilst the Lord Jehovah was entirely banished from the place. Then thought I of the word of the Lord, "The learned regard me no longer, and the pastors lead away the people from me; they are all become foolish, and regard not the work of the Lord." And an immense deluge inundated the land, boundless and interminable, consisting of pamphlets, books, and manuscripts. Many of them indeed bore the title of religious ; but on looking into them, I found the light had become darkness, the gold had become dim ; nothing but falsehood under the semblance of

truth; and the Lord Jesus was saluted in them
with a traitor's kiss. The spirit of unbelief and antichrist stared at me out of a thousand pages, and
blasphemed the Almighty· on his throne, by pretending to praise him, and ridiculed the word of
God under the pretence of saying fine things respecting it.

I mingled with the people. The whited wall of
specious appearances fell down; and oh what horrible abominations presented themselves to view!
Infidelity reigned universally; amongst the noble
and the great, it was called "politeness," and by
the lower classes "enlightening." The children
brought it from school with them, the young made
it their recommendation in the world. The men
regarded it as something to be proud of. The
women boasted of it as an accomplishment. The
righteous were pointed at with the finger, as fools;
and the pious were the scorn and contempt of the
people.

On looking deeper, I saw a vapor rise up out of
the yawning abyss, like a dense and poisonous ma-
laria, which spread itself over the whole country.
Ungodliness brought forth, and her brood was horrible and innumerable. Where shall I begin, where
end the numbering up of the sins of my people?
Shall I describe to you the evil spirit of speculation
amongst the merchants, the ungodly discontent
which pervades the class of mechanics, the licentiousness and immorality of the rising generation?
Shall I remind you of the irreligous eagerness for
pomp and show, for amusement and pleasure?

Shall I unfold to you the resorts of dissipation, and how they increase and prosper more and more? or open before you the gaming-houses, ball-rooms, and gin-shops, with their noisy assemblies; and those abominable haunts, in addition, which are of themselves sufficient to draw down the thunders of eternal wrath upon a land and nation?

"Son of man, dig now in the wall!" And I digged, and beheld all manner of wicked abominations, and saw "every form of creeping things, and abominable beasts," and many thousand idols, before which stood young and old, men and women, high and low, priests and laymen, superiors and inferiors; and every man had his censer in his hand, and a thick cloud of incense went up. Such is the state of things behind the wall. Therefore toll the bell for a fast, till the rope breaks. Let the whole country hear the sound, and all the people sit weeping upon ashes, if so be that the Lord may again have mercy!

But let us come nearer home. Shall I, according to the Divine command, dig through the wall, and conjure up, unveiled before you, what lies hidden in the darkness, and shuns the light? Shall I break through the wall of your families, and tell you of all the unhappy marriages amonst us, and the ill-conducted households in the midst of us? Shall I show you the eyes, red with weeping, of ill-treated females, the bodily and spiritual misery of neglected children?

"Son of man, dig now in the wall!" Shall I do so, and expose what takes place in your societies and assemblies? Shall I recount to you the idle talk, which there is heard, the scandalizing tongues which are there set in motion, and the poisoned arrows, which are there darted so uncharitably against God and our neighbor? Do you wish me to break through the wall of the specious appearance, which envelopes our religious assemblies, and point out to you the multitude of those, who are only here to tread down the sanctuary of their God, to fetch materials for uncharitable judging, or to find occasion for blaspheming the word of the Lord; or those, who loathe our manna as light food, and are filled to satiety with the most costly things which Heaven can bestow? Or, finally, shall I also break through the specious wall of an outward respectability, behind which so many amongst us creep, and shall I set before the eyes of these whitewashed sepulchres their pharisaic self-righteousness, and unveil the corrupt and sinful recesses of their hearts, and lay open and bare the pestilential ulcers of their souls? Oh no! I beseech you, excuse me from doing this. Let it suffice for me to assure you, that every thing which is able to cause the curse of God to descend upon a people, exists in our native land, and even in this congregation, so richly favored for so long a period. Only dig through the wall, and behold! The sight is truly appalling; how, then, can the prospect be otherwise? "He that hath ears to hear, let him hear."

When Ezekiel had dug through the wall, and seen the wicked abominations which were practised in Jerusalem, the Lord opened his mouth and said, " Therefore will I also deal in fury ; mine eye shall not spare, neither will I have pity ; and though they cry in mine ears with a loud voice, yet will I not hear them." So saying, he himself dug through the wall, through that which hid the future from the eyes of the prophet, and let the seer behold the dreadful judgments and horrible tempests, which should ere long disburden themselves upon the devoted city.

My brethren, our knees would also tremble, and our hair stand on end, were it to please God for a moment to remove the wall which conceals the future from us, and place before our eyes the judgments which are perhaps already determined upon in the council of the invisible watchers, one day to fall upon the Laodicean Christianity of this country. Much forbearance has already been exercised towards the lifeless church, and it has been allured to repentance in every way, by kindness and severity. " Go up," said Elijah once to his servant, " and look towards the sea ;" and he went up and looked, and said, " Behold, there arises a little cloud out of the sea, like a man's hand." And Elijah said, " Go up, say unto Ahab, Prepare thy chariot, and get thee down, that the rain stop thee not." Do not we also perceive, in the distance, something similar to that which Elijah's servant saw ? God alone knows how and where the rod is to be made ; but it certainly is preparing. His anger must kindle ! That God, who gave up Jerusalem to the spoilers, and in his wrath did not even spare his Israel,—he who is certainly merciful, but must also continue just in all his ways, will not always keep silence; for he weighs with a just balance, and the mountain of our sins reaches unto the skies. Oh, my country, that thou wouldest consider what belongs to thy peace! Oh earth, hear the word of the Lord; consider thy ways, and repent!

But let us turn our eyes away from distant objects, and direct them again upon ourselves. What have we to expect, should ungodliness and frivolity continue to burst their barriers, and set at defiance all the invitations and admonitions of the Almighty? What will become of us, with this predominant Laodicean lukewarmness, this obtuseness and disgusting satiety which prevails amongst so many? The word of God here digs through the wall for us. As saith the Lord, Hosea v. 12, "Therefore will I be unto Ephraim as a moth, and to the house of Judah as rottenness." By this is pointed out the manner, in which an angry God is wont to visit churches like ours; churches in which his candlestick is placed, and where his light and truth reside; where there is still left unto him a seed, and many a Noah and Daniel lift up noly hands to him in heaven. He is not wont to dash such churches to pieces with a stroke, nor to lay them waste with a tempest; for there are righteous amongst them, who must not be swept away with the unrighteous. To such churches he does not come as a lion, suddenly to tear them in pieces; nor does he judge them like Korah's troop, who were swallowed up by the yawning gulf; nor like the Philistines, who were buried by one tremendous fall, when Samson, taking hold of the pillars of the temple, rent them in his rage. In churches like our own, he is "to Ephraim as a moth, and to the house of Judah as rottenness." His curse then eats its way very secretly and gradually; and the fall is like that of a worm-eaten beam, and of a ruinous, or maliciously undermined building. Instead of fire and brimstone, a destructive mildew falls upon it from above; and it descends upon it like a pestiferous vapor, which at first is scarcely observable; and the church expires, not as beneath the axe or sword, but as by a secret epidemic and an evil insinuating disease. Then is imperceptibly fulfilled what the Lord said to Isaiah, "Make the heart of this people fat, and make their ears heavy, and shut their eyes; lest they see with their eyes, and hear with their ears, and understand with their heart, and convert, and be healed." The preaching of the Gospel then becomes an opiate to the people, yea, a pool of stagnant water, from whence arises a savor of death. The little flock of the righteous gradually enter their eternal home; but their vacant places remain unoccupied; nothing flourishes any longer on that soil. Awakenings and conversions are no longer heard of, nor any pe culiar manifestations of the Spirit; but a death-like silence reigns, and an awful desert permanently extends itself over the field of spiritual declension. Zion's harps no longer sound, the rust consumes their strings; the temples of God are deserted; the paths of Zion lie waste; the priests bear their testimony discouraged, and lament in her courts; and it is not long before they too are gone, and their places are filled by false prophets and lying priests, invited by the people to prophesy smooth things to them. The candlestick is now removed from the sanctuary, and the people are without a king, without an offering, "and without teraphim," and the Lord has returned to his place. No one any longer knows him; nothing more is perceived, felt, or tasted, of his gracious presence. All connection with him is at an end. The heavens are like iron and brass. The clouds are forbidden to rain upon the vineyard; and no intercession avails to turn away the wrath of the Almighty. The Lord says, "Though Moses and Samuel stood before me, yet my mind could not be toward this people." Hell receives one victim after another, and no one takes it to heart that they are carried away like chaff, and like shadows which the wind dispels.

Thus it is, that the Lord is to impenitent Ephraim as a moth, and to the house of Judah as rottenness. O God, who art a consuming fire, and an avenging God, how terrible art thou to those that hate thee! How awful is the path of thy feet, when thou walkest forth in thine anger! The hills smoke with thy wrath, and the earth trembles at thy rebuke! O Lord, trembling comes upon us, and our bones quake. Turn away thy rod, and take thy terrors from us. Lord, spare thy people, and let not thine inheritance be put to shame, lest the heathen mock at them. Thou knowest, O Lord, our frame. We prostrate ourselves before thee, not on the ground of our own righteousness, but of thy mercy. Let mercy triumph over justice, and have compassion upon us! But then, O Lord, teach us also thy ways, and make straight our paths, and hear us when we entreat thee, saying,

Thy life, O Lord! to us impart,
  Draw us with mighty power above;
Write thy commands upon our heart,
  And fill them with thine ardent love.

Thine image may we all express;
  Our souls supply with heavenly food;
Then shall the world with truth confess,
  Thou cam'st with water, and with blood.

III.—JONADAB AND HIS HOUSE

ONE of the most consolatory passages in the book of life, is, the Divine invitation recorded in Isaiah lv. 1: "Ho, every one that thirsteth, come ye to the waters, and he that hath no money; come ye, buy and eat; yea, come, buy wine and milk without money and without price." What a garland of the most valuable consolations from the garden of Divine grace! Certainly, it is not intended for those who are spiritually rich, self-sufficient, and powerful; it belongs only to those, who, like the woman in the Gospel, have expended all their substance on physicians, and yet are not healed. But there are doubtless many amongst us, who, no longer "riding upon horses," would heartily rejoice, if some compassionate Samaritan would set them on his mule and bring them to the inn of Divine mercy, attend upon them there, and pay their expenses. May the bosoms of such triumphantly expand at the glorious words, "They shall be abundantly satisfied with the fatness of thy house; and thou shalt make them drink of the river of thy pleasures;" and may the tongues of the former be loosened, to exclaim with Esau, "Hast thou but one blessing, my father? Bless me, even me also, O my father!"

The invitation we have quoted at the commencement, begins with an exclamation well calculated to excite the attention, and rouse the feelings. They are not the words of man, but sound down to us from the throne of the Almighty. The invitation is from the Lord God himself. Do not be horrified at this, ye sinners! It is not a summons to the bar of judgment, but an invitation to sacred blessings and eternal joys. You exclaim with astonishment, " We?" Yes, you who feel that you are transgressors. For know, that the cheering invitation does not descend from the skies as an arbitrary announcement; but rests on the wonders of Bethlehem and Golgotha. The Divine message is written in your Surety's blood; and hence, when Divine grace prepared it, the holiness, justice, and truth of God countersigned it.

Those to whom this heavenly invitation is addressed, are designated as "thirsty," and "without money." There is no need of any further qualification to enter the Lord's sanctuary. Thirst is a necessity, painfully felt. We are all thirsty and needy by nature, but we do not all of us know it, and willingly hear of it. The world, as respects the majority of its children, is like a lunatic asylum, where the maddest fancies exercise dominion; where, for instance, beggars dream that they are kings; cowards that they are heroes; and slaves sing liberty songs. Who shall heal them of their delusions? Human art avails not. Each one con-

tinues his folly, till God steps in, and with his
" Ephphatha!" dissolves the charm.   The dominion
of the imagination then terminates, the foolish fancies, depart, the naked reality unveils itself and in
the soul, thus come to itself, a thirst unknown before
enkindles, no longer for the stupefying draughts of
the world's pleasures, but a thirsting after the living
God and his mercy.   To the necessitous of this
kind is the invitation addressed.   To the spiritually
weary and heavy laden are the words of eternal
love directed.

The Divine invitation finds the people assembled
as at a fair ; shop upon shop presents itself to our
view ; signs all around in the most party-colored variety; noises on all sides, and pompous commenda-
tion of the wares on sale. Here a moralist of the most
modern fashion is seen abundantly provided with
" mirrors of virtue" for the higher classes ; promising " cheerfulness of mind," and a " meeting again
after death."   And what is the price of such valu-
ables ?   A modicum of propriety, and a little charity towards the poor.   And what is the inscription
on his sign ?   " We all believe in the same God,"
is his kind and all-conciliating, all-amalgamating
motto.   Here is another from Gamaliel's school.
" If you wish to go to heaven," is his language,
" say your prayers, attend church, read daily por-
tions, and keep fast and feast days."   A great
crowd surrounds this pedler's shop, and every one
commends the cheapness of his wares ; and before
we are aware, a spiritual rosary is seen in the hands
of many of them.   There is another in monkish

attire, with a gloomy visage, and downcast eyes ; and what are his directions ? " Renounce all pleasure, assume a sorrowful look, leave the world, and fast in sackcloth and ashes. The crown shall then be yours." Here comes a fourth, more worthy of attention than the former, though less popular, soon recognized as a disciple of Moses, with the words upon his sign, " Do this, and thou shalt live ;" and whoever could pay the price, would certainly gain his end. A perfect obedience to the Divine law, says he, will secure the crown. But who can furnish the sum required, since poverty has become so general ? He that would attempt the payment. would only reap the consciousness of his insufficiency. But look yonder at a fifth, who promises salvation to a perfectly matured faith in the Lord Jesus, and an ardent and active love. He is nearer the truth than the rest, and yet still very far from it. But mark how many of those, who surround his booth, are desirous of attempting to comply with the requirement. You perceive, however, how others hang down their heads, and with a sigh exclaim, " Where lies the mine, from which such faith and love are procured ?" The latter have already vainly attempted to furnish the sum required.

Hear a sixth, exclaiming. " Overcome the world, yourself, and Satan with his crew !" And many prepare for the fight, and triumphantly exclaim. " We will be kings in our own right, and according to the principles of rectitude and the laws of the kingdom, ascend from one degree of holiness to another, till we gain the crown." "Go on," is our response; make the attempt, and let us see the result. A seventh—but this may suffice. You see, the one requires this—the other that. Requirements are made by all; there is neither measure nor limit to them; and the confusion is great. But which of these advisers is to be believed, and which of the ways, thus recommended, are to be entered upon? Inquiry is made, and investigation instituted. On a sudden, a mighty voice resounds through the noisy fair. It is the voice of God. "What are ye bargaining for with each other?" exclaims the Lord. "Wherefore do ye spend money for that which is not bread? and your labor for that which satisfieth not? Hearken diligently unto me, and eat ye that which is good.—Come, by wine and milk, without money and without price." This call becomes a storm, which overturns all the booths of the tradesmen, and, where it is understood, alarms the market-place. For what else is it, but the final decision, that all this bargaining is but deception, and that salvation is not obtainable at any such price? The payment for eternal blessings has been made; and that which we have to do, is only to accept and appropriate them. The tree of life is planted; we have only to shake it, and eat of its fruit. The hunger of the soul is the valid claim to the Divine provisions. The New Testament belongs to the poor in spirit. The publican and sinner, with the wounded soul, possess the kingdom of heaven. They are kings, and many dwell in peaceful tabernacles. Oh, great and blissful thought! Our present meditation, as well as the following one, will tend to draw aside the veil still further.

2 KINGS X. 15

" And when he was departed thence, he lighted on Jehonadab the son of Rechab, coming to meet him; and he saluted him."

To judge from appearances, it would seem that we should soon reach the close of our meditation on that portion of the history we have selected; and yet this brief and limited text presents to us a richer harvest of ideas than we shall be able to reap and carry home in a single hour. We have now no longer to do only with Jehu, the Lord's dreadful scourge, but form a new acquaintance, which I think will afford us greater pleasure than that of the furious character, whose appearance filled us only with astonishment and dread. Jehonadab, the Rechabite, meets us. Let us, for the present, turn our entire attention to him; and consider, first, his person; and then the society he established. And may the Spirit of the Lord God breathe fructifyingly and animatingly over our thoughts and words!

I. We have arrived, as you will remember, at a portentous period of Israel's history. Jehu, in consequence of a Divine message from the Lord, has been anointed king—has received horrible commissions—and is instructed to open the sluices of the foaming flood of Divine vengeance against the house of Ahab and the priests of Baal. He has already begun his work. Streams of blood have been shed. You have already heard of the fall and dreadful end of Joram, Ahaziah, and the female abomination, Jezebel. You have also been told how Ahab's seventy descendants fell a prey to the sword in Samaria, and how the same fate befell two-and-forty of Ahaziah's relatives, at the shearing-house. Thus was Ahab's family swept away from the earth, both root and branch, and the awful inscription glowed, in gloomy and flaming characters, over the tomb of the slain, "Who can abide his wrath, or stand when he is angry?" "It is a fearful thing to fall into the hands of the living God."

On Jehu's victorious return from the sanguinary attack upon the last who had fallen, he is met by the individual with whom we have at present to do. "Jehonadab" is his name; "the son of Rechab," his description. Who is this Rechab? According to 1 Chron. ii. 55, he belonged to the tribe of the Kenites. But this little people, in their peculiarities, deserve to be better known. Let us therefore search for them in the sacred page; we shall soon find traces of them.

We meet with them, first of all, in the second chapter of Exodus. Moses, with a holy but mistaken zeal, had slain an Egyptian, whom he saw illtreating one of his Hebrew brethren; and on perceiving that the affair became known, he fled, from the wrath of Pharaoh, to Midian, a district in Arabia, which lies east of Sinai. After solitarily wandering for a time in the desert, he at length finds, at a well which he reaches, the first signs of population, and his supposition becomes certainty on the approach of a bevy of damsels, who were driving before them a flock of sheep, and bearing in their hands pitchers and buckets, with which to water them. At the same moment, a troop of rude shepherds rush forth from the bushy wilderness to drive away the young girls, and to make use of the well themselves. Moses now stepped forward on behalf of the oppressed females, and rebuked these turbulent sons of the desert so severely, that they retired to a distance astonished, and no longer ventured to prevent the stranger from drawing water for the damsels himself, and helping them to water their flocks. Most agreeably surprised by the unexpected assistance of the benevolent stranger, the maidens hasten back to their encampment, and the first person they meet, in its vicinity, is their grandfather Reguel, who expresses his astonishment at seeing them return so early. They do not leave him long in suspense about the cause of it, and circumstantially relate the terror they were in, when an Egyptian man protected them against the rudeness of the shepherds, drew·water for them, and, with his own hand, watered their flocks. The old man, on hearing this, was grieved that, forgetting the sacred duties of hospitality, they had suffered the obliging individual to pursue his way, instead of inviting him to their father's tents ; and after having seriously reproved his granddaughters, he sent them back, saying, "Go and look for the man, and if you find him, urge him to come and eat bread with us." The damsels yield a willing obedience, and have not penetrated far into the wilderness, before they are again met by the friendly stranger, who is easily induced to accept their invitation. On their return to the tents with their new guest, they meet their father Jethro, and having also informed him how nobly and boldly the stranger had taken their part, the latter is cordially welcomed by the worthy people, and urged to continue in their quiet social circle as long as he pleases. How gladly is the invitation accepted by the stranger, who had never imagined, that in this remote part of the desert he should have met with such a reception; for it is not long, ere, to his great and joyful surprise, he ascertains that he is not only amongst kind and sociable people, but that he has entered the circle of those, who are companions in the faith, and partakers of the same spirit. The little tribe know and worship the true God. Jethro is even a priest of God and a preacher of his name. Moses, who had never had an idea of a church of God out of Israel, feels greatly surprised, having believed that this wilderness was inhabited solely by savage idolaters—but now sees himself surrounded by brethren in the Lord, and feels himself under the influence of a Divine life and a sanctified love. His satisfaction is great; and that of the amiable family, after a mutual commmunication of their inmost thoughts, not less so. Their guest naturally wishes to know in what way Divine truth had reached them; and learns that this favored tribe are descendants of Midian, the son of Abraham and Keturah

He hears that a rich vein of Divine manifestation had been handed down to them by their forefathers, although it was scarcely any longer visible amongst the majority of the people, from the mass of heathenish error which had attached itself to it. In one family, however, that of the Kenites, it had been preserved pure and unmingled; and to this family, which must not be confounded with the Canaanitish Kenites, they were privileged to belong.

Moses listens to this statement with emotion and astonishment, and with his new found brethren, praises the Lord and his faithfulness. He feels, at the same time, that he will not soon be able to leave these dear people; and in a short time becomes united to them by other bonds than those of the same faith. He becomes attached to Jethro's daughter; she returns his love; her father joyfully grants them his benediction, and Zipporah becomes the wife of the beloved stranger. Moses, rendered thus happy, praises the Lord for his guidance with an overflowing heart. When afterwards seizing at early dawn his shepherd's crook, and joyfully leading forth the flock; when reclining on the quiet and herbaceous pastures of Horeb, surrounded by his fleecy charge, and yielding himself up undisturbed to a train of thought; when returning with the flocks in the evening, he is welcomed half way by his beloved Zipporah, and then, with those that belong to him, is able to give vent to his thoughts in holy discourse or animated hymns of praise, the harp of his heart continually resounds with songs of thanksgiving and rejoicing. The wish to return to

Egypt is silent in his breast; the idea of passing
the remainder of his life in this pleasing solitude,
satisfies his soul. But if he suppose he has really
found the object of his vocation in this harmless
sphere of life, he merely dreams a pleasing dream.
In the council of the invisible watchers it is otherwise decreed; nay, the time is already arriving,
when the peaceful shepherd's crook in his hand must
give place to a staff of a very different kind.

The word of the Lord goes forth to him out of
the bush, which burned and yet "was not consumed,"—that significant type of the church of God
here on earth, which is continually exposed to the
fire of persecution, but never consumed, because
God is in it. Moses is commanded to exchange his
beloved shepherd's crook for the wonder-working
staff of the chief in command over Israel, and the
quiet flowery meadows for the scene of conflict.
He returns to Egypt, inflicts, in the Lord's name,
horrible plagues on the land, and during the execution of these judgments, gives the signal for departure, and brings forth the Lord's host from
thence with a high hand. The Lord is visibly with
them. The Red Sea grants a dry passage through
its wavy walls, in order afterwards to bury their
pursuing foes, both man and horse, in the floods.
The bitter spring of the desert is miraculously rendered sweet, and fit to drink. At the proper time,
Elim, with its palm-trees and cool springs of water
unfolds itself before them, as a testimony of Jehovah's kindness and grace. The clouds rain down
manna to the hungry; the smitten rock presents

the desired refreshment to the thirsty; Amalek is quelled by the lifted hands of Moses; and Israel victoriously encamps at the foot of Horeb.

Here Moses was one day surprised by a most pleasing visit. Jethro, his father-in-law, appears in his tent, and in his train, Zipporah, who had remained behind at her father's, together with their two sons, Gershom and Eliezer. Moses gives them a most cordial welcome, and immediately begins to relate to them "all that the Lord had done unto Pharaoh and to the Egyptians for Israel's sake, and all the travail that had come upon them by the way, and how the Lord delivered them." And Jethro, deeply affected by all the kindness which the Lord had manifested towards his people, breaks out aloud into Jehovah's praises, exclaiming, "Blessed be the Lord, who hath delivered you out of the hand of the Egyptians, and out of the hand of Pharaoh! Now I know that the Lord is greater than all gods; for in the thing wherein they dealt proudly he was above them." And Jethro "took a burnt-offering and sacrifices," and offered them in thankful adoration to the Lord. And Aaron and the elders of Israel came thither to eat bread with Moses' father-in-law before God. But the next day, when Moses sat to judge the people, and Jethro saw the fatigue which his son-in-law underwent, and felt convinced that he could scarcely get through the work, he gave him some advice with respect to the administration of his rule in Israel, the wisdom of which Moses recognized, and therefore lent a willing ear to it.

After Jethro had spent several happy days in the camp, he departed, and leaving Zipporah and her children with Moses, returned to Midian, not to remain there, but soon, at the request of his son-in-law, to join himself with Israel for the future. Moses had said to him, " We are journeying unto the place of which the Lord said, I will give it you : come thou with us, and we will do thee good : for the Lord hath spoken good concerning Israel.— Leave us not, 1 pray thee ; forasmuch as thou knowest how we are to encamp in the wilderness, and thou mayest be to us instead of eyes. And it shall be, if thou go with us, that what goodness the Lord shall do unto us, the same will we do unto thee." Such were the words of Moses, and they produced their effect in the sequel, although not immediately. It cannot be clearly ascertained whether Jethro himself returned ; but Jethro's house, his family, his relatives, and others of the tribe of the Kenites, believers like himself in the only true God, forsook their native land, and joined the wandering train of the chosen race, never to leave it again.

Hence we find, from that period, in the retinue of Israel, a people, who, though not in reality belonging to Israel, were nevertheless most closely and intimately connected with them. We meet with them also in an advantageous position, participating in every thing of a pleasing nature which Israel enjoyed. With them they dwell under the shadow of the sacred cloud ; with them they partake of the bread from on high, without sharing in their burdens ; with them they drink of the refreshing stream, which flowed so wondrously from the rocks; and repose with them under the pinions of the same Divine and protecting grace. They are like the swallows, which build their nests under the cornices of the temple. They share, gratuitously and without trouble, in every thing with which Israel is favored.

When the Israelites took possession of the promised land, the Kenites were not wanting there. They likewise walked dry-shod over the bed of the Jordan, without participating in the previous anxiety respecting the mode of passing the rapid stream. From that time, as appears from Judges i. 16, they connected themselves, by preference, with the tribe of Judah—doubtless because of the great things promised the latter—and selected their district for their habitation, but modestly kept themselves on the extreme boundary, where they lived a patriarchal life in the greatest simplicity, moderation, and unassuming manner. They did not even build houses, but continued satisfied with tabernacles, or movable tents, as if they intended to give expression to their views of the present state of existence, as a pilgrimage and a journey homewards, by the manner of their outward life in this world. Many of them seem to have given a preference to intellectual occupations; for in 1 Chron. ii. 55, they are called "scribes," or learned men. Hence, in their position as connected with Israel, they might almost be compared to the historiographers, naturalists, and painters of modern times, who frequently attach themselves to some great expedition for con-

quest or discovery, not with the intention of sharing
in the conflicts, dangers, and fatigues connected
therewith, but only to profit thereby intellectually,
scientifically, and artistically, with this exception,
that the Kenites were in pursuit of a nobler object:
and in the footsteps of the people whom they followed, plucked flowers which exhaled Divine per-
fume; and from Israel's experience, collected paint-
ings, the colors of which have not faded in the
stream of time. The Kenites, as appears from a
variety of hints given us in the Bible, continually
cherished a vigorous and active life of faith; and
not unfrequently presented, in the days of religious
desolation, the only verdant oasis to be met with
in the large and dreary spiritual waste. Though
Israel revolted, yet they never polluted themselves
by the service of strange gods; and yet we find no
trace of Israel's being ever hostile towards them;
so that it appears, on the contrary, that they always thought highly of these guests of theirs, and
with pleasure entertained them.

In the sequel, a family sprung up amongst the
tribe of the Kenites, which pre-eminently shines
forth in the severity of its faith, and the riches of
its spiritual endowments. This the family of the
Rechabites, which gradually increased to a considerable community. Its patriarch was Rechab, a
venerable and extraordinarily enlightened individual. But he, who, as we shall subsequently find,
impressed the stamp of a regularly established spiritual fraternity upon his highly favored kindred,
was " Jehonadab, the son of Rechab," the same

whom we see, in the portion of the history at present under consideration, meeting with Jehu, and greeted and treated by him with such undissembled veneration. But even the Rechabites themselves were not admitted into Israel's citizenship and covenant of circumcision; of which, however, they were the less desirous, the more acutely they were able to distinguish between Israel after the flesh, and the spiritual Israel; between the outwardly typical, and the essential inward circumcision. They were satisfied with being tolerated amongst the Israelites as guests and neighbors; and they had reason for being so, since the burden of the law fell solely upon the children of Israel, whilst their fellowship with Israel limited itself almost entirely to the enjoyment of the favors which God was wont so abundantly to bestow upon his people. How gloriously does Jehovah's faithfulness manifest itself in this little people, in honoring and blessing his friend Abraham, even in his seed by Keturah! What a hopeful light also does this people afford us with respect to the whole heathen world, whilst inducing us to think, that many a living stream may have, at that period, flowed through it, and many of God's real children have existed in various places, who, though they did not adapt themselves to the forms and customs of Israel, were, nevertheless, permitted to claim an equal birthright with reference to the spirit and to faith.

II. We shall not regret making a closer acquaintance with the Rechabites. The Scriptures present us with the desired opportunity. Let us unite its scattered traces into one description. We have already heard from whence the Rechabites took their name. They inherited it from their venerable progenitor, Rechab the Kenite; but their rules and regulations were given them by Jonadab, Rechab's worthy descendant. But what rules? Jeremiah, chap. xxxv. gives you information respecting them. The prophet there, by Divine command, adduces the Rechabites to the children of Israel, as patterns of faithfulness and obedience. He publicly addresses the Rechabites in the presence of the people; on which, the former, with amiable simplicity, unfold the whole of their peculiar mode of life. They had existed for three centuries, as a regulated and closely united community in Israel, during the whole of which period, they had continued what they were; and amidst all the vicissitudes of circumstances and situations, to which they were exposed, they had remained firm in spite of the imitable spirit of the times, in their adherence to the statutes and ordinances of Jonadab their ancestor. The nature of these statutes we have from their own lips. "Jonadab," say they, when the prophet offered them a goblet of wine, to give them an occasion for stating the secret of their bond of fellowship: "Jonadab the son of Rechab our father commanded us, saying, Ye shall drink no wine, neither ye, nor your sons for ever. Neither shall ye build house, nor sow seed, nor plant vineyard, nor have any; but all your days ye shall dwell in tents; that ye may live many days in the land where ye be strangers. Thus," continued the Rechabites, "have we obeyed the voice of Jonadab the son of Rechab our father, in all that he hath charged us, to drink no wine all our days, we, our wives, our sons, nor our daughters; nor to build houses for us to dwell in: neither have we vineyard, nor field, nor seed. But we have dwelt in tents, and have obeyed and done according to all that Jonadab our father commanded us!"

Here we have, therefore, the rules of the Rechabites, in which there is something strange and striking; for they prohibit the use of things, which God has not forbidden; and make a mode of life imperative, whose yoke is nowhere imposed in Scripture on the children of God. What opinion ought we to form of such statutes, and how ought we to think of a community, which unreservedly submits to them and binds itself to them for the whole of their lives? Apparently, we have here to do with a tendency, which, to speak of it in the mildest manner, must be termed legal and sectarian; but on closer examination, this enigmatical phenomenon will be found to be something very different, and even extremely pleasing.

It is true, there have not been wanting in every age, and even amongst believers, those who were dissatisfied with the scriptural method of grace, because it was either so internal or so simple, and who therefore presumed to alter and deform it, in a variety of ways, according to their own ideas. The rule, which the word of God prescribes to the man who seeks salvation, only requires that he

should come as a poor sinner to Jesus, inwardly lay
hold on him, live and dwell in him, without delay,
and with renewed satisfaction, daily plunge himself
deeper into him, and into the wondrous depths of
his mediatorship. Joy in the Lord will then be his
strength, and faith, the victory that overcomes the
world ; whilst patience, hope, and holy resignation,
will be the fruits of faith, and love constrain him to
seek the Lord's glory and to walk so as to please
him. But what is there so particularly striking in
such a mode of life ? Little or nothing for inex-
perienced observers. It is a life which is hid
in God. Where is the wonder, therefore, that
in all ages many have lusted after a more prominent and striking form of godliness ? Whether it
was that they wished, for their own satisfaction, to
possess, besides that which was purely spiritual, other
more tangible marks of their Divine adoption, and
imagined they should the more surely attain their object by endeavoring to give their essential difference
from the world a more obvious external impress ;
or that they thought they could accomplish their
sanctification, attain a superior meetness for heaven,
and become more acceptable to God in this or that
particular way more rapidly than in the path pointed
out to them in the Scriptures : be this as it may,
they arbitrarily devised a form of godliness, which
was certainly more imposing than that quiet and
faithful imitation of Christ, in which the Scriptures
place the essence of true Christianity, and entered
upon a self-selected mode of life, which chiefly consisting in the denial of things not in themselves sin-

ful, certainly presented a greater appearance of holiness than the worship of God in spirit and in truth brings with it. In this manner arose monkish orders, and conventual fraternities; in like manner also the congregation of penitents and self-torment-ors. Thus grew up the hermitages in the depths of unhabitable wilds and forests, and sects increased, in which it was again said, " Touch not, handle not; live by such a rule; no marriage, no connection with the world; a hair shirt, a hard bed, bare feet, fasting, austerities, penances." And these kinds of saints are not quite extinct. They are to be found, though in more subtle forms, even in the bosom of the Protestant church. These contracted people have their rules, which say, " You must pray so many times a day, must pray on your bended knees, and for so long a time together. You must refrain from laughter, speak little, avoid company, limit yourself to the most simple furniture. You must only sing psalm tunes, read nothing but the Bible and prayer-book, and speak only in a pious tone. Give your apparel this particular cut, and hold your head and eyes only in that particular manner. Renounce this and that convenience; reject, as sinful, enjoyments which are not strictly ecclesias-tical; let mourning be the fundamental impress of your outward appearance; and as an essential mark of the true Christian, let silence and sighing form a prominent part of your deportment." Yes, we know those who act in this manner. We will not rebuke them for so doing. In an age like the present, when the reins of sacred gravity hang loosely, we are easily reconciled to such strictness. It is better to exceed the measure in this respect, than to draw down Christian liberty into licentiousness. And shall we judge our serious friends, when what they do is done with a faithful intention towards God? Although their forms may be self-selected, they may, nevertheless, rest upon a sacred basis, and have their root in pure simplicity of heart. And though they were really aberrations proceeding from religious mistakes, yet we ought not to infer from this, that they may not be rea' children of God. But if such people, in consequence of their particularities, wish to lay claim to a higher degree of holiness, we must regard them as deceived, and accuse them of lamentable blindness. Were they to suppose, that the favor and good pleasure of God connected itself somehow or other with their eccentricities, they would require instruction, as being under the influence of a dangerous error. Or if they regarded their peculiarities as marks of their adoption, we must still hope they knew of better proofs of their state of grace, or else we should be compelled to strike them out of the rank of Christians, as being entangled in horrible self-deception. If they looked upon an observance of their rules as something that, at least, assisted in justifying them in the sight of God, they would have fallen from grace, and Christ would have become to them of none effect, as in the case of the Galatians. Had they wished even to elevate their rule to an universal law, without the observance of which there could be no real religion, they would justly deserve being censured for going about to establish an after-birth of self-selected, narrow-minded sanctimoniousness and pharisaic formalities in the place of evangelical Christianity. The Gospel nowhere burdens its confessors with such-like things, and is so far from re-introducing its disciples to a new species of Judaism, that it affords, on the contrary, the greatest freedom for the manifestation of their inward connection with the Lord. Do not we hear Paul say, " The kingdom of God is not meat and drink ; but righteousness, and peace, and joy in the Holy Ghost ?"

As regards the " Rechabites," however, it would be doing them great injustice to number them with pharisaic religionists, or even with legal formalists. They never had the idea of impressing upon their peculiar mode of life, the stamp of an universal rule ; much less did it occur to them to propose it as a way, by which the Divine good pleasure might be procured, or even as the mark and sign of the true servants of God. They were well aware that God's good pleasure towards poor sinners, rests on incomparably superior conditions, and that the seal of adoption is to be sought for in something very different to outward apparel. They perhaps distinguished more minutely than many of us, between a Divine ordinance and a mere human agreement ; and with freedom of spirit adhered to their hereditary rule, because they acknowledged it to be appropriate and salutary. Thus they continued far from that slavish attachment to tradition, which blindly mingles Divine and human things together,

and from that false libertinism, in which throwing
away the kernel with the shell, war is declared
against every ancient usage, as such, because it is
not founded upon a definite command. We rejoice
that in our churches, many things which were formerly regarded as essential to Christian morals, are
now better estimated than was perhaps formerly the
case ; but we must, on the other hand, at the same
time, painfully regret, that the exhortation to " prove
all things," and " hold fast that which is good," is
not always practised as it should be. If our believing forefathers, without prejudice to the freedom
of their religious life, thought much of regular
family worship, mutual preparatory devotions for
the Lord's supper ; of simplicity in their domestic
arrangements, as well as in their dress ; of strict
abstraction from worldly society and its forms ; of
a grave and serious deportment where company of
that kind could not be avoided ; and of an universal cheerful confession of the name of Jesus, and an
almost painfully conscientious sanctification of the
Sunday, and many other things of the same kind ;
we should be acting, to say the least of it, super-
ficially, unjustly, and rudely, if, without further
cause, we should accuse them of a judaic legality.
We should do better, at least, were it but for once,
to inquire whether, amongst many of these individuals, this more severe and formal mode of life did
not well consist with the most unfettered position
in the element of grace ; and then search into the
hidden causes by which, although well aware of
their justification in Christ, they felt impelled to

limit their mode of life in such a manner, and confine it within firm and definite bounds. May we all learn to regulate our lives by that rule, which the apostle mentions at the conclusion of his Epistle to the Galatians, and may " God forbid that I should glory save in the cross of our Lord Jesus Christ, by which the world is crucified unto me, and I unto the world," seeing that " in Christ Jesus, neither circumcision availeth any thing, nor uncircumcision, but a new creature. And as many as walk according to this rule," whatever colors they may wear, to whatever regulations they may adhere, whatever mode of religious life they follow, "peace be on them, and mercy, and upon the Israel of God."

IV.—JERUSALEM WHICH IS ABOVE

"Our conversation is in heaven," writes the apostle to the Philippians, iii. 20, 21, "from whence also we look for the Saviour, the Lord Jesus Christ, who shall change our vile body, that it may be fashioned like unto his glorious body." What confidence in the language! How beneficial to our hearts is the expression of such a decided consciousness of the heavenly calling! Hence we see that it is certainly possible, even in this world, to gain a footing above it; and that the idea of its being impracticable for any man, with reference to his superior interests, to soar above the fleeting vapory region of mere desire and anticipation, is entirely without foundation. And if the person, who speaks with such confidence of eternal things, is a man of such decided strength of mind and depth of understanding as the pupil of Gamaliel, it adds the greater weight to his testimony, because it justifies the supposition, that his invincible confidence does not rest upon frail support, but upon good and tried ground. It is to such ground that the anchor of the hope of all believers cleaves; and hence they may freely and boldly make the apostle's words their own.

Real religion, which is wretchedly misunderstood when thought to be merely a system of doctrine, apart from the life, forms new creatures, and pervades, with its Divine and sanctifying power, the whole being of its disciples. The life of real believers is already a heavenly and beautiful life, even on this side eternity ; and if you inquire after the source and origin of this beatitude, I reply, first, the consciousness of a great and present possession ; next, a daily renewed experience of the risen Lord ; and lastly, the hopeful contemplation of an unspeakably blissful futurity.

Paul writes from Rome, a prisoner, and yet a free man ; trodden under foot by the world, and yet triumphing over it ; and even in the anticipation of his approaching decease, full of good courage and of holy joy. This indeed is great. But true greatness presents itself to the world as deeply veiled. The worlding may also rejoice, but no longer than " the flower of grass" flourishes. If the day of their earthly good fortune declines, how soon their courage fails ! Paul's sun rises in the evening, and when his earthly roses fail, he walks between the blooming fields of paradise. He leads a twofold life ; he is a citizen of earth like as ye—but his earthly citizenship, so far from limiting the sphere of his existence, forms, on the contrary, only one side of his position, a provisional and transitory one. The apostle belongs to another order of things ; and is at the same time established in and heir to a kingdom, which lies far beyond this outward world, but which nevertheless projects into it—a kingdom from which sorrow and sighing are forever expelled, and where that which is partial is swallowed up by that which is perfect.

"Our conversation," says Paul, or more literally, "our citizenship is in heaven." It *is*, says he, and not it will be; and this points it out as something present. He here expresses something very different from what the world calls the "hope of a future existence." Paul is now conscious, although his foot still rests on this transitory sphere, that he is a citizen of heaven. And oh, think what happiness and what a treasure it must be, to carry such a consciousness about with him in this poor dying world! Yet Paul can do so, and his faith reposes on a more immutable basis than that of so many of our contemporaries, who have no other foundation for their hopes than that which is presented to them by natural reason from her poor reservoir of ideas. Had this been the case with the apostle, he would not have said with so much certainty, "Our conversation is in heaven;" but like the children of the present age, he would only have said, "Heaven? Is there really a heaven?" and with them have exclaimed,—"Immortality! may not that be a delusion?" just in their manner. But the most important affairs of mankind are no longer a matter of doubt to Paul. He is above these "rudiments of the world," as the Scripture terms these inquiries of reason. He is a pupil of that revelation which emanates from the truth as from an elementary principle, with which, in the best case, as with its choicest product, philosophy concludes. Philosophy is at its acme in proving that there is a God; whilst the Scriptures tell us that "the fear of God is only the *beginning* of wisdom." Paul knows that a heaven exists, and that a possession in it is bestowed upon him. And he knows this so surely, that nothing would ever be able to shake his conviction of its truth.

How did he attain this knowledge? What, must you still ask such a question as this? There appeared unto him One, in the gloom and darkness of this earth, a high and lofty and mysterious One, who uttered the words, "I came out from the Father, and am in the world;" and on being asked, Who art thou? replied, "I am the way, the truth, and the life." On its being said to him, "Show us the Father," he answered, "He that seeth me, seeth the Father;" and when one of his disciples called him his Lord and his God, he confirmed and sealed it by saying, "Thomas, now thou believest." The dumb, whom he made to speak; the blind, to whom he gave sight; the dead, whom he called forth from their tombs to bear witness of him, confirm it; and repeatedly he exclaimed, "I am from above," and confirmed it anew, not only by forgiving sins and claiming Divine honor for himself, but also no less, by majestically commanding all the powers of nature, and finally, by casting away from him the bonds of death itself, visibly ascending to heaven, and sending down the Spirit, the Creator of a new world.

After the apostle had become acquainted with this high and lofty One, and acknowledged him, not only as the revealer, but also as the Mediator, he knew, with irrefragable certainty, that he had become a citizen of, and proprietor in the kingdom above; and all who share his faith, being cleansed from sin by the same blood, are also justified in cherishing the same conviction.

Place yourselves now, in spirit, in the social sphere of individuals planted in such a soil, and then say whether you do not learn to believe in a superior light, which must be shed over their existence. Certainly, this halo, by which they are surrounded, is not of this world. The outward appearance of these blessed individuals manifests itself indeed, occasionally, in a manner sufficiently mean, and even profoundly obscure. The glory rests within the temple; light beams in the depth. Oh precious knowledge, blissful consciousness! These happy individuals behold the boundaries of this world broken down, and angels' pinions are attached to their souls. If night reign here below, it is forever light and bright above. If the road be rough and thorny, " We are going home," is their motto; " our names are there written in a book; there are the friends who know us, and there resides our greatest Friend." Such is their language, and this view of the subject is not mere poesy, but the most real truth, founded on the words, work, and example of Christ. Thus they possess each other in God, and know that they do so forever. Oh, could you form an idea how much this consciousness must ennoble love, shed light upon the life, hallow every connection, and alleviate pain! Each earthly tear reflects thy light, eternal father-

land, and from every trial I receive the consciousness, that my best and real life is not here, but
above.

"Our conversation is in heaven," says the apostle, and continues, "from whence also we look
for—" whom, I need not tell you. You who do
not know the Lord, are also expecting something;
but woe to the wretched object of your desire,—
to the frivolous life you lead, incessantly carried to
and fro between anxious hope and painful deception! Your poverty-stricken wishes and expectations do not ascend above what the world is able to
give; and what can proceed from such a miserable
source? If, on the contrary, we resemble Paul,
how widely the region expands, through which the
searching eye is directed! With him, we wait for
the Lord Jesus from on high, and not merely for
the day of his great second coming, but daily,
hourly, and never in vain. We experience that
we are in the living God; and this experience becomes a second source of that supernatural glory,
in which the earthly existence of God's children is
arrayed. In this case also, there is no outward
appearance or splendor; but what glory in the inmost part, what lustre in concealment! Every
morning his coming is invoked; and he comes in
reality. Every prayer for help and deliverance is
graciously answered. His traces are perceptible
through the whole course of our lives, and his salutations meet us, first in one way, and then in another. Oh, how faithfully he keeps his word, "Lo,
I am with you alway, even unto the end of the

world !" and how he stands to his promise, "Come unto me, all ye that labor and are heavy laden, and I will give you rest!" His name pervades the whole of our guidance, and we have no need to wait for proofs of his Divinity, but daily rejoice in its manifestations.

One evening, an individual was descending the neighboring hills. The partner of his life lay at home on her death-bed. He looked up to the calm and solemn canopy of heaven, and ejaculated, "Lord Jesus, comfort, save! She 'whom thou lovest is sick.'" And looking tearfully upwards to the spangled sky, no gate indeed opened itself to his view, yet he thought within himself, "Oh, how strange it must be, to know with undoubted confidence, that a soul with whom one is so closely and intimately united on earth, is become a resident there! How does such a thought make us intimate with heaven, and loosen us from the earth! And in thee, O Lord, there is no separation! The soul that is called away from this world, lies in thy bosom above; there I also lie, though still wandering here below!"

It was on the pinions of such-like thoughts as these, that the musing spirit of the worthy man was borne, as upon the rosy clouds of the morning, over the heights of the earth, and heavenly light increased within him. He returned home with joyous feelings, as though he had seen the glory of the Lord. He greeted the beloved sufferer; on which she whispered, "I am dying." "God forbid!" exclaimed the startled husband. "Lord Jesus, do not forsake us: help, comfort, and save!" The dying woman sank exhausted on her pillow. Her hour was come. One more inquiry of the dear departing soul, one question more amidst a flood of tears: "Is your mind in peace?" "Unspeakable!" was the reply breathed forth with her last breath; and with a blissful smile she repeated, "Unspeakable!" Oh, the Lord was there, no other! How real is his mercy and his presence! "Lord Jesus," ejaculated the husband, "wilt thou really tear from my arms the dearest thing I have on earth?" During these words, she fell asleep. He was then able to imprint on her forehead the parting kiss, and fold his hands over the beloved corpse, and say, in a loud and firm tone, "I thank thee, Lord Jesus Christ, that thou art 'the resurrection and the life.' He that believeth in thee shall not see death, but is passed from death unto life. Blessed be thy name!"

Such are the scenes, which are witnessed in the tabernacles of the righteous. It is there we wait for him, and he is not slack concerning his promise. He is like a roe on the mountains. "Behold, he standeth behind our wall, he looketh forth at the windows, showing himself through the lattice." And how often are we ourselves seen coming forth from gloom and darkness, with shining countenances; and the lustre on our foreheads is lovelier than that of Moses. Nor do we spread any veil over it; for this radiance terrifies no one; on the contrary, each feels a gentle consciousness, that "the home must be sweet in which we dwell;" and it is so in reality. The Lord has appeared unto us. " I have loved thee with an everlasting love : therefore with loving-kindness have I drawn thee." This is the reason why the clouds have been dispersed, and this is the circumstance which makes us so cheerful and happy.

To the consciousness of having a possession in heaven, and to the daily experience of the living God, must be added, finally, as the third point of glorification in the life of the children of God, the hope of an incomparably blissful futurity. " From whence also," saith the apostle, " we look for the Saviour, the Lord Jesus Christ : who shall change our vile body, that it may be fashioned like unto his glorious body ;" and significantly adds, " according to the working whereby he is able to subdue all things unto himself." Oh blissful prospect, refreshing expectation ! A mighty image of the future presents itself amongst the shadowy forms of earth before my spirit. I see myself, perfected both in body and in soul ; a citizen of a new world,—a world, in which the Lord's kingdom is embodied, and where eternity and time essentially mingle together. The universe, pervaded by the brightness of heaven, stands before me as a radiant memorial of the redeeming power of the blood of Christ, and of the regenerating operation of his Holy Spirit. I see nothing disproportioned, discordant, or profane ; but everywhere a healthy, sanctified, and divine life ; " death is swallowed up in victory," and that which was in part, terminated by that which is perfect. I suffer not from the sorrows of earth ; I have that which mightily consoles me for the fading and perishing things of time. I know what a wondrous spring behind the storms of winter is approaching, to which the present material world is subject. I perceive in all that is truly beautiful in the kingdoms of nature, art, or imagination, only a slight reflection of that glory, which shall eventually expand itself over every thing that exists. By faith I include this bright futurity in the present, and thus its dawn, although with a still feeble ray, already plays on the front of my pilgrimage here below.

Truly, it is a benign and peaceful sphere, in which the citizens of Jesus' kingdom move, even whilst on earth. If you are desirous of looking still more deeply into it, and of seeing the way thither unfolded before you, follow the thread of our present meditation. "Jerusalem which is above" opens before us her golden gates.

2 KINGS X. 15

" And when he was departed thence, he lighted on Jehonadab the son of Recbab, coming to meet him."

WE are about, the second time, to direct our attention to an historical trait, which, however inconsiderable it may appear, is well worthy of a more minute consideration. By it we are made acquainted with an individual, who, as the founder of one of the most noble and spiritual orders the world has ever beheld, demands our liveliest sympathy. In reality, we scarcely know what to admire the most in his character—the heavenly-mindedness with which he is inspired; the singular wisdom which is so peculiar to him, and abundant in him; the free, unbiassed view which he takes of every thing, and which enables him to judge them spiritually; or the enlightened, tender, and calculating forethought, which we see him exercising for his house. With regard to all these advantages, it follows of course, that the glory belongs alone to Him from whose fulness of grace they originally emanated. God had chosen him, before others, to be the depositary of these superior gifts; and hence this remarkable personage remains a highly important phenomenon, to which, as often as reference is made to "the wisdom of the just," or to forms and manners in which the life of godliness on earth may express and manifest itself, an inquiring and scrutinizing attention may be directed, since in this instance there is abundant opportunity afforded for the formation of a sound judgment upon those points.

Let us then, in our present meditation, resume the subject, where we recently broke off, and consider, first, the Rechabites as an evangelical people under the old covenant; and secondly, evangelical Christians as the Rechabites of the New Testament.

I. Jonadab, as you will remember, although a believer, was not an Israelite, but a Kenite, and consequently, belonging to the tribe, which attached itself to the Israelites during their wanderings through the desert, from the land of Midian. The connection with these interesting guests had continued almost six hundred years, when Jonadab, the

son of Rechab, arose amongst them, for the purpose of exalting the manner of life, which his countrymen had hitherto observed, more from necessity
than from mature consideration, to an express order and decided rule for his family, the so-called
Rechabites.   You have heard the nature of this
rule.   They were not to build houses, " nor sow
seed, nor plant vineyards," nor possess them, and
to dwell continually in tents, that they might " live
many days in the land" where they were " strangers."   And this rule, however severe its conditions, had always been punctually fulfilled on the
part of the Rechabites.   At the period referred to
in the thirty-fifth chapter of Jeremiah, almost three
centuries had elapsed since Jonadab's time ; but
still they had not deviated in a single particular
from the ancient rule.   " Thus have we obeyed,"
say they, " the voice of Jonadab the son of Rechab
our father, in all that he hath charged us."

The question now presents itself, what it was
that induced Jonadab to institute the rule now
under consideration, and it will well repay us to
investigate the matter more closely.   It is scarcely
necessary to premise, that he was influenced by no
aimless and arbitrary motive.   We are likewise
agreed, that he just as little thought of pharisaically
attaching a greater degree of sanctity, or even of
merit, to the severe manner of life which he established.   He did not wish it, even to be regarded as
a way to holiness, or as a means of growth in grace.
Every idea of a monkish institution, penitential sect,
or anchorite fraternity, must be left entirely out of

the question. It did not occur to Jonadab, either to send forth his testamentary ordinance in any other name than his own, or to attach importance to it except as a measure of sanctified prudence and parental provision for his descendants. The latter did not submit to it from compulsion, as a painful but Divinely imposed and therefore indispensable yoke; but they freely and cheerfully bound themselves to the observance of the rule— not from the belief of being thereby enabled to establish a righteousness of their own, by no means; they did so merely with the salutary intention, which, with a penetrating look, they clearly perceived beneath it, and this intention was the following.

Imagine to yourselves, that these strangers had led a different life on the borders of Israel, than that which their rules prescribed; and that instead of tents, they had built themselves durable and even elegant habitations, had acquired possessions, accumulated riches, assimilated themselves to the more wealthy in Israel, or even taken precedence of them as regards property, luxury, and family splendor; what would have been the consequences? That the amicable understanding between them and the people, whose hospitality they claimed, would at length have been broken in upon, and that language to the following effect would soon have been heard in Israel:—"What shall we now do with these intruders, since they threaten gradually to rise above us, and appropriate to themselves the best part of our country before our eyes? Why should we suffer these luxuriant, parasitical plants to grow any longer in our soil? Prudent forethought for our children and grandchildren demands that we send back the strangers to the place from whence they came."

In this manner would jealous Israel infallibly have reasoned ere long, and the Kenites would have been compelled to pack up and be gone without further ceremony. But these peaceful neighbors had nothing of the kind to fear, so long as they unassumingly remained, as before, in the background; and by their life of poverty, and their moderate requirements and necessities, secured the unenvying favor of their protectors. They were, of course, gladly permitted to bring to market the milk and the wool of their scanty flocks, as well as the productions of their limited agriculture and horticulture upon a leased soil, and with the product of them make their modest purchases of Israelitish tradesmen; whilst their faithful attachment to Israel and Israel's creed and Divine service was observed with pleasure, and acknowledged with esteem. Jonadab's penetrating eye wisely foresaw all this; and on this very account, he prescribed to his descendants, by virtue of his paternal authority, for every succeeding age, that form of life, which never suffered them to exceed the bounds of a simple and modest pastoral life. And the Rechabites submitted the more willingly to the self-denial and privations connected with it, the more glorious the privileges they thereby acquired. By these means, they permanently secured to themselves the blissful connection with the people of God ; and, at the expense of a handful of earthly enjoyments, procured an abundance of the most valuable privileges and blessings.

The intention of this family-rule of Jonadab's is therefore no longer enigmatical. We are now convinced, that there was not even a distant idea of a narrow-minded imposition of a yoke, or of a hypocritical separation. Every thing was based upon a voluntary agreement, formed by the true " wisdom of the just." A prudent limit was fixed upon, as being a low price for invaluable blessings. What think ye, brethren in the Lord, if, during our whole lives, we were not to hear another evangelical discourse, unless we could resolve to renounce all the superfluous conveniences we enjoy ; should we hesitate long before we consented to make such a sacrifice ? And were we willing to do it, who would dare to reproach us with having fallen from grace, or with having come under the influence of a narrow-minded sectarianism ? As regards the Rechabites, the point at issue with them was something more than preaching would be to us. If this were wanting, we could still cleave, without sustaining injury, to the Bible, of which the Rechabites had only the few first pages. The Divine revelation, in whose noontide splendor we walk, was at that time incomplete. New prophets constantly arose in Israel, and announced either what had not been previously predicted, or illustrated more minutely what had already been uttered. The revelation was constantly confirmed afresh by new signs and wonders, or its mysteries still further disclosed. And how unceasing were the manifestations of Divine grace and favor, which Israel was permitted to experience, and the mighty helps and deliverances with which it was still favored! Testimonies and confirmations of eternal love and compassion were rained down, as it were, upon the highly favored race! Call to mind all the manifestations from the invisible world, which it was given these privileged people to behold; the personal appearance of Jehovah in the sphere of their public and domestic life, and the friendly angelic visitations with which they were surprised—first in one place and then in another; and all the other delightful and faith-invigorating events they experienced. In all these, the children of Rechab continually participated, in virtue of their connection with the Lord's people. How could they have refrained from making every concession, in order to retain and prolong such a blissful connection?

But what prevented them from formally incorporating themselves, as proselytes, with the Israelitish community? Nothing but the single circumstance, that they regarded it as more advantageous to continue in their liberty as neighbors. But to this it might be replied, that it was just because of Israel's religious privileges that they attached themselves to the latter. Certainly, it was their religious privileges, but not their religious burdens. If they were able to enjoy the former, without submitting to the yoke of the latter, they naturally chose the better part. An entire amalgamation with Israel would immediately have imposed upon them the whole weight of the Sinaitic law, and have forced them, no less than the Jews themselves, into the narrow limits of the Levitical ordinances. And the multifariousness of the ceremonial law would not only have been as a burden upon their shoulders, but also equally upon their consciences; for they were Divine commands, but applicable only to the circumcised. Hence, as long as the Rechabites were excluded from the commonwealth of Israel, they had no need to trouble themselves respecting them. You are aware how burdened the children of Israel were with the keeping of the Sabbath, the ordinances respecting eating and drinking, fasting, sacrificing, purifications, and the like. You also know with what difficulty they kept them, and in what constraint and bondage they were held by them. If they treated the matter lightly, they saw that they were accused, judged, and condemned by these laws at every step. Were they diligent in the due fulfilment of them, they were still only rolling, with perspiring brow, a ponderous stone, which, when they thought they had fortunately brought it up to the top of the hill, suddenly slipped from them again, and rolled once more down into the gulf below. Thus there was labor enough, but never the wished-for and satisfactory result. However sincere they might be, there was always something omitted; and, as the Epistle to the Hebrews expressly observes, they never attained to a purified conscience. Hence the Rechabites thought within themselves, "Let the

Israelites weary themselves in vain, we will mean while rejoice in God and his grace." And in reality, they were much better situated in their separate position, and enjoyed the glorious privileges of the children of Israel, without sharing in their toils. Whilst Israel had to observe the Levitical ceremonies, with their oppressive burdens and requirements, they took no notice of them except as being, at the same time, consolatory types and portentous symbols. Whilst the former were compelled to gnaw the shell, the latter refreshed themselves with the sweet and hidden kernel. Whilst the Israelites, with their sacrifices, were continually disturbed by the scruple, lest they should not possess all the requisite qualities, and lest the Eternal should be disinclined to receive them graciously, the Rechabites penetrated the covering to the true sacrifice, which only threw its shadow into the Levitical; and enjoyed the heavenly honeycomb of a New Testament peace, whilst the Israelites busied themselves only with the earthen vessel, which retained that flower of life and grace. If the children of Israel, on their sabbath days, were compelled at every step, from morning till evening, to inquire what was next to be done, the Rechabites were wont, meanwhile, to keep holy day, and blissfully repose in the prospect of salvation, which was unfolded to them also. And whilst the former could scarcely take breath under the burdensome authority of Moses and Aaron, the latter, to whom the Levitical law had no reference, were like birds in the air, and praised and called on the Lord whenever their hearts impelled them, and lived in the wide and bright expanse of the promises of grace, and feared neither curse nor punishment.

Thus you have, in these Kenites, an evangelical people in Old Testament times, a people that only plucked the grapes in the vineyard of the Is-raelitish church, and left to others the labor of digging and breaking stones; a people that en-tered upon the pasture, as a horse divested of its furniture, whilst Israel panted on its steep path, like a heavy laden animal, and Issachar was like "a strong ass, couching down between two burdens." All that Israel possessed that was valuable, was also the property of the Rechabites. Israel's pros-pects and promises, Urim and Thummim, seers and prophets, all belonged to them, and they to God alone ; all the blessing, help, and protection from on high, which Israel experienced, was also for their benefit ; and whatever of that which was sweet, life and soul-animating, and strength and refresh-ment-affording, which the Old Testament economy contained, they wisely divested of its shell and outer-covering, and left what was binding, depress-ing, discouraging, and heart-oppressing therein, as far as being uncircumcised, they might entirely to the Jews. Thus they clave to the social and serene character of the patriarchal age, whose wings were not yet paralyzed by the subsequent ceremonial law. Quite in Abraham, Isaac, or Jacob's man-ner, living as free and happy children in the ele-ment of Divine love, they trod with light and easy steps over the clods of this world, and breathed, in blissful anticipation, the atmosphere of the brighter period towards which they were hastening. Like those patriarchs, they symbolically expressed, in the form and manner of their outward life, the sentiment, "We have no abiding city here," as the basis of their conviction and feelings; and remind us more of a ship's crew, steering cheerfully homewards, with well-filled sails and flying streamers, than of colonists, who, anxious for their descendants, busily measure out the ground, which they cheerfully greet, as their new and only fatherland.

But let this suffice concerning the Rechabites. Permit me to make only one not uninteresting additional remark, namely, that the Rechabites, although more or less degenerated and fallen into heathenish errors, exist, to the present day, in the practice of their ancient mode of life. Not a long time ago, a missionary is said to have found them out in the heart of Asia, and has given the following account of the circumstance. One day, he was met in the depths of a distant wilderness, by a splendidly attired horseman, arrayed and armed after the Arabian manner, of martial bearing, who on the missionary's inquiring who he was, hastily and haughtily replied in a powerful voice, "A son of Rechab." The missionary on this presented him with an Arabic Bible, printed parallel with the Hebrew text. On which, the son of the desert turned to the prophecy of Jeremiah, and read in Hebrew the 35th chapter, which treated of his order. Being further interrogated by the stranger, as to his abode, and if there were many of his tribe, he invited him to visit them in their tents, which were near at hand, and to bring with him as many Bibles as he could spare. He then turned his horse about, gave him the spurs, and disappeared in the wide and pathless desert.

The missionary followed the direction, which the son of Rechab had taken, and met, not far from Mecca, with the tribe which had been indicated to him. He found them dwelling in tents, as of old, and spread over three fruitful and verdant districts. Their number amounted to several thousands. They strictly adhered to Jonadab's rule, and to their forefathers' manner of life; built no houses, drank no wine, professed to belong, as far as they understood it, to the Jewish persuasion, and possessed a large portion of the Old Testament as the standard of their faith. They fought for their laws against Mohammed, sword in hand: and although conquered, were not subdued. They continued true to their creed and their traditions. The other Asiatic Jews think highly of them, and believe, that whenever they shall return to the promised land, the Rechabites will act an important part, and join them as valiant confederates.

This intelligence of the continued existence of the Rechabites will not fail to produce a beneficial effect in strengthening our faith, when we compare it with the promise, which the Lord gave to the Rechabites in Jer. xxxv. 19: "Jonadab the son of Rechab shall not want a man to stand before me for ever ;" that is, to serve me, and be my favorite. See now, how Jehovah keeps his word. Because he has promised it, the Rechabites continue to the present day, although more than two thousand years have elapsed; and though they may not be spiritually what they were, but, estranged from the sentiments of their forefathers, have come under bondage to the letter, yet the hope of the Asiatic Jews, that a peculiar time of grace will eventually arrive for these Rechabites, must by no means be rejected as an idle dream. Oh, pray for the peace of Jerusalem, to Him who keeps his covenant and his promise to a thousand generations, and who will at length constrain his whole people to bear witness to the truth of Joshua's testimony, in its greatest extent and universality, "that not one thing hath failed of all the good things, which the Lord your God spake concerning you; all are come to pass unto you, and not one thing hath failed thereof."

II. That which the Rechabites were in the Old Testament—evangelical Christians—their antitypes—or more particularly, those who have been made free in Christ, the little flock amongst the believers, whom the Lord so strikingly honors, and who walk worthy of the Gospel, according to the apostolic rule—are in the New. The people who, looking "into the perfect law of liberty," do not mingle law and gospel together, but let law continue law, and gospel gospel, and who have no longer their lives in their own hands, but live, out of themselves, in Him, with whom they feel eternally incorporated in one body, as with their exalted Head; the people who know that on Calvary is the grave of all

their sins—in Joseph's garden the Divine receipt
for the payment of all their debts—in the obedience
of Christ the discharge from their united obligations, and who, by Christ's offering, are forever perfected and in the full possession of all the righteousness which they could ever require ; a people who,
richly assured of the Divine good-pleasure, are divested of every anxious care about their well-being
in eternity ; a race, which has been freed from the
hireling yoke of legal self-working, who live to the
Lord, not with eye-service, but in sincerity, from
the impulse of love, not from servile compulsion,
not because they are afraid of otherwise bringing
the curse upon themselves, but because they find
it blessed to yield themselves up to him ; a people,
who devote themselves to him, not as to one who
requires first to be propitiated, but as to a God long
since and forever reconciled in Christ. This order
of free knights under Zion's banner, with the inscription on their shields, " Thanks be to God, which
giveth us the victory," with the watchword, " All
things are ours," on their joyful lips, and with the
royal consciousness in their breasts, that if they live,
they " live unto the Lord ;" if they die, they " die
unto the Lord ;" so that whether they " live therefore or die," they " are the Lord's,"—these are the
people, this is the order, which presents to our view
the Rechabites of the New Testament.

Of these New Testament Rechabites, the Apostle
Paul speaks in the fourth chapter of his Epistle to
the Galatians, the 20th verse ; " Jerusalem, which
is above," says he, " is free ;" by which he means

not so much the city of God beyond the clouds, as in opposition to the earthly Jerusalem, or the legal Jewish state, the church of the living members of Christ upon earth, and especially those amongst them who walk in the perfect light of the New Testament. For what reason this people, chosen out of the world, are so frequently called " Jerusalem," and thus compared with the temple city, which was a city of God, like none beside, is abundantly evident. The church in Christ is now, as Jerusalem once was, the place of Jehovah's manifestation and residence on earth. In her he walks and dwells. His heart is in her. She rejoices exclusively in his beatific proximity. The wings of his tenderness and mercy are expanded over her ; and those only join her, who desire to participate in that blissful protection. Beyond the limits of this Divine Zion, it is not safe. There lie the gloomy provinces of the prince of darkness ; there brood the thunder-clouds of wrath ; there resound the curses of Ebal, and threaten eternal perdition.

The apostle may well call this church a " Jerusalem which is above," because its full glory does not manifest itself here below, and because it has certainly to expect its best things above. Those who do not belong to it, he very properly designates as a city here below, and this because they boast themselves of having here below the ground of their hope, which they introduce into the fabric they call their righteousness. And if these latter are not merely legally-minded, but even unconverted, they have, certainly, their all below—their affections, their desire, the object of their longing, their deities, and their heaven. That which we, who are Christ's, possess here below, is always incomparably more than what they have. Though here below, yet we have a heart, which hates sin like the heart of God, and is inflamed for all that is holy,—which possesses a peace, which the world knoweth not of; an escort incomparably dignified ; brethren connected with us by "bonds of perfectness ;" privileges exceeded by none which earthly potentates can bestow ; bubbling springs, which remind us of the glories of Eden ; and much besides of what is lovely and beautiful. But our chief treasure is not on this side eternity. Beyond is our fatherland ; there stand our native homes ; there glitter our crowns; and the righteousness itself, of which we boast, is not below, nor do we possess it in our hearts or lives, but it shines resplendent above, even in Christ. His obedience intercedes for us ; clothed in his virtues, we stand before the Father. Hence it is, that this wonderful people, although still wandering here below, pervade the world, and are better known above than below. Attend to their inmost thoughts, meditations, and wishes. Where do you meet them ? You may seek them here below a thousand times in vain. They soar above, on wings of faith, and lead, at times, the life of angels, whilst still in the body. They lie at the threshold of paradise, contemplating their future glory, or on the steps of the throne of grace, breathe out thanksgiving and prayer. Their "conversation is in heaven."

The apostle further presents to us the church

thus rooted in the Gospel, as a "mother," and certainly she proves herself to be such, beneficent in a thousand ways, and causing joy. Look around you, and you will see how wondrously her holy hands are employed in laboring and blessing. At one time, these hands are folded in order to draw down streams of life from the heights above; at another, they break bread to the hungry, which refreshes the heart and satisfies the spirit. Now they stretch themselves out into the heathen world, in order, with the torch of revelation, to light the way towards Zion, to the children of the night. See them founding Bible Societies, establishing missionary seminaries, and opening hospitable asylums for the destitute and the orphan. See them wiping the tear from the eye of a weeping brother, with the napkin of the Divine promises; or carrying those who have been smitten, plundered, and left for dead, by the law, into the gracious fold of the good Shepherd; or boldly and resolutely unfurling the imperial standard of Christ in the provinces of Satan. Do you know these hands? They are not those of the world, much less those of antichrist. They are maternal hands, the hands of Jerusalem, the true and invisible church.

You also meet on earth with two eyes, beaming with lovely and benignant light. They shine with joyful brilliance, when children are born to the Lord, as dew from the womb of the morning; and their tears abound when the paths towards Zion lie waste. They are radiant with affection and kindness, as often as a man of God enters their sphere of observation ; and they are frequently seen lifted up on high, that " the heavens may hear the earth." Oh tell me, to whom do these eyes belong ? They are not those of the blind, self-infatuated multitude ; no, they are maternal eyes, the eyes of the holy church, the daughter of Zion, the Jerusalem of God.

Oh, be conscious also, that there is a heart in the world that beats more faithfully than any other on earth. How comfortable it is to rest upon such a heart ! No serpent lurks behind the roses there. No specious appearance of a love without reality deceives us there. There the sincerest good intentions are joined with the wisest advice ; and the most hearty offers of service and assistance are united with the most heartfelt sympathy, both in joy and in sorrow. In whose bosom beats this expansive, affectionate heart, concerned for the salvation of thousands ? Not in the bosom of the self-seeking world. It is a maternal heart ; it is thy heart, O Zion !

If no such Zion existed on the earth, who would be able, with the key of prayer, to open the sluices of heavenly blessings ? Who would mourn for the wound of Joseph ? Who would call down the Spirit's vivifying streams into this vale of death ? Who would receive the new-born babes, and nourish them with milk or strong meat ? What would the world, the whole world, have lost, if deprived of this church ? She would have lost a mother, a dispenser of blessings in a thousand different ways the only interpreter,—for who, besides the daughter of Zion, can pray in such a manner as to pierce the clouds?—and the only preacher of the name in which is salvation.

But may not the church of believers be called a mother, even in a more peculiar sense than that above mentioned? Is it not she who bears spiritual children unto the Lord by the power of his grace, by which he is wont to fructify her testimony and example? Is it not written concerning her in Isaiah liv. "Sing, O barren, thou that didst not bear; break forth into singing, thou that didst not travail with child: for more are the children of the desolate than the children of the married wife." The world would be deprived of its salt; yea, the earth's pillars would be shaken, if a church of saints no longer existed upon it.

The apostle further speaks of the church as "free;" comparing it with Sarah, the mistress in Abraham's house, in opposition to Hagar, the bondwoman, the Egyptian slave. And truly, the Lord's people are free. Were I commissioned to prepare a coat of arms for them, I would portray it much as follows:—I would draw it in the form of a trophy of victory, and would fashion its border out of shattered lances, broken bows, and riven chains. I would paint within it a serpent with a bruised head; for Satan has nothing more in these people. Opposite to it, a fugitive skeleton, with a crown hurled from its head; in other words, death, which no longer exists as a king of terrors with relation to this people. Moses must also take his place in the picture, holding a palm-branch, instead of the oppressive rod in his hand, and kindly and complacently inclining himself before a man who embraces a blood-besprinkled cross; for Moses is reconciled unto these people by this cross. Under the feet of the man embracing the cross, I would draw a writhing monster, which, though it shows its teeth, is on the point of expiring. And over all, a blood-red banner should be unfurled, on which should stand written, " He whom the Son makes free, is free indeed :" and on the staff, from Rom. viii. 34, " Who is he that condemneth ? it is Christ that died." And on the border to the left, " O death, where is thy sting? O grave, where is thy victory?" On the border to the right, " We are more than conquerors, through him that loved us—and hath given himself for us."

Thus would I portray the arms of spiritual Judah, and yet I should only have scantily traced the outlines of the manifold rights and glories of this people. Truly, they are a free people ! You cannot form too great and exalted ideas of the liberty to which they are called. That which the enthusiastic admirers of liberty in the present day would fondly strive for, as the highest imaginary form of human felicity, is truly found in these people in a spiritual and glorified state. If freedom of speech be claimed by the world ; it is fully possessed in our Jerusalem, where the King may be applied to every moment, and on every occasion, by day and by night. If a reduction of taxes is desired ; in worldly matters, nothing is demanded as a tribute in our Divine state, except what grace has previously presented to us, out of its fulness. If a participation in the government, by the people, is thought desirable in the affairs of this world; the citizens of Jerusalem assist by their prayers and sighs in governing the world. If even the desire is excited for equality in possessions; in the city of our God, where the motto is universal, "All things are yours!" this community of goods really exists in a sacred sense. If, in the world, it is thought desirable to be bound by laws, to which we have ourselves subscribed, or which we have even promulgated; we really find ourselves so situated, that we submit ourselves to the laws of the everlasting King for this very reason, and because our inmost will is in unison with them. Tell me, therefore, where is there a constitution comparable to that of this spiritual kingdom? He that desires true freedom, can find it only in our Zion. Out of it, even though outwardly in the freest conceivable position, he is only a poor captive servant, and a slave.

There are, however, only a few Christians, who attain the full freedom to which the Gospel calls them, and justifies them in seeking. The most of them suffer themselves, by a natural inclination to the covenant of works, to be again taken captive, more or less, under the yoke, which Christ does not impose upon them. To this the apostle expressly refers, in the course of the chapter from which we have already quoted, when bringing seriously before the Galatians, that they are not children of the bond-woman, but of the free.

The comparison of the children of Zion with Isaac has its depth, as well as its reference to believers generally. If he is a vital Christian, his own image is vividly represented in Isaac, whether he be in bondage or free. He will recognize in Isaac's character, the peculiarity of his own spiritual state; In Isaac's experience, his own guidance ; in Isaac's privileges, his own prerogative. He that does not recognize his own features in those of Isaac, must not imagine that he is a partaker of Isaac's grace.

Isaac was born according to the promise. His birth was a Divine miracle. Such is also the case with the descent of all God's children. But there are professed Christians amongst us of human fabrication. Instruction in the nurture and admonition of the Lord is frequently very efficacious; religious society is not less beneficial ; a powerful resolution often produces a moral and religious deportment, which may even appear to an experienced eye as true piety, and as being born of the Spirit. But all this is by no means sufficient. There must be a consciousness that something has taken place in thy heart, which neither thou nor any other individual has brought about, and that it is infinitely more than the best of that which thou hast had to thank men for ; something, whose origin and basis lies in an immediate operation of Divine grace. If thou art able to explain to thyself thy conversion, without having reference to that which is above mere human nature, thy conversion is dubious ; thou mayest be a bastard, but not a child at home. Sayest thou, How can I know that I am a Christian by Divine operation or by human preparation? Compare thyself again with Isaac, as thou findest him on mount Moriah. What the son of Abraham there typified is essentially experienced by every one who is born of God. By the influences of the Holy Spirit, each one is brought to a similar state of resignation to that which we admire in Isaac. He lays himself on the altar of the Lord, as a willing sacrificial lamb; gives up his old man, together with its affections and lusts, to the Divine sacrificial knife; submits himself, with all that he has, in the most unlimited manner, to the dispensations of the Almighty; and says, from his inmost heart, " Here am I, Lord! Do with me as seemeth thee good! Wilt thou slay me, or tread me under foot, do so ! I will not let thee go any more; for 'whom have I in heaven but thee ? and there is none upon earth that I desire beside thee.' What is the price which shall make thee mine? Is it my will? Behold I resign it to thee. Is it my reason ? Gladly would I become a fool for thy sake. Is it my worldly reputation ? Willingly will I be regarded as the offscouring of all things, if I may only possess thee. Is it my property ? Place me, like Job, upon its ashes; but only let me, like him, experience thy presence within me."

Now, if thou art conscious of having, in thy inmost soul, accomplished such an act of self-resignation, then only art thou justified in numbering thyself with Zion's children, and art an Isaac. In Isaac's portrait thy own must be reflected. Art thou really born in the spiritual Jerusalem, thou needest to be nothing more, in order to be at the summit of happiness and glory. What kind of a lot has fallen to thee, may be recognized in Abraham and Sarah's child of promise. Thy name, like his, is also "Isaac," for thou art a child of joy—a son of delight, as the term implies. There was joy in heaven at thy birth; there will be joy over thee when thou departest hence; the heavenly hosts will fetch thee home with acclamations, and welcome thee with crowns of glory. That which Isaac was to Abraham of old, thou art, and in a still greater degree, to the eternal Father—a son whom he loveth—the apple of his eye—his crown. Like Isaac, thou goest freely in and out—lookest in his face with childish affection—and castest thyself, with a filial "Abba, Father" on his bosom—hast evey thing to hope for from him, and nothing to fear, not even the smallest thing.

And if, for the time, thou art like Isaac in Canaan—a stranger here upon earth—yet thou belongest to the number of those, who are described as "having nothing, yet possessing all things." The earth on which thou dwellest, regarded through the eye of faith, is thine, as was Isaac's, the land which bore his tent. And though thy path through this world may be, like Isaac's pilgrimage, thorny, beclouded, beset with troubles, lonely and desert; nevertheless, it will be eventually said to thee, as of old to him, "Now we see that the Lord is with thee." In a spiritual sense it may also be said of thee, as is recorded of Isaac, "And the man waxed great, and went forward, and grew until he became very great; for he had possession of flocks and herds, and great store of servants." And when

Abimelech, with reference to Isaac, exclaimed, "He that toucheth this man shall surely be put to death," so with reference to thee, the King of kings has declared, that he who curseth thee shall be cursed; but he who blesseth thee shall be blessed.

But the most important point of comparison between thee and Isaac still remains to be mentioned. It lies in the legacies—in the inheritance bequeathed thee. You know what Isaac inherited from his father. It was not merely house and land, but also the whole of the promises, which the Lord had given to Abraham. And not only are these promises, which rejoiced Abraham and Isaac, made over to thee; but all that God ever uttered, in blessing, upon his people in general, or on individuals of them. It is when thou regardest them as entirely addressed to thee, that they are received in the manner in which thou art justified in receiving them. Accustom thyself to this mode of considering them. Isaac laid hold of the promises, which rested upon Abraham, and treated them, not as if they had been sworn to Abraham, but to himself. Go and do likewise with all the promises of Scripture—write them together in a book, and bind them upon thy heart. Use them as drafts on the Divine treasury, and thou shalt not receive a repulse. They were thrown to thee like a golden chain, wherewith to bind the Lord of heaven and earth. Bind him with it for thine own peace and welfare, and that of those whom thou lovest.

Now tell me, can there be any thing more desirable, in heaven or on earth, than the lot of the people of Jerusalem which is free ? But how few of them realize their happy position ! and how small is the number, even of those, who attain, here below, to the full enjoyment of it ! The ancient covenant of works continues to cleave to them like a heavy weight on their feelings ; and retains them, notwithstanding their noble rights and filial privileges, in vassalage and slavery. There are legal as well as gospel Christians in Zion—children of the bondwoman, according to the words of Paul, although incorporated into Christ, as well as " children of the free." If amongst the former it is said, " When thou hast found Christ, show thyself worthy of the grace thou hast attained," the motto of the latter is, " On finding Christ, rejoice in the Lord always." If the former say, " God's faithfulness connects itself with ours," the latter maintain, " If we believe not, yet he abideth faithful : he cannot deny himself." If the former think, " I *must* now do good works," and go about under the urgency of this feeling, and yet accomplish nothing ; the latter do the works freely without constraint. If the former fall from their fortress, on discovering any unfaithfulness in themselves, and think to atone for it by a certain degree of penitence, and thus heal the broken bond—the others lament their relapses deeply, but in a childlike manner. If the legally-minded are inclined to linger chiefly at that which they have become in themselves—the inclination of the evangelical Christian leads him to view himself more out of himself, in his exalted Head ; and, with all his infirmities, he is thus enabled to be of good courage. If the legally-minded speak of prayer, as of a service or a duty—the evangelical Christian considers prayer degraded by such names, and exercises it as an unspeakably high privilege, and as a blissful employment. If the former are wont to impose upon themselves churchgoing, reading the Scriptures, and speaking of Divine things, as a command, with the strict discharge of which their peace is cemented—the latter also perform all these, because love impels them as free men, to whom, in these things, no law is given. If the former believe that the right of appropriating the blessings of the covenant depends upon a certain degree of personal sanctification—the latter find this in God's free grace, and regard the enjoyment of these blessings, not as a reward, but as the source of all real sanctification and all good conduct.

In these two characters you have the New Testament Jews and Rechabites; those who are impelled by love, and those who are urged on by resolution; those who make holiday in grace, and the hirelings under the commandment; free-acting men of faith, and fettered slaves of dead rules and observances. And as the two characters meet us externally, so does every Christian find them in his own bosom. How often does a workmonger stand forward there to prevent us from prayer, from a free access to the throne of grace, from hope and from joy, because we have not yet attained to some particular height of worthiness! But away with this non-commissioned slave-driver, who darkens the glory, and lessens the merits of Christ; who knows nothing of the Divine economy, and desires to mingle together what God has obviously put asunder. "What saith the Scripture," asks the apostle; "Cast out the bond-woman with her son; for the son of the bond-woman shall not be heir with the son of the free-woman." So then, brethren, we are not the children of the bond-woman, but, as Issac was, the children of promise.

V.—JEHU AND JONADAB

PAUL, in writing to the Corinthians, exhorts them, "as workers together with him," not to receive "the grace of God in vain. For he saith, I have heard thee in a time accepted, and in the day of salvation have I succored thee. Behold, now is the accepted time; behold, now is the day of salvation." 2 Cor. vi. 1, 2.

This passage has its mighty promises, since it is immediately connected with the well-known and very important chapter, in which the accomplished work of our purification in the mediation of Christ is announced, almost more unequivocally than in any other part of Scripture, and the ministerial office which preaches the atonement is so highly spoken of. The disclosures, messages, and entreaties of this office had penetrated even to Corinth, and had not failed of their effect in many instances. Nevertheless, the apostle still finds room and occasion enough for the exhortation you have just heard, and which I do not hesitate on this occasion to make my own to you, and not to you only, but, in the Spirit, to the whole of the churches of this district.

The apostle begins, "We then, as workers together with him, beseech you," by which he designates the lofty position appointed for every faithful minister of the Gospel, to labor at the same work with the King of kings, in a vocation, which far exceeds in sublimity and glory all the most brilliant offices of this world. To many amongst you, the intimation of human instruments in the extension of God's kingdom, as "workers together with him," may certainly appear strange, and little in accordance with the axiom, according to which, grace alone works every thing, and we are capable of nothing. But here again you have an instance, how the holy apostles, in the choice of their expressions, were ignorant of that narrow-minded and anxious foresight, which is, in general, so peculiar to us ; and that they were just as far from our human anxiety, as regards system, as from the partial views with which we are too much accustomed to apprehend Biblical truths. They knew, however, how to defend what they said, and whereof they affirmed, to an iota ; and their freedom of speech was no loose mode of expression, but on all occasions one that was under the influence of Divine truth, and of that alone, which was its only measure and its only limit. The Lord works, in the sphere of spiritual manifestation and development, certainly alone ; but it pleases him, in numberless instances, to accomplish the erection of his kingdom on earth, not immediately, but by our instrumentality. He does so in order, in this manner, to prove his condescending love towards us ; and how great a favor is it, that he should place in our hands his wonder-working rod ! He does so to give, even on this side eternity, a vital and powerful expression to the wonderful incorporation into him, to which his believing people have attained ; for how essentially is this incorporation manifested, when his almighty, saving, and gracious powers stream through us ! He does so, in order again and again to confirm it, that he is really ever with us ; for how tangibly are we conscious of this truth, when we see our poor words falling, either as fiery bombs into Satan's fortresses, or descending as miraculous and healing drops of balm into the deadly wounded and comfortless soul ! He does so, to join us together in sacred bonds of love ; for how tenderly and affectionately, with a love which the world knoweth not, do our hearts beat for those preachers and friends, by whom Divine grace rescued our souls from destruction, or successfully warned, or effectually reproved, or cordially cheered and refreshed us, though it were but in one solitary instance !

" As workers together with him," continues the apostle, " we beseech you." Scriptural exhortations are enlisted into the service of Divine grace, as well as Divine promises. If it be the place of the latter to comfort us—that of exhortation is to bring us to the feeling of our need of comfort. If it be the province of the former to unveil to us the salvation, which God has vouchsafed to us—that of the latter is to shed light upon the way to that salvation. If the object of the former is to unfold to us the treasures of mercy—the latter reveals to us the will of Divine mercy, in accordance with which, we would gladly live, after having experienced the grace of God. Are the promises given us to serve as angels of peace, in pervading our melancholy state—the exhortations serve as lights, in those seasons of gloom, in which we do not rightly know what God requires. Do the exhortations then belong to the Gospel? Were you ever able to doubt it? Even the words of the original include in them the idea of friendly entreaty, and even of consolation. Therefore, my " brethren, suffer the word of exhortation."

But does the apostolic exhortation admit of an application to our particular condition and circumstances? Assuredly, in the most abundant manner. For if Paul speaks of the grace, which was vouchsafed to the Corinthians, the same has been communicated to you also ; to one more, to the other less. Does he speak of an accepted time, in which the Corinthians rejoiced ; the same period has poured forth upon you its copiousness, and accumulates upon you its blessings and its benefits. The apostle has in view, first of all, the New Testament times in general. He quotes from Isaiah xlix. 8, the words, which the Father spoke to his Son, the Messiah, with reference to a great and eventful period that was to come, saying, " In an acceptable time have I heard thee, and in a day of salvation have I helped thee." And it was when the Father heard the voice of the blood of his Son ; when he heard the Lamb of God crying unto him, "Father, forgive them !" when he listened to the

voice of our Surety, when on the ground of the
satisfaction rendered he exclaimed, " I will that
they also whom thou hast given me, be with me
where I am ;" and the infinite merits of the Divine
High Priest, when crying for mercy for poor sinners ; and when the Father delivered his Son
" from prison and from judgment—crowned him
with glory and honor," and thereby gave him the
public and unequivocal testimony, that he had am-
ply fulfilled the work of his atonement and Mediatorship—then was the " accepted time" accomplished, and " the day of salvation" brought near ;
that happy day, which during eighteen centuries
has shone upon a benighted world ; which, instead
of the twilight of typical shadows, surrounds us
with the full blaze of resplendent truth, and places
that in unveiled glory before our eyes, which the
ancients saw only afar off: the cross, and the handwriting that was against us nailed upon it ; Jesus'
empty sepulchre, and in it, the sealing of the accomplished mediatorial work ; the throne of grace, and
on its steps, the blood of the ever-valid sacrifice ;
the open heavens, and on heaven's throne, our
Brother and our Head. This day, which announces
to us, as already brought to pass, that which presented itself only as remote to the view of the
fathers ; this period, which brings with it lucid
Gospels and intelligible Epistles, and no longer de-
tains us with dark prophetic riddles and hieroglyphics , this time " is the day of salvation," an " accepted time," which expanded its radiant, bliss-dis-
tilling wings over the Corinthians, and in whose

lovely splendor we also have been born and brought up.

But the apostle likewise speaks of " the accepted time" evidently in a more limited sense, whilst including in it, at the same time, the pleasing period of the youthful days of the Corinthian church, the days in which the church of the saints was in its growth, in which the apostles addressed them, and in which Paul himself gave them to drink immediately from the heavenly springs of revelation, and was able, with parental kindness, personally to watch over and attend to them. And are you not able, my brethren, to tell of a similar " accepted time ?" Oh, think how delightful was the season, when your own religious life first burst the bud, and the glory of the Gospel, so fully laid open to you, shone upon you with all the splendor of its vernal radiance ; how delightful, when you knew no sound more welcome than the church bells, and when you hastened, in crowds, with joyful expectation, to the house of God ! And the word never returned void. There was a rain of the Spirit which descended upon you—a shaking amongst the dry bones which ceased not—and children were born to the Lord, as dew from the womb of the morning. Oh, how vividly do I still remember how animatedly and joyfully we sowed the seeds of our mission in the field of youthful piety—that germ, which is now grown up to a tree, that extends its beneficent boughs far over the ocean ! How present it still is to my mind, how, with beaming countenances, we celebrated the first festival of our spiritual triumphs—how a host of youthful preachers presented you with garlands of the most fragrant vernal blossoms of their inward life—how from the threshold of our vale to its furthest extremity, the waters of the sanctuary flowed so rapidly, and the spirit of Divine testimony assailed your hearts, against whose force it was necessary for the man to be doubly armed, who would continue in his unbelief! Yes, this was "an acceptable time," during which our valley became a city set upon a hill, which was seen far and wide. During this period, the holy fire went forth from our churches, surrounded the neighboring hills, and kindled blazing fires both far and near. During this period, the beauteous crown of reproach for Christ's sake was woven for us by those that were without, and which adorns us even to the present day. And will it be asserted, that this "acceptable time" is past? Oh no! it still continues in more than one respect. In the preaching to which you now listen, certainly, maturer faith is presented to you, than at that time; you are being more deeply initiated into the word of truth; you are more fervently exhorted to be reconciled to God; and you still attend your places of worship, where souls are occasionally overpowered by Divine grace, and where many a cheering festival is celebrated.

But whilst I am endeavoring to prove to you, that "the acceptable time" still shines upon you, a melancholy feeling steals over me, lest that happy period should be already on the wane. But I will say no more; and however inquisitively you may look upon me, I conceal no secret, except that of my mysterious grief, my sorrowful foreboding. But "the Lord will provide." Suffice it to say, that the present may still be called an "accepted time;" but a more acceptable period has already passed. Abundant grace has been vouchsafed to you. It would be dreadful if you had received it in vain. I know, alas! respecting not a few amongst you, that the droppings of heavenly dew have fallen only on a heated stone, and the solar ray of Divine beneficence has only met with closed doors.

Yes; you need the apostolic exhortation, "We then, as workers together with him, beseech you also, that ye receive not the grace of God in vain." I look upon those amongst you, who saw the stream of blessing to which I previously alluded, rush past them for years together; but their feet alone were moistened by it, their hearts remained untouched. I fix my eyes on others amongst you, who have listened to the invitations of ardent love, and to those sacred and solemn admonitions which, for years together, proved a witnessing spirit amongst you; but the inward death, which you brought with you into "the accepted time," you also take with you out of it. God be merciful to you! I think also of those, who were favored with being spectators of the rich series of delightful festivals of adoration and triumph which, at one time, bloomed among us, but whose knees have never bent before the Lamb. Oh that they may not forever remain unbent! I look likewise upon you, who have witnessed so many wonders of Divine grace and spiritual revivals amongst us, but never vitally experienced the reality of that life, which is from God, nor of union with Jesus. Oh, how often did the net of Divine truth close around you; but ye rent it, because you preferred darkness to light! How often did the arrow of conviction pierce you; but you violently wrenched it from your breasts, and healed the wounds with the deadly salve of wilful self-deception, or with the darkness-causing spirit of worldly lust! Oh, how often has the lightning flashed over the abyss, on the edge of which you sleep! How frequently has the fire-bell rung in your ears, and yet your feet are still walking, as before, on the road that leads to the eternal flame! You have received "the grace of God in vain;" and worse than this could not have happened to you. Oh, awake, even now, from your lethargy! An evening ray, and perhaps a parting one, of the day of salvation, still falls upon your heads! Grace still invites! Oh, "kiss the Son, lest he be angry, and ye perish from the way!"

But God be praised, that all of you have not in vain received grace, even as also the Corinthians, to whom the apostle wrote, and who, as far as they knew the truth, and had devoted themselves to the Saviour, were certainly safe, both for time and eternity. But Paul, nevertheless, addresses his exhortation to them also; from whence it is evident, that the grace of God is effectual to the peformance of other works, besides that of initiatory conversion; and that we, if we are living in strife and contention, or regard each other with suspicion and self-exaltation, or are again becom-

ing conformed to this world, or have fallen back
into apathy and indifference, have ourselves received the grace of God in vain, in so far as it is
not merely an enlightening and a genial influence,
but also one which inflames our love, lifts us above
the world, promotes peace, and quickens us. We
do not deny that, latterly, there have been fewer
contentions amongst pious people, and the points
of doctrine, with which they formerly assaulted
each other, have, by the word of God, been con-
siderably blunted. Both parties have acquiesced
in a more unconditional submission to the whole
of God's word, and yielded to sounder ideas, particularly with respect to the relation between justification and sanctification. Those who thought
legally of the latter, have penetrated more deeply
into the heart of the Gospel, and glory with us in
free grace. Those who refused to hear of sanctification, confess, that the entire glory of the Gospel
has risen upon them only since they perceived
how Christ undertook the twofold task of presenting, mediatorially in himself, the church as un-
blamable to the Father.

But since there has been a cessation of hostilities
amongst us, and opposites have begun to assimilate
themselves to each other, other dangers menace
us, and give us urgent occasion to address to
many amongst us the words of the apostle, " Ye
did run well; who did hinder you?" for we see
them going about among us inflamed, puffed up;
devoid indeed of hatred, but equally destitute of
the freshness of love; no longer inflamed with the

fire of party spirit, but abandoned by the fire of holy zeal, and listless, slothful, inert, and apathetic. Hence the word of exhortation is suitable for us: "We beseech you also that ye receive not the grace of God in vain." You have received grace for the purpose of exhibiting to the world that church, which should render needless all other apologies for the Christian religion, because it was to be a living commendatory epistle, written not with ink, but with the Holy Spirit, actually representing to every beholder, the Divine and sanctifying power of the Gospel; that church, in whose features, he who runs might read, besides the inscription, "Behold, I make all things new," the words, "He that believeth on me, as the Scripture hath said, out of his belly shall flow rivers of living water," the risen Jerusalem-church, in which the Holy Spirit abides.

But how far are you at present from exhibiting any thing like this picture, notwithstanding so much pains has been taken in cultivating the soil, and although the building materials have been so abundantly provided! Woe, woe unto you, if ye have received "the grace of God in vain!" Luther says, "The Gospel does not tarry much above a man's age in one place, it then travels further." May the narrative, which we are this day met to consider, operate upon you still more effectually than these preliminary observations!

2 KINGS X. 15—17

" And when he was departed thence, he lighted on Jehonadab the son of Recbab, coming to meet him; and he saluted him, and said unto him, Is thine heart right, as my heart is with thy heart? And Jehonadab answered, It is. If it be, give me thine hand. And he gave him his hand; and he took him up to him into the chariot   And he said, Come with me, and see my zeal for the Lord. So they made him ride in his chariot. And when he came to Samaria, he slew all that remained unto Ahab in Samaria, till he had destroyed him, according to the saying of the Lord, which he spake to Elijah."

Our two last meditations were exclusively confined to Jonadab's person and rule; let our attention, on the present occasion, be directed to the scene of his meeting with Jehu. Upon this apparently barren passage, we shall nevertheless find traces of hidden riches, and doubt not that gain will reward our trouble.

In pointing out the principal features of our present meditation more particularly, we shall consider, I. The Divine scourge; II. The intimacy; III. The zeal for Jehovah's honor; IV. The triumphal chariot; and V. The journey taken. May these five points serve, as so many steps, to lead us up to the Lord's sanctuary, and to the light of his countenance !

I. The words we have read, introduce us into a solitary district of the Holy Land. A simple tent, over which the branches of the terebinthine tree extend themselves, rises up before us. A little flock grazes quietly and peacefully in its vicinity. We approach the unassuming tent, and are met by the venerable old man, with silvery locks, and simple pastoral attire, with whom we have already become acquainted, namely, Jonadab, the chief of the Rechabites. Here he dwells, far from the bustle of the world, happy in God and his love. Here he himself finds pasture on the ever-verdant meads of Divine promises, and with sabbatic feelings, rejoices in the prospect of that city, in which he believes, and "whose builder and maker is God." Oh, how pleasing is the appearance of such a one, who, before his hour arrives, has cheerfully settled his account with this life, is lying, ready to depart, on the borders of eternity, reflecting already the dawn of a future world upon his forehead, and waiting, in peaceful hope, for a favorable wind, which at length shall impel him towards the object of his most ardent desires! How much more important is the expression of such a state of mind, than a thousand of what are called rational arguments for the immortality of the soul! What a greater abundance of truth, and how much more powerful proof it carries with it than the most brilliant declamations respecting our eternal existence, and a meeting again in another world! That which is the most noble, the most exalted, and the most venerable in the world would be a lie, if the intellectual elevation of such an individual were founded on nothing but a pleasing dream. Nay, a God could not exist, if a hope, which is so willing to renounce the most valuable things this world offers, for the sake of the kingdom of heaven, were not in reality provided, for a state corresponding with the idea formed of it. There ought not to be a single believer who does not anticipate the hour of his departure as the best of his life. But in most cases,

alas! the fashion of this world still exercises a
mighty influence, even over the children of grace;
and there are only a few, who are entirely weaned
from the soil of mutability, and the magic influence
of a specious appearance. Many feel themselves
more at home in this mazy wilderness, than their
prospects of future glory warrant. An immoderate
desire to depart would be a heavy legacy for him,
who had still far to travel through this vale of tears;
we ought, however, all to be inwardly-minded, as
Paul was; the world ought not to have an anchor
in our hearts, and we ought to throw into it only
that of a believing resignation to the Divine will,
and be willing to continue in the circumstances of
our temporal vocation, because God, in his holy
counsels, has so decreed it; whilst the fundamental
principle of our hearts should be, that "to depart,
and to be with Christ," is far more delightful and
desirable than to remain in the flesh. The representation of our inmost feelings should be seen in
those migratory birds, who, on their way to south-
ern zones, may possibly alight upon the verdant
summit of a tree, but without permanently settling
here, keeping fixedly their home in view; for,
truly, the prospect which is opened out to us in
Christ, is delightful, and the hopes we are permitted
to cherish, rest on an immutable basis.

The aged Jonadab had just cheerfully stepped
forth from his pastoral dwelling, boding nothing ill,
when a chariot rolled rapidly towards it, in which
a man in martial attire rose up, who immediately
made himself known as the newly elected king, as

Jehu, the Divine scourge. He came as a treader of the wine-press, and from an awful vintage. The blood of two kings, a queen, and a whole host of their progeny, cleaves to his sword, and yet he has not completed the work of destruction for which he had girded himself. Nevertheless, he goes out of the horrible slaughter pure, because he did not draw the murderous steel from an inherent thirst for blood, but in the name of Him, who occasionally makes his servants storms, and his ministers flames of fire ; who appoints the martial Jehu his executioner, and hides in him the lightning of his holy anger against a degenerate and thoroughly depraved princely family.

Angels of this kind are also still occasionally sent forth, Divinely commissioned from the throne of Jehovah. Not all his ambassadors come with peaceful palm branches ; they also sometimes appear with the bloody banner in their hands—death and destruction in their train—as the Lord's embodied maledictions—as arrows of Divine vengeance, disguised in flesh and blood. We have still to look forward to the appearing of Jehu in the latter character. These ambassadors will rise up in a much more imposing manner, in order, first of all, to bring upon the church of Christ, the awful hour of trial and purification ; then, blindly raging against their own power and dominion, in order to overturn the proud edifice of Satan—the Babel of a thousand years ; and finally, to fall a prey to the two-edged sword, which proceedeth out of his mouth, and inflicts incurable wounds. Oh that the great and triumphant song already resounded, " Babylon the Great is fallen, and is become a habitation of dragons!" Oh that the still more mighty acclamation might soon roar through the world, " The kingdoms of this world are become the kingdoms of our God and of his Christ, and he shall reign forever and ever!" "The Spirit and the bride say, Come; and let him that heareth say, Come!" He that testifieth these things saith, "Surely I come quickly, Amen! Even so, come, Lord Jesus!"

But they are not the worst kind of Jehus, who come with the sword, and can only shed the heart's blood of the body. There are still more dangerous messengers of wrath, who ride through the world, and I fear, alas! ride round our borders, or, at least, have begun to do so.

There is one, first of all, who travels about very softly, and bears upon his banner the inscription, " Peace, peace ; there is nothing to fear ;" and caresses the people, and sings them flattering songs. But beware! They are magical songs, with which he lulls the souls of people to sleep, so that they neither observe that the time is fast passing away, nor hear the solemn tones of an approaching eternity ; and it seems to them that every thing continues as it was. The Scriptures call this destroyer, the spirit of carnal security and of deep sleep.

Another steals through our ranks, whose breath is cold as the breeze of the north pole, and blows upon the people with a chilling, a petrifying effect. Then it suddenly surrounds their hearts like a brazen wall, and not a word, either of warning or invitation, penetrates through any more; and even the fire of love, on Calvary, is no longer able to melt it. The Scriptures call this assassin, the spirit of judicial hardness.

A third scatters a horrible seed into the human heart. He sows lies and strong delusions. When he accomplishes his work, the ability to distinguish between day and night ceases, and error clothes itself, in the eyes of the unhappy mortal, in the radiant robe of truth, and is thus driven into them fimly and forever, as a dreadful nail, by the hammer of the Divine wrath. May God preserve each of us from the attacks of this horrible visitant!

A fourth announces himself to sinners, when in their last agonies. He then approaches, and unfolds before them the record of their lives and the register of their guilt, whilst he veils from their sight the view of Christ and his cross. He causes the terrified mortal to hear the curses of God's broken law; but he prevents him from hearing the voice of that blood, which "speaketh better things than that of Abel;" so that nothing remains for the agonized soul but the despairing cry of Cain, " My punishment is greater than I can bear!" and the appalling path which Judas took. And we see them descending into the pit, alive to all its horrors.

A fifth carries a vial, and from it drops poison into the heart of man—a poison prepared in hell. The individuals are then inflamed with furious rage against Christ and his cause. They know not why it is; but they hate Jesus above every thing; blind, foaming, and inexorable is their hate. Jesus is the only one who could save them; but they hate him. The spirit of bitterness has seized them. Oh, horrible assassin, from whose secret blows no blood indeed flows down, but souls are murdered—no skulls are fractured, but poison is imbibed, which brings eternal death. Hear what alone can protect and save. In Ezekiel ix. we meet with those destroyers. Every one of them has a dangerous weapon in his hand. They come from the way of the north, and by Divine arrangement, are on the road to Jerusalem. Oh, woe to the holy city! The hour of its visitation is come. But what do I behold rising up, together with these terrible ones? Another kind of appearance, venerable and glorious, standing likewise in the presence of the Lord, but coming also from the north. Not a destroyer, no; "I am not come," testifies the lofty One, "to destroy, but to save." Hence, instead of appearing in military array, he is attired in white linen, signifying the spotless righteousness with which he himself is adorned, and may adorn others. Instead of a sword, he has writing materials at his side. He is the writer and recorder of God, to whom the government of the kingdom, and the office of judge of the world, is committed. His name is Christ. "Go through the midst of the city," saith unto him He that sitteth upon the throne. But what does the Divine voice direct further? "Go mark the men that sigh and cry for all the abominations that are done in the midst of the city." Observe those who

mourn over sin; those whose hearts are heavy, because of their own sins and those of their brethren.
But what has the man with the inkhorn to do with
them ?   " Set a mark," saith the Eternal, " on their
foreheads !"   This is, therefore, his office.

" Set a mark !"   In this, my friends, there is a
depth and a mystery.   The words literally mean,
Mark them on the forehead with a Tau.   The tau
is the last letter of the Hebrew alphabet, and had
the form of a cross, and from which the Greek and
Latin T take their origin.   Thus the interpretation
of the passage is easily discovered.   He is commissioned to mark them with the cross, even as of old,
the blood of the lambs in Egypt was a mark to the
destroyers to pass over and to spare.   But who are
they, who have this cross on their foreheads?
Those who dwell beneath the cross, so that it every
moment casts its shadow on their countenances—
who have clung to it, wrestling and weeping, until,
so to speak, the cross impressed itself upon them—
those who publicly boast of the cross, as the only
plank on which they escaped uninjured from a
dreadful shipwreck—on whom, as poor sinners, the
bloody mediatorial cross impressed itself so deeply,
that whatever else might fade away in their hearts,
the cross would not,—those who possess nothing, as
the basis of their salvation, but the blood of their
crucified Surety, and bind themselves, with their
whole souls, freely and privately, to the banner of
the Man of Sorrows, and cling to this blood-besprinkled banner, in order to live and die beneath it ;—
these are the characters who have the mark of the

cross on their foreheads—the man with the inkhorn has himself impressed it.

Happy are these people, for they are safe ! For what does the Lord say to the destroyers? "Go ye after him through the city, and smite. Slay utterly, both old and young, both maids, and children, and women. But come not near any man that has the mark." Be of good cheer, therefore, ye distinguished people of God, beneath the protection of the cross of Christ. How well are ye preserved, protected, and sealed unto the day of glorious reward ! Wherever your lot may be cast, he will forever know you, for it is his mark which you bear. Be concious therefore of the full privilege of your lot, and enter into that sabbatic rest, which is prepared for you.

But as to the rest, the dread command is gone forth, "Slay them utterly!" May it cling to your heels, and follow you wherever you go ! Be it as the awakening sound of a trumpet, may it ring day and night in your ears, until, with humility and contrition of spirit, you sink, imploring mercy at the throne of grace, and languish to have the mark of that cross, in which alone is salvation.

Jehu has now reached the son of Rechab, who would not have lost his presence of mind, even though the dreaded chieftain had appeared with a hostile intent, instead of as now, with the most friendly sentiments. What would have been the result ? He might have killed the body ; but this would have been only Jonadab's gain, who would then have been spared a further pilgrimage, and with one step, would have found himself in the city, which was the object of his most fervent wishes and ardent desires. What can exceed the assured and privileged position of the children of God? No destructive power or influence can any longer affect them. Mention whatever hostile force you please; these men of God stand beyond the range of their shot. And if they come into collision with each other, their encounter with them, in the worst case, is only like that of the ore in the furnace, which eats away nothing but its dross. It is true that grave visitors occasionally knock at their door; but all that is then necessary is, that the good people be found at their posts, under the shadow of the cross, and in the peaceful tabernacles of grace; there is then no longer any cause for terror or affright, whoever may appear. If the images of sins committed present themselves, tell me, ye who are out of Christ, whither would you flee to escape from these spirits of darkness? You can only find a momentary refuge behind the shield of falsehood and self-deception. We, on the contrary, regard them with a feeling, which is not unlike the pleasure of a wanderer, who beholds the poisonous serpents, which had just before threatened him with death, lying crushed at his feet. If Moses present himself with his Divine injunctions, "Thou shalt," and "Thou shalt not,"—you, who are without Christ, what have you to prevent you from feeling alarmed? Nothing but the groundless idea, that he does not mean to be so strict and severe. We, on the contrary, calmly unfold before

him the sumptuous robe of our Redeemer's righteousness, and ask what is wanting, when arrayed
therewith.   If conscience announce itself as an accuser, what remains for you but despair, or disgraceful
stupor ?   We, on the contrary, willingly permit the
inward judge to speak, and justify all his accusations against us ; but no sooner is he desirous of
pronouncing sentence and condemning, than we
accuse him, before a higher tribunal, of presuming
to recommence a suit, which was long ago decided
in our favor on the cross, and eternal silence is
imposed upon the unauthorized accuser.   If the
angel of death announce himself, you can only
shudder and stand aghast, who perceive beyond
the grave merely a dark, horrible, and starless
night.   We exclaim, "Welcome, heavenly deliv-
erer !   Though others tremble before thee, we do
not.   Thy hand no longer wields the sword of
wrath.   A friendly God dispatches thee to us, and
hope walks brightly at thy side.   Unloose these
bonds of dust and clay.   Open the dungeon of
mortality, and present to us angelic pinions for our
upward flight."   Such is the language which is
heard in the tents of Israel, when the wind blows
from Calvary, and the sun of grace sheds abroad
its wondrous rays.

II. Jehu, however, is so far from intending any
evil to Jonadab, that he meets him, on the contrary,
with all the fidelity of a friend, and offers him a
heartfelt salute and greeting.   It might even be supposed he was of a kindred spirit with the pious Re-

chabite. But although it might be said of him, as of king Herod, Mark vi. 20, " He obeyed God in many things," yet he did not belong to the truly converted, as his subsequent conduct evidently proves ; for he feared the Almighty only in so far as he could do so without sacrificing his own self-ishness. Men of this kind are everywhere to be found, who are certainly desirous of having a good understanding with the Most High, but with a strange peculiarity, they retain their ritual, which, minutely examined, consists only in ceremonial ob-servances, and possibly in some pious feelings. Nat-urally, their carnal man has nothing to fear, since not a hair of him will be touched, much less a cross erected for him. These people, as an assistant to their devotion, have " Devotional Hours," and as a surrogate for self-denial, they offer religious com-pliments, and in their deep delusion are scarcely able to comprehend why the service of God and decided worldly-mindedness, should not be most happily joined together.

Jehu, in consequence of circumstances, had at-tained to that fear of God, which induced the Lord to favor him with the crown of Israel. Woe unto any one, who would not, from that time, honor such a God ! " Away with the Sidonian and Philistian idols. Not Baal, but Jehovah is God ! Let him be worshipped ; let temples be built and sacrifices of-fered to him !" Alas for the conversions, the ori-gin of which is solely to be found in the experience of temporal benefits ! Are they generally any thing else than the emotions of carnal pleasure, disguised in pious attire; or as the more or less anxious attempts of human prudence to secure itself against a possible deprivation of the benefits obtained? True conversion is founded on Divine grace inwardly experienced. The individual has obtained forgiveness of sins, and from this cause, the true God of gods is worshipped. He is assured of the love of God and his favor, and therefore he cleaves to him at all hazards. Having found in him his chief good, he desires nothing in heaven or on earth so much as him; he commits all that he is and has to his unlimited disposal; carries his own individuality as a voluntary sacrifice to his holy altar; and desires no wisdom but that of his word, and wishes only one thing, that his gracious will may be done, and his holy name be praised by him, whether in life or in death.

Jehu's conversion certainly sprang not from such a spiritual germ. It was formed of coarser materials, and would scarcely be considered as conversion when weighed in the balances of the sanctuary. At least, it by no means follows, from the fact of Jehu's showing kindness and affection for Jonadab, that truly pious man, that he had himself experienced a thorough renovation of heart. The Lord's words, "The world hateth them, because they are not of the world, even as I am not of the world," sometimes find an exception. There are believers, in whose outward manifestation the ray of their inward life diverges into such pure and multiform lights, and in whose persons so much gentleness, so much sanctified kindness and true humility is reflected, that in reality they do not displease even the world, which is ensnared by that which is earthly. The world observes in them only the outward bloom and fruit of their inward life, and cannot fail to perceive its beauty and supernatural grace. But the hidden ground of heavenly-mindedness in the heart, of which the amiability and moral lustre exhibited in the outward deportment of these people is only a slight reflection, the blind world sees not ; for wherever this is surmised, it immediately confirms, even with respect to the most select of the saved, the word of our Lord to his disciples, "The world hateth you." Such characters, though applauded by the world, have only to lift the veil which covers their interior, and gently whisper to their uncertain friends, "That which you think beautiful in us, is nothing but grace vouchsafed, and the fruit of our fellowship with the Lord Jesus, of our life of faith in his blood," and immediately the world's friendship is at an end, and instead of the wonted expression, "They are a good sort of people," very different appellations and judgments are uttered. It is invariably found, that as soon as the Christian manifests himself no longer as a "well-meaning man," but at the same time as a Christian, that is, as a man in Christ, than he is to them that are without, as "the offscouring of all things," and a "savor of death unto death." "If ye were of the world," saith our Lord, "the world would love its own ; but ye are not of the world, therefore the world hateth you."

The chief motive, which lay at the foundation of

Jehu's gracious visit to our pious shepherd, was, as the history places beyond a doubt, policy and worldly wisdom. It was of great importance to the newly-crowned monarch, that Jonadab should approve of his ascending the throne, as well as of the bloody catastrophies, which necessarily preceded it, and also publicly testify this approval. How great must have been the respect, in which this unassuming man stood with all the people, to make Jehu believe, that when he had obtained Jonadab's approval, it would be, at the same time, a testimony in his favor, which would be regarded, in the eyes of the Israelites, as a Divine sanction! Hence it was that Jehu had made his calculation, thus to make use of Jonadab, as a beautiful robe and a sacred dress, and to add the friendship of the Rechabites to the customary phrase, " We, by the grace of God," as a new seal, which should glitter in the eyes of every one.

The same thing occurs at present also, although in a manner less justifiable, by unconverted characters, in districts where, as with us, true Christianity, according to general opinion, is still of value. They seek the friendship of persons of acknowledged godliness, and boast of it, but only from selfish motives. Some even go so far as to deceive, not merely others, but themselves also, by surrounding themselves with believing Christians, as with priestly holiday garments, and seek, by means of their intercourse, to cause their religious nakedness. They use the love, which pious individuals show them, and the favorable opinion they pass

upon them, and the social intercourse with which
they favor them, as a covering, and boast of them
as infallible marks of their belonging to the people
of God, and being children of his kingdom. But
even such-like coverlets are, in the Lord's sight, but
as cobwebs, and constitute just as little the beauteous array, which availeth in the judgment, as Adam's fig-leaves did. Know, ye deluded mortals,
that even the most enlightened Christians are not
searchers of hearts, and may be very much deceived in their judgment of you. The last and de-
cisive sentence to be passed upon your state is left
to Him, whose eyes are as a flaming fire, who seeth
not as man seeth, but who trieth the heart and the
reins.

After the king had most graciously saluted
Jonadab, he puts the question to him, "Is thine
heart right, as my heart is with thy heart?" By
which he means to say, "Are thy intentions as
sincere towards me, as mine towards thee? and
dost thou approve of my proceedings? speak."
Jonadab replies in the affirmative. "Give me
then thy hand," continues Jehu; and Jonadab con-
sents, and reaches him his hand. You see here a
regular treaty agreed upon. The condescension
shown, on the king's part, to the simple shepherd,
does honor to the former, even although he might
take it for granted, that by it he would run no
danger of losing any of his dignity with respect to
an individual, who regarded the potentates of the
earth, and especially those of Israel, as irradiated
by a far superior glory, than that which a mere

human convention afforded them. We may take it for granted, that Jonadab's yielding submission was wholly free from any impure mixture. There has never been any want of faithless shepherds and hirelings, who regarded it as a small thing to sacrifice truth and conscience to the favor of the gods of this world; but Jonadab, at least, was not one of these miserable beings. For one who enjoyed the eternal friendship of the King of kings, the hand of a mortal, however elevated might be his station, could not possibly be too highly valued. An Israelite, in the real sense of the word, whose predominant feeling was that of being a pilgrim, and who dwelt, with all his hopes and desires, in the city of golden streets, and who stood day and night in the presence of the Lord, such an one, in virtue of this his inward position, was more than secure, notwithstanding all the reverence with which his heart might be filled for the vicegerents of God upon earth, against the magic influence of earthly grandeur, whether it shone upon him in the department of civil authority, or in that of genius and intellectual endowments. Had not Jonadab been most deeply convinced of Jehu's Divine calling, both to be king over Israel, and to the work of destruction, nothing in the world, and the kindness of the monarch as little as his threats, would have been able to make him utter a word for the mere purpose of obliging him. That he is of the same mind with him, and that he approves of Jehu's cause, is solely because he clearly perceives, from the object he has in view, and the entire direction his life had taken, the counsel of Jehovah, and his judicial arrangments. Hence we behold him equally as free, whilst consenting, approving, and rendering homage, as in other circumstances he would prove himself to be, were he obliged to express his disapprobation, censure, and condemnation. The liberty which consists in not swearing, nor being willing to swear, beneath any other flag than that of truth, is alone worthy of its fair name. But there is only One who can thus make us free; it is the eternal Son. He alone teaches us the great art of loving and esteeming none in earth or heaven but himself.

III. Jehu requests his silver-haired friend to seat himself by him in his chariot. "Come with me," says he, "and see my zeal for the Lord." This is a high sounding speech; but he was justified in uttering it. There might indeed, were we to seek the solution of his zeal in its fundamental principles, be found a tolerably large substratum of mere carnal energy for the establishment of his own power and glory; but still there would remain so much of what is commendable, that he would continue sure of the fair title of a "zealot for the Lord."

"Zeal for the Lord!" Oh, why is it that in the garden of our church, we so seldom meet any longer with this fiery lily of heavenly origin? Here and there I perceive a glimmer; but it is not that beauteous flower, but only its earthly shadow and vapory form, although luxuriating at the altar. Consider the encampment of our believing divines.

I greet with pleasure this well-equipped force, and observe how it has closed its ranks against the standard-bearer of a God-and-Christ-denying philosophy. I mark their zeal ; but what becomes of it on closer examination? Alas! in most cases, our friends are desirous only of a *scientific* triumph over an opposition, which was bold enough to accuse them of ignorance ; and although they burn fiercely for the maintenance of their system against the attacks of objecting reason, yet they give little evidence of a holy indignation against their foes as an ungodly and blaspheming troop, who dare to touch the honor of their supremely beloved Lord. They glow only with a human fire; and refer indeed to the examples of Nadab and Abihu, but not to such warriors as Moses and Elias. There stand our sharpshooters in array against the host of rationalists. They draw their bow, and aim bravely, and burn with martial fury. We bless their banner beneath the colors of truth. But of what kind are their witticisms and their raillery? "This is flat, and that devoid of spirit, and that yonder, obsolete or scientifically null and untenable." Such are their arrows, such their glittering swords. But we seldom hear from them the words, "This is wicked, absurd, or blasphemous," forced from them by a sacred pang, and accompanied by a shudder at the appalling and awful position of their opponents. They strive indeed for the good cause, but only as light infantry ; whilst the real armor, the Divine, prophetic, apostolic panoply of a pure fervor for the Lord's kingdom, as such, seems a strange and unknown thing to them. Our regards fall on the representatives of the Protestant cause. They stand well armed, in rank and file, and their heavy ordnance against the old lying edifice of the seven hills does not fail of the mark. How they uncover the nakedness of a canonized irrationality! How do they anatomize the errors, which have lasted a thousand years, to the very nerves and fibres! How do they draw forth priestly deception, out of its mummery and its sanctimonious decorations, to the light of day, and think highly of themselves, and rejoice with a triumphant joy! Well, we rejoice with them; but there is one thing we would gladly not miss in our heroes. We look for a tear of sacred grief over such "abomination of desolations;" for the pure fire of Divine indignation at that which is antichristian, demoniacal, and dishonoring to God and his Anointed in the mighty lie; for the sigh, originating in profound and tearful grief, ejaculating, "Oh that the Lord would graciously look upon it, and put an end to such horrible desolation!" It is for these we inquire; but in vain. We perceive, indeed, the struggle for truth against error; but where is the divinely-begotten zeal, the inward weeping over the desecration of his name, the life-consuming ardor that God may be glorified, and that to him every knee may bow?

Nor do we refuse our gratitude and heartfelt thanks to the antagonists of frivolous axioms, refined worldly-mindedness, and the immoderate love of dissipation and enjoyment, exhibited in the present day; but we should promise ourselves an infinitely greater effect, and a much more considerable result from their well-furnished declamations against a world sunk in materialism, if they were pervaded by as much of holy and indignant grief, at the impiety of this modern mode of life, of as that bitter satire, which is wont to inflame them against its vanity, inanity, and beggarly vacuity. Alas! our prophets themselves have more or less partaken of no inconsiderable drop of the intoxicating cup of that homage, which is paid to outward appearances by the present age, and carry with them still too great a remnant of a sympathy, never overcome, which operates like a hidden magnet, when proceeding to the attack against those vain pursuits. Still too excitable and susceptible themselves, either for the honor of being regarded as philosophers, for the charms of art, or for that which the world calls intellectual, ingenious, and original, they stand, beforehand, crippled on the battle-field; and only remind us of the well-known heroes at the brook of Sorek. Delilah's anger has passed over their heads, and it never occurs to the Philistines to be afraid of the menaces and blustering of men, whose inward heroism remains behind in the hands of the wanton. O ye ancient heralds of the kingdom; ye zealots for the Lord, with your pure, genuine, heartfelt earnestness; ye who stood forth with the all astounding lamentation, "Oh that my head were waters, and mine eyes a fountain of tears, that I might **weep** day and night for the slain of the daughter of **my** people!" ye, with the dead-awakening trumpet-sound, " O earth, earth, earth, hear the word of the Lord !" with the rock-rending word of thunder, " Why will ye die, O house of Israel !" O ye walking flames of zeal, armed as with threefold coats of mail against the enervating influences of a corrupt age ; ye who, for the honor of Jehovah and his kingdom, were wont to greet the reproach of Christ as your fairest crown, and regarded the world's laurels and its glories as dung, for the excellency of the knowledge of your Lord—Isaiah, Jeremiah, Daniel, Paul, Luther, Calvin, Knox, and whatever your names may be—yes, ye are the individuals whom such an age as ours requires ! Men formed out of one piece, one mould, with that lucid vision which no enchantment could trouble : men who soared on eagles' pinions above the heights and depths of their century, and whose only passion, which glowed in their sanctified bosoms was, that Immanuel might reign, and be magnified and glorified. Oh, rise from your ashes, ye venerable forms! return, and restore a degenerate race to a renewed consciousness of what is meant by being baptized with fire from on high, and how, where perfect faith exists, the grace of Christ shows itself powerful in human weakness !

" Zeal for the Lord !" There is no want of the appearance of this zeal amongst us. Oh that from the appearance we could always infer the reality ! There have latterly again appeared amongst us, many bold confessors of the name of Jesus, warlike opponents of the false prophets, active promoters of missionary and Bible associations ; but it would be too rash an inference to conclude, that with all of these, the glory of the Lord is the bride, whose suitors they are. It is, alas! too manifest, that there are, at least, not a few amongst them who do not seek in all things the glory of God. Whilst hanging out the sign of the purest humility, they are still not always able to conquer the desire to be something themselves in the Lord's cause. Only put them to the test, and inform them, in accordance with the truth, that in and through themselves, they neither are, nor possess, nor can effect any thing which can stand in the sight of God; and that their salvation depends just as little on their willing and running, as that their enlightening, conversion, and justification, as well as their sanctification and preservation, is an unmingled work of free grace, to which they have neither contributed, nor are in a state to contribute of themselves—a work of grace of such a kind, that in case the Lord were inclined to take back what he had freely bestowed, not an iota of self-acquired good would be left to them: it is only necessary to preach this to them, and what would be the results? You would see very many of your brethren alter their feelings and demeanor towards you, and partially take up arms against you, with an excitement, compared with which, that wherewith they opposed infidels and the enemies of the Gospel, was scarcely felt by them. I would call to many amongst you, and say, "Do you wish to prove your zeal for the Lord and his glory, manifest it first of all by unconditional submission, by approving of his word in every respect, and by leaving to his grace the splendor of his majesty, by which it appears everywhere surrounded in his word. It is not enough that you place yourselves, with pious mien or religious phraseology, at the corners of the streets; nor does it suffice to approach, with splendid offering, the poor's-box, or the altar of heathen missions. Go, first of all, to the altar of burnt-offering, on which the individual presents himself to the Lord. Slay before him there, the last remains of the foolish idea, that you possess any wisdom, righteousness, and strength of your own. Acknowledge, in profound humility, that unless you are held, borne, and cared for, by Divine grace, from one moment to another, you would perish, notwithstanding your professed conversion; and that if it did not freely bestow upon you every thing needful for life and godliness, you would neither be nor possess any thing—nay, less than nothing, if that were possible. Do as I have now said, and we will boast concerning you, that you give God the glory. The motto by which true zeal for the Lord is always made cognizable, is found in the well-known words of the Baptist, " He must increase, but I must decrease."

IV. Jonadab accedes to the king's proposition, and places himself at his side in the chariot. He would not have seated himself on his throne, could this honor have been purchased with even the slightest betrayal of the truth. If it be of importance to Jehu, Jonadab is ready, on his part, freely and openly to testify his approval of his acts, because

he knows that he is furnished with the Divine sanction.   That abominable flattery, which places the
most sacred convictions, like figures on a chess-
board, in the hands of the mighty of the earth, had
not desecrated Jonadab's breast.   Sooner would he
have laid his neck beneath their axes, than nod as-
sent, to please them, in disgraceful eye-service to
any thing whatever, of which the voice of conscience disapproved, and which it condemned and
rejected.   It was, nevertheless, an unwonted position, to which the simple shepherd was suddenly
exalted.   But one who really lives in the Lord, and
walks in the light of eternity, will never be defi-
cient in any situation of life, even the most ensnar-
ing, in that which we call manly bearing, presence
of mind, and real tact.   In the same plain and sincere manner will Jonadab have rendered to the
monarch at his side what was his, and what was
due to him ; but in other respects, have been just as
far from that mean-spirited, awkward, and mind-
confusing embarrassment, which is wont so easily
to disturb characters of an inferior kind in the presence of earthly potentates, as he was near in spirit
to the throne of the King of kings.   He certainly
considered it an honor, when seated by Jehu's side,
to be even a mute witness to the truth, that it was
God who had now girded himself for judgment.   But
the honor afforded him by the uncommon condescension of his monarch, was only valued by him in
the degree, in which it applied to the Master whom
he served, whose cause on earth he represented,

and the promotion of whose glory was the most fundamental and vital desire of his heart.

The two, then, are seated side by side. How strangely matched! The one a mysterious enigma; the other its radiant signification: like a dark thunder-cloud, gently illumined by a promising rainbow; as if law and gospel had embodied themselves for the purpose of exhibiting living allegories—Jehu, the "woe" of Divine justice upon all ungodliness; Jonadab, the guide-post upward to the throne of grace. Both emblematical figures at the temple-gates of the eternal sanctuary; expressive testimonies of the one thing needful.

The true church, indeed, boasts of a still sublimer alliance and fellowship than that of earthly potentates. Did not He elevate her with him on his triumphal chariot, who is called the Prince of the kings of the earth, and who will never rest, till he has laid all her foes low at her footstool? But his time of waiting is not yet expired. The order of Divine justice demands, that before the kingdom of Satan experiences the destroying stroke, space should be given it for a certain degree of development and expansion. The seed of ungodliness must ripen, ere the sickle be put in. But how rapidly does it hasten, in modern times, towards this maturity! How complete becomes the general declension! How anti-christianity strips itself of its coverings, more and more, in which hitherto a certain apprehension of public opinion, or "a pious prejudice," as they call it, had retained it! How does infidelity rise to the most decided atheism; pride to the maddest deification of the human mind; carnality to the most refined materialism! Is there a man in the present day, whose heart is engaged in the cause of Christ, who does not become alarmed and terrified? Faith, however, is not afraid; but goes about already triumphing over these manifestations, because it discovers nothing in them, but the signs that the day of the Lord is at hand, and the triumph of the adversary is near its end. "The Bridegroom cometh; the great Treader of the wine-press girds himself!" That which a hopeful faith joyfully anticipated, now becomes matter of record, and the historical account of our Kingdom's triumph, the history of its final, glorious, and everlasting completion.

V. After the Rechabite has taken his seat in the royal carriage, they drive off at full speed to the commission of a new tragedy. The priests of Baal are, this time, devoted to be slain. The sight of the pious Jonadab, by the side of Jehu, does not fail of its desired impression on the minds of the people. The doings of Jehu all at once appear in the light of a superior sanction; his executions bearing the stamp of Divine approbation. Jonadab's position doubtless caused him pain and sorrow enough. How much would he have preferred overthrowing Jehovah's foes by the power of converting grace, than by that of destroying wrath! But the Lord's counsel was opposed to this, and Jonadab's self-denying submission to it was a greater virtue than, notwithstanding its superior appearance, a misplaced and disapproving pity would have been in this instance. It is foolish to suppose that every thing in the world should proceed according to the effeminate sentiment which we call love. The well-known saying, "Every sinner shall be forgiven, and hell be no more," is as wicked as it is popular, notwithstanding all its absurdity, with this volatile and insipidly religious age. "Damnation," says a sentimental lady, "is a joyless, and therefore an incorrect idea." If any thing be incorrect, it is the assertion which denies sin, as such, and robs God of his holiness. Light is not conceivable, except as in struggling opposition to darkness, nor God, except as in decided opposition to evil. A legislating God, who is not at the same time a judge, would be the most absolute contradiction, and a nonetity. To fear God, is to confess, on our knees, that his name appears equally glorious in the flaming characters of infernal punishment, as in the bloody ones of the work of redemption, and the rosy ones of grace. A psalm, which glorifies him, is the hallelujah of the redeemed in heaven; and the despairing moans of the lost in the eternal wastes, also bespeak his glory. It becomes his children, when he condescends to and favors sinners, to offer up the severity of their hearts, as much as their insipid and human tolerance, when he rejects and punishes.

Jehu and Jonadab thus sitting together, remind us of another connection of a more spiritual nature and kind. They remind us of the old and new man in every true Christian. How seldom does the Spirit manifest itself in his works and occupations, without the flesh mingling itself with them! But how rarely, on the contrary, does nature alone act, so that grace, or the new Divine man, does not operate at the same time! When Moses hurled the stone tablets of the law upon the ground, and broke them in pieces, his unrenewed nature manifested itself together with the new man, as it were in one and the same cloud. They appeared, as in one chariot, in the case of Elijah, when he called upon the Lord his God, under the juniper tree, that he would take his life from him, because he was weary of this miserable existence. How intimately connected did they appear in Peter, when he seized his sword in Gethsemane, in order to attack his Master's foes! And I should be glad to know, my dear friends, in which of our performances they are not seen together in us. Do you imagine it is not the case when we give alms, or are angry with unbelievers, or express ourselves eloquently on spiritual things, or promote religious undertakings, or approach the Lord in prayer? Alas! even in our holiest moments, it is very rarely that Christ ascends in us alone; the old Adam always associates himself with him, in some way or other, and our best works remain partial and imperfect. But because the old man sometimes receives a borrowed glimmer from the divine beauty of the new, he does not, on that account, cease to be what he is, a disgusting creature, on whom sentence of death is passed; or that because in the performances and actions of the new, the old often mingles something of his own, is the former polluted, and ceases in the sight of God to be perfect and pure. However, the longed-for time will come, when the new man will be left alone, and the old taken from his side forever. For he only sits near the former now, as a dying guest, long marked by the Lord for the sword, and already carrying the germ of death in his members.

The two, as we have already heard, are hastening to Samaria, to a fresh scene of bloodshed. Jonadab will only be a spectator of it; the sword-bearer is king Jehu. In the more desirable position of Jonadab, ours is reflected, although in a slight degree, so far as we are in the faith. The King of kings has elevated us to his seat, and continues to fight for us, as he once did in our stead. Why should we care? Let us be tranquil and joyful. That which is still opposed to and leagued against us, he will subdue and destroy for us. All that we have to do is, to wave our colors, and cry, "Victory!" Let us never forget the position which is appointed us. If any thing comes to terrify us, let us touch Him who sits by our side, and whisper in his ear, "Lord, take thy sword!" and then be confident, and wait for the deeds of his arm. We shall unfailingly keep the field. They that wait on the Lord shall "never be put to confusion."

Before the new massacre begins, the two allies make an excursion over the battle-fields, where the enemies of Jehovah are already lying in their blood, and remind us thereby of our own prerogative, since we also are justified and enabled to make in the Spi

rit, similar excursions on the chariot-wheels of faith.
We ride forth, and touch, first of all, upon a mysterious hill.   An awful sign is raised upon its summit.   Oh, how many slain here cover the field!
They are the sins of our lives.   They are overcome, slain, and put away before God ; not indeed
with the sword, but, strangely, by the blood of a
sacred Lamb.   A voice resounds over the scene
of slaughter, "Christ hath redeemed us from the
curse of the law, being made a curse for us : for it
is written, Cursed is every one that hangeth on a
tree !"   Lovely ride !   We breathe the air of peace.
"Who is he that condemneth ?"   We continue our
excursion, and arrive at a garden, where an open
and empty sepulchre meets our view.   Hallelujah !
A mighty giant here licked the dust !   Here a triumph was celebrated over the king of terrors,—
"Death is swallowed up in victory.   O death, where
is thy sting !"—life and immortality are brought to
light.

Our spiritual chariot carries us further ; and we
see before us, with joyful eyes, a ruined dungeon.
It is the castle of the prince of darkness.   His sceptre over us is broken, and although, for our purification, a little space is allowed him, yet all right
over our souls is taken from him, and his head is
bruised.   The wicked one shall touch you no more.
We follow our path, and lo, what a spectacle presents itself !   Even Moses, with his commands and
requirements, not slain indeed, but in the most holy
and legitimate manner overcome, and compelled to
do homage to us, sinners, to acknowledge us as

righteous, and to take back all the curses which he had heaped upon us. "Christ is the end of the law—he that believeth on him is justified."

We go forwards, and halt at the temple. It is Pentecost. See ye the little flames of fire descending? Another victory. Death in us is also overcome by life from above. The force of gravity in our nature is annihilated by the fire of a spirit soaring heavenwards. "If any man be in Christ, he is a new creature." "Old things are passed away: behold, all things are become new."

We hasten further, and a beautiful blooming meadow stretches itself out before us. It is that of the Divine promises; but this scene likewise is covered with the slain. Our cares are the foes, which here lie breathless, powerless, and even slain upon the ground—our anxieties about our daily bread—how we shall get through the world—as well as those about spiritual nourishment, preservation, and protection. They have here together found their graves. "Be careful for nothing!"— "Be of good cheer; I have overcome the world!"

Thus are the hostile powers trodden down, as regards those who are in Christ Jesus. Let us also, my brethren, become more vividly and constantly conscious of the lofty position, which we have attained in Christ, and learn to tread the ground more firmly. Whilst concealed in his wounds, why should we fear the terror by night? Covered by his wings, the wings of his grace, why should we dread "the destruction that wasteth at noonday?"

VI.—JOASH

HEAR ye the testimony of the apostle John: "That which was from the beginning, which we have heard, which we have seen with our eyes, which we have looked upon, and our hands have handled of the Word of life; (for the life was manifested, and we have seen it, and bear witness, and show unto you that eternal life which was with the Father, and was manifested unto us;) that which we have seen and heard declare we unto you, that ye also may have fellowship with us; and truly our fellowship is with the Father, and with his Son Jesus Christ." 1 John i. 1—3.

What words! A stream of light and life, swelling above its banks, pours itself out in this passage. Oh, what a mixture of love and holy rapture is heard in these words! You hear how the apostle struggles for language, and how our poor human sounds are much too circumscribed for him, and too scanty to afford a suitable expression for that which affects his inmost soul. You perceive that, for this reason, he is even on the point of breaking off at the very commencement, as well as that he is not master of his feelings, and how his full heart breaks every barrier, and bursts every bond. Here we have the beloved disciple before us in the most peculiar aspect of his character. Like an eagle of the sun—young and vigorous—he soars, with majestic pinions, above the world, and rises to the throne of glory. His forehead shines with the rays of eternity; and his language sounds down into the world like the thunder, which, though it causes its voice to be heard, does not come forth from the clouds betwixt which it is enthroned.

"That which was from the beginning," writes the apostle, at the commencement of his epistle. He has elevated his wings, and shaken the dust of the earth from his feet. The eagle eye of his enraptured spirit rises above all the bounds of time and space. Behind him lie the limits of all that has been—low beneath him vanishes the world of human ideas. He flies into the boundless past—far, far beyond the manger and the cross—beyond the hoary ages of the promise and the law—beyond the days of the patriarchs, and of creation itself—into the infinite, the commencement of all things—into boundlessness, where no time had been measured, no moons had waned, no years flown past like an arrow. He is in eternity; an infinite void is around him, where worlds now revolve. No earth is yet verdant in the depth; no firmament radiant in the height, telling of the glory of God; no seraph dwelling in eternal light. One alone reigns—even He who ever was, and whose years know no end, the all-sufficient, the alone blessed. And in his bosom rests his only-begotten Son.

"That which was from the beginning," exclaims the apostle. His voice sounds to us like that of a spirit, and transports us, not merely to the throne, but to the heart of the eternal Father. Christ was from the beginning. Whilst as yet there was nothing, the great idea of redemption was already conceived in the heart of the Father. That which should afterwards be, in the course of future ages, was present with him. He already saw the world, called forth out of nothing; the fiery spirits, still uncreated, as already created before him; the blissful pair already walking in the sweet shade of the palm-trees of Paradise; and saw the serpent lurking amongst the flowers; and the creation, with man, its lord, fallen a prey to sin, death, and the curse. And lo! the ocean of eternal mercy is already sounding, and Divine love stretches out the saving arm to the fallen. The question resounds through heaven, "Who will go for me?" and the Son presents himself, saying, "Lo, I come to do thy will, O God;—for thy law is within my heart." The apostle sees it in spirit; and exclaims in blissful astonishment, "That which was from the beginning!"

He then continues, "of the Word of life." Thus he denominates Christ. Oh what a depth is in this name! The incomprehensible connection of the Son with the eternal Father is thereby signified; and thus discloses to us, although with a stammering tongue, and under an earthly figure, the fact, that Christ is truly God, and one with the Father, with respect to glory, nature, and being. Even as the word, which proceeds out of our mouths, reveals and expresses the hidden thought of our souls, and differs from the thought, and is yet one therewith, and comprehends it within us: so the hidden God was bodily made manifest in Christ, on which account he is called "the face of God," and "the God of manifestation." Even as the thoughts of my heart come to thee on the wings of my words, so the all-sufficient God has visited us in Christ. As by means of the word, thy soul becomes intimately connected with mine, so that thou art now at home in my soul, and the latter has poured itself out into thine, so Christ is the Mediator between God and us, by whom we are re-introduced into fellowship with God, and God again dwells lovingly in us. In short, the apostle means to say, that the Man in Joseph's workshop and on the cross, is God, and born of God; that he it is through whom, and for whose sake, the world was created; by whom alone it exists; and from whom it receives every blessing from on high.

After having designated him as the centre of all evangelical preaching, he then brings forward the infallible certainty of his testimony regarding him, and continues, "We have heard" that which we announce to you of him. In the word "we," he includes the whole cloud of departed and still living witnesses for Christ. He sees the spirits of patriarchs and prophets—these wandering light-houses in the night—the seven that landed on Ararat, the man of gigantic faith from the grove of Mamre, the successful wrestler with God, the eagle beneath

Sinai's trumpet, which flapped its wings, even into the darkness where the Almighty dwells, and the royal harper on mount Zion. He sees these ancient heralds, to whom Jehovah spake by word of mouth, and challenges them, in the spirit, to make known that, which they once heard, from the clouds, of the Lion of the tribe of Judah, of the Sun of righteousness, which should arise upon the darkness of the earth. And besides them, he beholds his brethren the apostles, who sat with him at the feet of the Prince of peace, were with him on the holy mount, and heard with him the majestic testimony from on high, "This is my beloved Son, in whom I am well pleased; hear ye him!" and who, with him, beheld his glory, "the glory as of the only begotten of the Father, full of grace and truth." He sees the shepherds, who heard the hallelujahs of the angels above the hills of Bethlehem, the comforted and beatified sinners, to whom the gracious words were addressed from his lips, "Your sins are forgiven you; go in peace," and who, from that hour, had all the wounds of their souls healed. This happy host of witnesses, whom no man can number, he sees in spirit, and joining himself with them, he exclaims, "The Saviour has appeared, for we have heard him!"

"And have seen," continues he; "seen with our eyes;" and oh, the never-to-be-forgotten periods which then presented themselves to his inward view! He sees him walking once again upon the earth; and fiery traces of a new life wait upon his steps, and death and woe flee before him, and deeds of omnipotence and love mark out his path. Here storms are silent at his high behest; there the billows form a firm footway beneath his steps; yonder flee the powers of darkness before him, and awestruck implore him not to banish them into the deep. John recalls all this, and exultingly exclaims, "We have seen him!" Seen? no, continues he, "we have looked upon." By which he means, we do not testify of Christ from a transient manifestation, which passed before us with the rapidity of lightning; no, we feasted upon him quietly and delightfully, have associated with him, have for days and years together dwelt in the light of his countenance, and sunned ourselves in the wondrous splendor of his beauty.

Yes, "our hands" continues he further, "have handled him!" Oh, what delightful remembrances affect his heart at these words! He here not only calls to mind how frequently they sat around him in the social circle, how he laid their hands in his, their fingers in his wounded side; but those hours especially present themselves to his view, when he, in particular, enjoyed the bliss of reposing on the bosom of the fairest of the sons of men; when, with his bodily ear, he heard the beating of the compassionate heart of the sinner's Friend, and felt upon his face, that Divine breath, which brought health and cure. On these things thinks the apostle, and his meaning is, "He manifested himself to all our senses, and filled our eyes, our ears, and our hands with his glory."

Oh, if the ancient kings and prophets had been

permitted to see and hear that, which the apostle
John, and even ourselves have seen and heard!
But their days fell in the period of waiting and hoping.   Oh, how difficult was it occasionally for them
to maintain their belief in Him, who was also their
sole comfort in life and death!   What privileges
are vouchsafed to us, in comparison with those
children of the Old Testament!   The narrative we
are about to consider will render us more conscious of this, and convince us, that our relation to
Jesus, compared with that of the Old Testament
saints, will show that we have every reason to rejoice with the apostle, and say, "That which ye
greeted at a distance, we have heard, seen, and handled of the Word of life."

2 KINGS XI. 1—4.

" And when Athaliah the mother of Ahaziah saw that her son was
    dead, she arose and destroyed all the seed royal.   But Jehosheba,
    the daughter of King Joram, sister of Ahaziah, took Joash the
    son of Ahaziah, and stole him from among the king's sons which
    were slain; and they hid him, even him and his nurse, in the
    bed-chamber from Athaliah, so that he was not slain.   And he
    was with her hid in the house of the Lord six years.   And Atha-
    liah did reign over the land.   And the seventh year, Jehoiada sent
    and fetched the rulers over hundreds, with the captains and the
    guard, and brought them to him into the house of the Lord, and
    made a covenant with them, and took an oath of them in the
    house of the Lord, and showed them the king's son."

THE event, the commencement of which you
have just heard, does not indeed belong to the history of Elisha, but occurs during his lifetime, and must
certainly have deeply and pleasingly affected the
man of God.   But occurrences which, tending to

strengthen, elevate, and animate our faith, have had
their influence upon our minds, justly occupy a
place in the portrait of our lives, however far they
may have lain out of the sphere in which we moved.
Permit me then to interweave this affecting, as well
as consoling and referential circumstance, as a
pleasing episode, into our meditations, and speak to
you of the wondrous king Joash; the imminent
danger which menaced him; as well as how gloriously he was preserved, and how highly honored.

I. The scene of the event related in our text, is
not Samaria, where Elisha was residing, but Jerusalem, the metropolis of the kingdom of Judah.
You know what deep wounds the Divine avenging
sword, in Jehu's hand, had inflicted on the royal
house of that kingdom.   Judah's ruler, Ahaziah, together with his cousin Joram, the king of Israel,
had fallen the same day in Israel; and the same
fate had befallen two-and-forty of his nearest relatives, during their journey to Israel, as they were
approaching the summer pavilion of their royal
friend.   The throne of Judah thus became vacant,
and opportunity was afforded to Joash, the younger
son of Ahaziah, who at his father's death was
scarcely a year old, to succeed to it.   But an evil-
boding star, with baleful ray, shone on this youthful
scion of royalty—the envious and jealous eye of his
own grandmother on the father's side, Athaliah.
This proud and idolatrous woman had inherited all
the sins of her father Ahab, and her mother Jezebel, of scandalous memory, and from the latter had

received, as a dowry, that insatiable thirst for rule, in which she could not brook to be the second, when it was denied her to be first.   Scarcely, therefore, had Athaliah received intelligence of the death of her royal son, than the flagitious desire of seizing the reins of government glowed in her breast, instead of grief and sorrow.   She soon stood immutable in her resolution to satisfy, at any price, the demands of her pride, although, in order to reach the throne, it were necessary to pass over the slaughtered bodies of her grandchildren.   She soon perceived, that there was no other path, than that of murder, for the attainment of her object, and therefore assembled around her her favorites and intimates ; hinted at her intention ; divided, doubtless under promise of costly rewards, the bloody part, which each was to act, amongst them ; and in one night, a piece of wickedness was enacted in Jerusalem, at which the very stones might have trembled and been horrified.   The young sons of Ahaziah were suddenly attacked in their bed-chambers, and stabbed without pity, before the eyes of their horrible grandmother, and perhaps by her own hand.

And did the Almighty God keep silence at this deed, and permit the dreadful crime ?   We are surprised, especially, when we consider what an important and significant place these massacred children occupied in the chain of the Divine economy.   In them the stock was verdant, which the Lord crowned with the promise, that out of it should arise the mighty Seed of the woman, which should bruise the serpent's head; and how could this promise be fulfilled, if the root from whence the long-looked for Scion was to shoot forth, were laid waste? Thus the murderous hand was raised, not merely against the princes, but it gave, at the same time, the mortal blow, at least, apparently, to the most blessed of Jehovah's engagements—nay, even to the salvation of mankind. Probably, no massacre ever caused greater joy to Satan's kingdom, or to the little flock of believers deeper anxiety and distress, than that which took place in the palace of Jerusalem. According to all appearances, the serpent-bruiser was slain in the loins of his fathers according to the flesh; Satan's victory over Jehovah decided; the hope of the saints destroyed; and, alas! the truth and faithfulness of God placed in the most equivocal light.

So it seemed; but, God be thanked! it was not so in reality. How often does it happen, that the Lord himself walls up his way with hindrances, which, at the moment, never fail to throw us into the greatest consternation. But, however insurmountable they may seem, yet they never hinder the realizing of his counsels and his promises. Before we are aware, in order that his power and faithfulness may shine forth to our view so much the more brilliantly, the opposing objects are not only overcome, but even transformed into the means of promoting the Divine intentions. Do you require proofs of this comfortable truth? how richly are they afforded us in the human line of descent of the Mediator, and its history! How we find

ourselves irradiated there, by the unfolded glory of
all the Divine perfections! We welcome the occurrence in the palace of Jerusalem as a desirable
occasion to cast, if but a hasty look, on that genealogy. We are acquainted with every member of
it from the twofold document preserved for us in
Matthew i. and Luke iii. We here meet, indeed,
with only a bare genealogical table, and nothing
but names; but it is a tree which, on closer inspec-
tion, begins to bud and put forth luxurious foliage,
and will reward a still narrower investigation with
a thousand fragrant flowers.

Even the register itself, as placed before us in its
extension through thousands of years, necessarily
produces in us no small astonishment. There are
families amongst us, who regard it as a high honor,
and a claim to nobility, that they are able to reckon
back their genealogy to the eighteenth or twentieth
generation. In the family register of the Virgin
Mary, we have before us a pedigree, which looks
back through forty centuries, on one hundred and
seventeen ancestors, and touching the world's commencement with the last fibre of its root, specially
adduces, by name, each of its predecessors. This
itself is something unheard of and wonderful. This
of itself is a fact, which brings with it evidence of
a more than human arrangement.

At the time when our Lord was born, this genealogy existed complete in Israel. It was possessed
as a precious legacy, in the bosom of many a pious
family. The public archives also preserved it, upon
ancient parchments, as a treasure, with which

scarcely any other could compare. Who was the
editor of this wondrous family register? Who so
carefully continued it from one generation to another? It was indubitably done by a higher hand;
though not immediately from heaven, but through
human means and instruments. Contemplate, with
a devout feeling, this long-continued list of names
in Matthew, from Abraham downwards: in Luke
even from Adam to Mary. This wondrous chain
has been knit and connected together by precious
hands. The thread, on which these names, like
pearls and precious stones, are hung, though invisible to the naked eye, is on that account not the less
costly and golden. Hopeful faith is the thread, and
ardent longing and love ranged them upon it. The
ancients knew how unspeakable was the gift, which
the Lord so graciously intended to bestow upon
them. They knew that to them, though poor sinners, and broken by the law, a Saviour, a Prince of
peace, a sin-destroyer, would arise. "From Abraham's seed shall he come," was the promise in the
twentieth century of the world; and after this revelation, there was no end to the attention paid, the
investigation carried on, and the recording of every
birth in the line of promise. During the first centuries, it certainly was no hard matter to continue
the genealogy of the race, from out of which the
Messiah was expected. From Abraham, the hope
naturally connected itself with Isaac; from Isaac
to Jacob, whom the Lord plainly enough preferred
to his brother Esau. It was only till the dying
hour of Jacob, that it remained a secret, which of

the sons of Jacob would be selected as the ancestor
of Christ; for the spirit of prophecy opened the
mouth of the dying patriarch to utter the significant
words, " Judah, thou art he whom thy brethren
shall praise : thy hand shall be in the neck of thine
enemies." Judah thus became the first and most
interesting individual on earth; because the promise attached to his house. But on which scion of
that house? Before it was expected, even this, by
a Divine intimation, was made known. His son
Pharez was selected ; and his name was therefore
also immediately introduced into the tablet. In this
manner was observation and attention maintained.
The faithful never left the watch-tower. After
Pharez, his son Esrom was inscribed in the register,
because the Lord let there be no want of unequivocal marks, that he would form the next link in
this chain of promise. After Esrom, Aram; after
Aram, Aminadab; after Aminadab, Naasson; and
after Naasson, Salmon; after Salmon, Boaz; after
Boaz, Obed; after Obed, Jesse; after Jesse, king
David ; and so on. It might be deemed inconceiv-
able, that they should never have made a mistake
in the person; but this was prevented by Him, who
always knew how to indicate the heir of promise,
in such a manner as did not admit of an error. It
might certainly have once happened, that pious Israelites, ignorant of the time when the expected de-
liverer would appear, might have felt induced to
regard some infant son of one of those progenitors
with similar feelings and anticipations to those,
with which Eve regarded Cain, or Lamech his son

Noah ; and to surround the cradle of such an infant with feelings as if the long-desired Messiah had come, and the great year of jubilee commenced. But it was never long before the pleasing delusion vanished ; in which case, they comforted themselves with the idea, that though this time mistaken, the next might prove correct. The family, which had received the promise, ever produced fresh shoots, and this circumstance was of itself worthy, in a high degree, of joy and thankfulness. The children of Abraham regarded this genealogical table as their choicest treasure, next to the word of God. They added it to their last will, that their children might continue it. The names in the register sparkled, like bright and friendly stars, in the firmament of their lives, and you may well believe, that you do not see a single one, in the long list of names, on which a tear of sacred longing, love, and joy, from times the most ancient, has not glistened.

Thus stands this genealogical tree, as a wondrous monument of the faith and hope of the ancient fathers, and justly did the apostle engrave upon its bark, " They saw the promises afar off, and embraced them." From age to age, the fervent aspiration whispered through its branches, " Oh that thou wouldest rend the heavens, that thou wouldest come down !" and tears of thankfulness and delight bedewed its root. But in what a dreadful light does the decline in the religion of the present day present itself, when we compare its lukewarmness with the ardent desires of those pious ancients !

Oh, could the eyes of the latter have seen what we see! Thousands amongst us stand before the manger and the cross, gazing, as if they stood before dusty relics of hoary antiquity, which have become valueless with reference to the present age.

A second inscription beams upon us from our Lord's genealogical table, in addition to the one just named. It is the ancient Divine prediction, "I will put emnity between thee and the woman, and between thy seed and her seed." It is almost impossible to enumerate the manifold attacks and perils to which, before Christ's appearing upon earth, his human predecessors were exposed. The danger, by which we see it menaced in the words of our text, was by no means the worst and most considerable. It is dreadful to think how, from time to time, the adversary has rioted amidst the branches of that tree. There is scarcely a spot discoverable upon it, which does not bear the marks of the furious dragon's teeth. From the moment that he ascertained the line of descent of the conqueror, who was to bruise his head, he placed himself in the complete array of his cunning and power to oppose it : and his whole aim was directed to annihilate the hope of the faithful by the extinction of the race to which the promise attached, and at the same time to preserve and secure his own kingdom. Hence, he either plunged our Lord's forefathers into heinous crimes and sins, in order thereby to render them reprobate in the sight of God, and compel him to retract his promise in anger ; or else laid fatal snares for them, and brandished the murderous steel against them, in order to destroy both the plants in the germ, and in them the entire progeny, and lay the whole tree in the dust, before the dreaded Scion should shoot forth. On other occasions, the evil one sought to expose them to public shame and contempt, and to place them in humiliating positions, by which the faithful might at least be confused, and led to suppose that the Messiah could not possibly proceed from this or that individual. Had the father of lies succeeded in seducing the faithful to the keeping of a false register, he would, by that means, at least have caused this result, that when the Messiah really appeared, he would have gained no credence, because, according to popular opinion, he would not have proceeded from the true root. And though Satan was soon compelled to give up the hope of being able to destroy any single branch of the great genealogical tree, against which he directed his attack, yet he did not cease, on that account, to foam out, in every possible way, his hate and fury against it. Think only of Judah, and the abominable sin to which the devil enticed him; think of David, and of the spear, which the evil spirit, by the hand of Saul, hurled at his heart; think of the imprisoned and infamous Manasseh, and the horrible events which occurred to so many others of Christ's forefathers according to the flesh. What other sound rings in your ears from all this, but the roaring of the lion of the bottomless pit? What do you see blazing from it, but the fury and deadly hatred of the old serpent towards the Saviour?

But if the prince of darkness raged, even at that time, so dreadfully against the family of the Lord Jesus, how great must now his fury be, seeing that He is really come, who was to break his head, and daily make inroads upon his kingdom! Ah, the most dreadful and tormenting fire, which is prepared for that unhappy spirit, consists in this, that he eternally hates and must hate what is good and amiable, and yet, by his attacks upon it, never attains his end. It is, therefore, by no means a bad sign to be assailed by the devil. He leaves his own people undisturbed, and shows his teeth only against Christ and his seed.

If there be a third inscription on the genealogical tree of the Messiah, it is to be found in Isaiah lv. 3: "I will make an everlasting covenant with you, even the sure mercies of David." The faithfulness, with which the Lord has watched over the direly menaced and oppressed race of the promised Messiah, is equally as wonderful and great as the power. Satan's infernal plan was not permitted in anywise to succeed; and every thing remained fruitless that the arch enemy, in his horrible malice, undertook in order to thwart or nullify the Divine counsel of grace. The weapons and heavy ordnance of the adversary broke or burst, either on the Divine omnipotence, or on his grace and wisdom; and in the end, it will be manifest that, though he has assailed the Lord's cause for ages, yet he has not approached a single foot nearer to the object of his fury. If he plunged the Lord's forefathers into transgressions and sins, eternal compassion was always greater than the iniquity, and the promise did not fail on that account. If he lived in hopes of confusing the people, with reference to the person who was called to propagate the holy line, the Lord immediately interfered, and pointed out the true progenitor in a manner so unequivocal, that no one could any longer mistake him. If, in the intoxication of victory, the wicked one believed that he had eradicated the Messiah's genealogical tree to the last fibre of its root, on a sudden, a shoot, which had been placed in security, burst forth and developed fresh growth. Thus did God extend his protecting hand over the tree, and there was nothing ruinous or decayed to be seen upon it, however hell might exhaust itself in intrigues and open attacks upon it.

If you perceive a fourth device gleaming upon you from the genealogical tree of the Lord Jesus, it will be in his own words, "The Son of man came to seek and to save that which was lost," or else those words of the apostle, "Therefore he is not ashamed to call them brethren;" for what a gracious light plays upon the summit of this tree!— What a radiance of Divine love to sinners beams, like sunshine of Paradise, around its branches! Direct your attention to the individuals, who form the links in the Lord's genealogical chain. For what else are they but living hieroglyphics, full of sweet and comfortable significancy?

You will first observe, that the family of Christ

existed, the greater part of its time, as a mean and insignificant race in the eyes of the world. Who was Abraham, the son of the heathen Terah, before the Lord called him? Who were Boaz and Obed, those plain farmers of Bethlehem, and David, the shepherd of Bethlehem's plains? Certainly, the descendants of the latter were, for a period, born of the royal family, but only, in a short space of time, to sink back into the obscurity of their origin. After the Babylonish captivity, we again meet with them in the lowest sphere of citizens, such as artisans, carpenters, weavers, and the like. Thus we find, even in our Lord's genealogical tree, the meaning of what our Lord himself subsequently testified, "The poor have the Gospel preached to them;" and the words of Paul are also applicable to the progenitors of the great Friend of sinners, "Not many wise men after the flesh, not many mighty, not many noble are called; but the base things of this world hath God chosen."

The individuals, who form the genealogical tree, are altogether monuments of Divine mercy. They stand there as mementos and lofty monuments of Divine compassion. They are men, who began to be something, when it pleased God to ordain that they should be to the praise of the glory of his grace. By what means had Judah merited to be exalted by God to be a progenitor of Christ; and instead of him, why was not Joseph, or even Reuben preferred? How did Abraham become worthy of being called from amongst the heathen, and appointed an ancestor of the promised Messiah? What was

it that gained David the honor of hearing the Messiah called "David's son?" Look around at them,
and you will rarely find, in the individual himself,
the reason of the distinguished preference shown
him,—a circumstance, which certainly ought to
point out the fact, that the spiritual family of our
Lord consists of children of grace,—that no personal worth is taken into account, and no other
merit admitted than that of its glorified Head.

If we examine the list of our Lord's forefathers
more minutely, we shall find even heathens in it;
as for instance, Ruth the Moabitess, and Rahab the
Canaanite. There is a pleasing intimation in this
fact. The promised Messiah, on coming amongst
us, was designed, with his beatifying light, to break
through the barriers of Judaism; to be found of
them who sought him not; and to say unto those
who asked not after him, "Behold me, behold me!"
Even the savage son of the desert was destined to
see his face and live; and the abandoned infant, in
the shades of death, to rejoice and be glad in the
sunshine of his favor. Such a forlorn babe was
once our dear native land; and even further shall
the word of salvation penetrate, for it shall be said
to the remotest countries, "Arise, shine; for thy
light is come, and the glory of the Lord is risen
upon thee!"

Look at the predecessors of Jesus also, with regard to their moral character. What kind of persons
were they in this respect? Were they exclusively
saints, or rare instances of innocence and virtue?
It might have been supposed so. But how different

do we find it! Pass through the line once more, to its very commencement. There is Judah, who certainly does not meet us in the glistening robe of innocence. There is Rahab, and you know to what rank she belonged, before God accepted her. There is David, of whom it is very significantly said, " He begat Solomon of the wife of Uriah." There is Manasseh, the man with blood-stained hands, behind the grated windows of a prison. What say you to this company? See, the Lord of heaven is not ashamed to call these sinners brethren. That the Messiah should be descended from such people, loudly proclaims the great truth," Where sin abounded, grace did much more abound." How powerfully does this circumstance announce to the world, that the mission of Jesus was by no means founded on any human worthiness! How plainly does it exhibit the comfortable truth, that no sinner, even were he the vilest of the vile, has any cause or reason to deem himself excluded from Christ on account of his sins; and how impressively and encouragingly does it call to the fearful and timid on the frontiers of the kingdom of grace, " The Son of man is come to seek and to save that which was lost!" A person might certainly feel vexed at the chain of transgressors, which pervades the genealogical tables of Christ; we, however, are so little offended by it, that, on the contrary, we rejoice and delight in it. It affords to us an infinitely more refreshing sight, than if it had consisted solely of heroes in virtue and exemplary saints.

If we cast another look at the persons composing

the genealogy of our Lord, we make, in conclusion, a twofold remark. First, we meet amongst his forefathers many, who certainly had gone so far as to make a covenant with God, but who were carried away to apostasy in a considerable degree, and yet did not lose their places amongst the heirs of the promise. Does not this circumstance point out the truth, that Christ has received gifts, " even for the rebellious ?" Next, we find in this register, relatives of Aaron the priest, but none of Moses. This is a remarkable fact. In the Divine economy, legal principles and ordinances are not acted upon ; but grace rules there, and grace alone. " Christ is the end of the law for righteousness to every one that believeth."

How much of what was typical, and intended to find its chief fulfilment only in the members of the Lord's spiritual family, was included in the secure and honorable position, with which these forefathers of Christ were privileged ! Wherever they appeared, the profoundest reverence was shown them, and they were welcomed with mingled feelings of hope and love. How sorely would that man have had to repent of it, who wished to do them an injury ! Had such a one dared impiously to attack these supporting pillars of the kingdom of grace and depositaries of future blessedness, he would certainly and justly have been considered as guilty of the crime of high-treason, and something even beyond that. But to whom were these people indebted for this high respectability and secure position ? Not to themselves as individuals, but solely to their being members of Christ. The mighty Scion, which should spring from their loins, upheld them, and they shone with his radiance. But how significantly did they shadow forth, in this their connection, the incomparably more sublime and beatific connection, in the spirit, of the incorporated redeemed of Christ, who, endued with inexpressible glory, possess all that they have and are, not in themselves, but exclusively in him," who of God is made unto us wisdom, and righteousness, and sanctification, and redemption !" These now form the genealogical table of the glorified Jesus, except that Jesus appears here no more as a scion of the tree, but as the root, from which the latter shoots forth, and derives its vitality. It now sends forth twigs and branches, and we are those branches, even as many of us as have become partakers of his nature. Oh that its summit might become abundantly more verdant, and fulfil the Lord's promises, " Thy children shall be as olive-branches round about thy table." " Thy seed shall be as the stars of heaven !"

But let us return to the eventful scene at Jerusalem, where hell seems to have at length succeeded in its murderous attempt on the genealogical tree of the Messiah. Athaliah has executed her horrible design against Ahaziah's offspring. As far as she could tell, they all, including the little suckling, were lying, pierced to the heart, in their graves; but instead of mourning, the banners of joy and triumph wave around their tombs. Ah, what grief and lamentation must have been experienced by the quiet in the land, on hearing of the horrible occurrence! How must their deeply affected minds have complained and inquired, saying, "Keeper of Israel, dost thou slumber and sleep, and remember no more thy promise? Behold, our hopes are blasted, and we are entirely lost!" It was an event, not very unlike the subsequent massacre of the children at Bethlehem. Israel suddenly beheld its most blissful expectations drowned in a stream of blood. But no stream, whether of blood, or of flame from the bottomless pit, has ever been able to swallow up and carry away even an iota of that which Jehovah has once promised to his people. Appalling and awful waves may rush roaring over it; but that which is stronger than all, rising up again out of every depth, breaking through every dungeon, and overpowering every obstacle, is the word of promise, which he has once uttered.

II. This consolatory truth meets us, confirmed anew by the result of the portion of history now under consideration. It seems scarcely possible, since Athaliah really appears to have cut through the root of the Divine promises. A tender shoot however remains, even little Joash, whom she also believed to be murdered; and in him, therefore, the blessed race of David is, for the time, preserved. Prayer, or the desire after God, often becomes such a Joash to us, in the sphere of the inward life. With fearful apprehension we seem to ourselves to have lost every inward mark of regeneration, except this last sign of spiritual life. To it, our hopes of being still God's children cleave. Even as a miner, in the

the sepulchral darkness of his pit, anxiously watches the only lamp, which lights his way along the dusky labyrinth, so do we watch, feeling ourselves on the borders of despair, these last emotions, which are the only stars that shed a consolatory ray into our darkness.   But when it seems to us, as may possibly be the case, that they are also about to be extinguished, we are then like some anxious mother, who, dreaming that her only child is lying at the point of death, and, roused by the painful dream, springs from her couch, and taking the lamp in her hand, creeps gently to the cradle, bends tenderly over it, and listens long, in order to tranquillize herself, to the breathing of her darling babe ; and oh, how happy does she feel, on perceiving its regular respiration, and is then able to lay herself down again to rest, with the consciousness that it was only a painful dream, and that her darling lives !

In Joash, the family of Ahaziah and the race of David was to be preserved. The decision was made by God. Be not anxious, therefore, respecting the infant boy. Though the strong ones fall, the suckling in his cradle, the defenceless, the forsaken babe remains. Yes, slumber on in peace, beloved child ! However horrible is the night, which envelopes thee in its gloom, and however fatal the gleam of the murderous poniards around thee, slumber and fear not, beloved boy ! Thy brothers indeed are already weltering in their blood, and the steel is already whetted to pierce thy infant heart. Thy feet are yet unable to carry thee, thy little hands too weak to defend thee ; and childhood and tears are unable to touch a heart like Athaliah's. Nevertheless, sleep on, and take thy rest! Let no uneasy dream disturb thee; no fearful apprehensions approach thy pillow. Eternal love covers thee with its pinions, and no fortress can compare with that in which thou dwellest. Even were the world to be shaken to pieces, its ruins would only be permitted to form a protecting arch over thy cradle. And were the fiery billows of the abyss to whirl themselves over the earth, they would find, before thy couch, a barrier, against which they would only dash and break. O thou silent and yet powerful preacher of the safety of God's elect! We do not say that terrors may not assemble themselves around them, as well as about thee. More dreadful foes may environ them with their barricades, more dangerous daggers threaten, and more imminent perils assail them. But whatever may conspire against them, they may rest as unconcerned as thou. As the Lord liveth, who hath graven them in the palms of his hands, they shall come forth from every murderous den unhurt and whole; and they may beforehand attune their harps to as many thanksgiving psalms for the faithfulness of Jehovah as the number of threatening clouds which gather around them.

How was the rescue of Joash accomplished? Not by a miracle; if that may not be called one, when the mighty God descends with his Spirit into a poor human heart, and there secretly influences and inclines the senses, thoughts, and will, as he pleases. This time, Josheba, the high-priest's wife, was, in the Lord's hands, the instrument of his preserving mercy. Whether she lingered by chance, as it is called, at the very moment in the palace, or whether some official character enjoined it upon her, who was a daughter of Joram, but by a different mother than Athaliah, and was therefore a half-sister of the late king Ahaziah, to reside, at certain times, entirely at the palace, we are not informed. Suffice it to say, that the period, which Athaliah had fixed for the execution of her murderous plan, happily found the faithful Josheba under the palace roof. It was night. Every thing around was in deep repose. Josheba then awoke from her slumbers, in a state of alarm, either in consequence of a painful dream, or of the murderous tumult itself, and on awaking, it seemed to her—oh who can describe her horror!—as if she heard the agonizing groans of the dying princes in their chamber. She immediately anticipated what might happen; for she knew Athaliah. In reality, it was a crisis, which might have deprived the most resolute of their presence of mind. But Josheba did not lose her self-command. Her first thought was of Joash, and of saving him. Starting up from her couch, she hastened to the chamber, probably close to her, where the babe was reposing, under the protection of his nurse, and waking the latter, whispered to her the horrors that were taking place in the palace, and urged her immediately to quit the dreadful scene with the infant, and follow her. The terrified nurse delayed not a moment in obeying the hint. The little one was taken out of his cradle, carefully wrapped up and veiled, and thus was carried through a back door, out of the palace, to the temple, the extensive out-buildings of which surrounded Josheba's and her husband's dwelling.

Jehoiada, the high priest, not a little surprised at this midnight visit, after having ascertained its import, was deeply affected; but at the same time, rejoicing greatly, he adores the faithfulness of God for having delivered, in this infant, the blessed royal race from the murderous sword of hell, and points out to the nurse, in the background of the spacious priestly abode, a secret chamber, where, withdrawn from the world, and secure from treachery, she might nurse the hopeful child, till the hour selected by Jehovah.

There, in the most profound seclusion, close to the sanctuary and the altar, the gracious offspring of David grew up, and his abode there remained a secret, known to none but the three individuals above mentioned, Josheba, the nurse, and the high priest. There shot forth, as if inclosed by God in a sacred shrine, certainly the most valuable of all the treasures of the temple, the tender scion, which hid within it the germ of the mighty "tree of life," which, with its blissful shadow, was eventually to extend itself over the world. Athaliah had not the remotest idea that the babe was still alive, but imagined the bloody lot had befallen him also. She now arrogated to herself her son's throne, without any apprehension; whilst, unknown to her, in the secreted babe, the axe was already laid to the root of her usurped and murderous sway.

Oh how frequently, in later times, has the image of Athaliah and her position been renewed in that of anti-christian wolves and children of destruction! Their hearts also, intoxicated with the blood of the saints, exalted themselves in the proud conviction of having rooted out the kingdom of light from the earth, and that they now reigned alone. But, although it might not perhaps be in a temple, yet possibly in a convent, a workshop, or under the thatched roof of a rural cottage, or even in a shepherd's tent, a spiritual power secretly grew up, and attained strength, against which the pride of the enemy was to be shattered, and they with their triumph and dominion to be broken to pieces; because we had not yet become like unto "Sodom and Gomorrah," and "God had left us a small remnant." On the anti-christians amongst us, whilst reposing on their couch of carnal security, and on the crumbling thrones of their imaginary wisdom, righteousness, and virtue, lies the axe, which shall hew them down, in the temple of the Scriptures. It is Moses, it is the law, it is the words, "He that believeth not on the Son of God shall not see life, but the wrath of God abideth on him." They also dream of security and repose; but they shall fall by their own counsel. They are resting on a volcano, in whose bowels the threatening thunders already growl.

Athaliah now ruled in Judah, as her mother Jezebel once did in Israel. The worship of Jehovah is intended to be rooted out, and Baal to be God.

The high-places and groves were again had in reverence. Idolatrous revellings were the order of the day. The kingdom of truth seeemed on the point of sinking beneath the horizon. He that resolved to continue steadfast in Israel to the faith of his fathers, was no longer sure of his life. Oh, such a time of distress and tribulation, as that which we are now contemplating, had perhaps never been before experienced by the pious! For although days of great anxiety had broken upon them, yet the bright and benignant star of the promised Messiah illumined the gloomy sky, powerfully dispelling and brightening the shadows. But now, besides the oppressions brought upon them by an ungodly government, there was superadded the hopelessness with reference to the appearance of the promised one, which completed their wretchedness. They necessarily believed, that not a drop of blood of David's line remained; and thus the distress of the faithful bordered on despair. It is true, they again distressed themselves without reason. Believers then, as was formerly the case with Abraham, ought to have thought, " God, who is faithful and true, will sooner raise from the dead one of the slaughtered princes, than suffer an iota of the word of promise connected with them to fall to the ground." But the performance of the task of believing, where there is nothing to be seen, sometimes appeared, even to the strongest and most advanced among them, as an impossibility. But hear how comfortably the Scripture speaks on the subject: " If we believe not, yet he abideth faithful: he cannot deny himself."

III. Six years have passed away—years for Joash of silent preparation, by means of prayer and instruction in the history of his people—for the quiet in the land, six years of grief and terror. The high priest then receives an intimation from a higher hand, that the hour is come, which the Lord has chosen for the downfall of Athaliah, and for the appearance of the legitimate heir to the throne; and connected with this intimation are the Divine commands as to the conduct of the priest, the publication of the great secret, as well as the immediate anointing and crowning ceremonial.

Jehoiada, who for six years together had probably had enough to bear from his sweet secret;— for only imagine his situation, though able with one word to change the lamentation of the mourners in Zion into dancing, and yet to keep to himself, for six whole years, the most blissful intelligence—Jehoiada hears the command with exultation, and feels as if a mountain had been hurled from his soul, on seeing assembled around him, in the house of the Lord, the captains of hundreds, together with a host of well-disposed body guards and musicians, when he is on the point of informing them of the true state of things.

It was a solemn moment. Jehoiada sought first to ascertain the feelings of the assembled troop towards Athaliah, and her favorites and dignitaries, who had so audaciously contemned the nationality of Judah, and trodden it under foot. He then gently hinted at his secret, and after having assured himself of their favorable sentiments, he concluded

a solemn covenant with them, and in the sight
of the sanctuary and the altar, took of them an
oath, that in the event of his presenting to them
the rightful heir of Judah's sceptre, in a genuine
descendant of David, they would pledge themselves,
as the Lord liveth, to stand by him to their latest
breath, and also to employ their whole influence to
procure him the homage of the people.

After this introductory act, the high priest orders
the spears and shields, which king David had deposited in the temple, to be brought forth, bids the
men arm themselves with them, appoints to every
single troop its place in the house of the Lord, and
after they had occupied their posts, in anxious expectation of what was about to take place, he
opens a side door, and, under the escort of the
pious Josheba and the faithful nurse, the little
Divinely-protected prince steps forth from his cell,
a pleasing, healthy boy, Israel's blooming hope,
Christ's root according to the flesh.

Jehoiada, surrounded by his priestly sons, takes
him, reverentially and deeply affected, by the hand,
conducts him to the pillar, where the kings were
wont to take their seat, places in his right hand the
book of the law, the fundamental law of the Israelitish state, anoints his head in the name of Jehovah,
and then places upon it the royal crown.   The same
moment, the trumpets are blown, the armed host,
filled with joy, clap their hands, and the cry of
"God save the king!" rolls like a storm through
the temple.

The shout does not die away between the pillars

of the temple, but breaks through the open gates, into the streets of the city. The rumor of the extraordinary things that have just occurred, flies from house to house, and from mouth to mouth; and in a few moments, the hill on which the temple is built, appears covered with a crowded mass of people, as with a cloud. The shouts of homage increase every moment, and, like a roaring sea, they ascend from a thousand voices, heavenward. Wherever they are carried by the sound of the music, they find an abundant echo. There are only two places where the contrary is the case—beneath the roofs of the creatures of the queen, where only pallid faces and troubled aspects appear, and in the dwellings of the pious, where all are prostrate in the dust in adoration, and where at first, only tears of confusion, joy, and thankfulness are seen to flow.

Athaliah, in her palace, listens with surprise to the growing tumult, and hears something whispered of its meaning; on which she immediately sets out on the way to mount Moriah, accompanied by some of her favorites, who had continued faithful to her. She sees, standing by the royal pillar, the youthful king; at his side, the priests and trumpeters in festive array, and around him the rejoicing, shouting, and homage-rendering multitude. If, at this moment, the lightnings of heaven had been at her command, not a head in the temple would have remained unshattered, nor one stone have been left on another. But her own head was this time selected as the object of God's avenging thunderbolts. There she stands, and nothing is left her, in her impotency, but to tear her clothes, with gestures of the most desperate rage; and with the cry of "Treason! treason!" she descends from the blood-stained heights of her dominion, marked with accumulated disgrace and infamy.

Jehoiada, in the name of Him who is to his enemies "a consuming fire," commands the captains to lead forth the accursed woman from between the ranks, and calls upon them to slay, without mercy, any one who should take the queen's part. But no one ventures. Jezebel's daughter is seized, and led away, surrounded by the glitter of arms, to be slain with the edge of the sword at the horse-gate. In her blood, gleams the Divine inscription, "The light of the wicked shall be put out." And the words are visible over her corpse, "I have trodden her down in my anger, and have trampled upon her in my fury."

After this sanguinary scene, Jehoiada makes a covenant between the Lord, the king, and the people, that they should again be the Lord's people; and then between the king and the people, that they should be subject to him in the name of the Lord. After this, the multitude, full of holy zeal, rush to the house of Baal. The scandalous building is torn down, its sanctuaries and images are destroyed, and Mattan, the priest of Baal, is slain at his altars. After the high priest had appointed new officers in the house of the Lord, and again arranged the priests and Levites to perform their sacred service, as prescribed by the law, the youthful regent is conducted into the royal palace, and placed upon the

throne, and "all the people of the land rejoiced," as
the history goes on to state, "and the city was in
quiet." And Joash was seven years old when he
began to reign, and Joash did that which was right
in the sight of the Lord, as long as the high-priest
Jehoiada lived.

Such is the history. Where is there an event,
which tends more to the glory of God, and the
wisdom and faithfulness of his providence, than this?
How well he is able to unloose the most intricate
knots, and to prepare the way for the accomplishment of his purposes, notwithstanding apparently
insurmountable obstacles! Whatever he has promised—let it suffice thee, that he has promised it.
His assurances may travel through strange paths,
and pass through circumstances which appear the
most contradictory. But still they do pass through
them. Wait patiently! They rise up again out of
every threatening wave, and the conclusion impresses upon them, in obvious traits, the stamp of eternal
truth. The Lord's government proceeds on its quiet
but stupendous march. If, in the accomplishment
of his counsels, he sought only to glorify his power,
every thing would certainly reach more rapidly and
obviously its aim, and many cares and anxieties
would be spared us. But all his perfections are destined to find, in his procedure, the candlestick on
which their brilliance must shine forth; and hence
it is that the threads of circumstances and events
frequently pervade each other so manifoldly, and
succeed each other so wonderfully. His omnipotence demands opposition as a striking contrast;

his faithfulness, danger; his wisdom, intricacy : his favor, obvious unworthiness of him to whom it is shown ; his mercy, oppression, distress, and misery. The more variously the diamond is cut and polished, the richer will be the colors which the light of the sun reflects in it, at one and the same moment of time.

However deeply disguised thou mayest wander, my brother in the Lord—however scanty thou mayest seem to thyself with respect to spiritual gifts, let nothing prevent thee, O thou that feelest thy own poverty, but hopest in Jesus ! from perceiving in Joash thy image, in his history thine own.   Continue unknown to the world ; be even to thy brethren partially disguised ; yet in the gloomy chrysalis state of thy infirmity thou art still a king's son, who has found an asylum, though it be in a hidden back room, instead of before the altar, yet nevertheless in *his* temple, and art attended to by the hands of a great high priest.   I know not what may have been ordained concerning thee, but the hour will at length arrive, though it may be the last of thy earthly existence, when the gate of thy tearful cell shall open, and thou shalt hear the voice of Him, whom thou dost not trust in vain, blissfully exclaiming, "Come forth !" and messengers, in dazzling robes of light, approach to invest thee with the attire and crown of that King David, whose dominion is infinite ; and the host of those who have overcome, which no man can number, shout a thousand times, " Welcome !" It is then hell's turn to hold down its head ; Athaliah's—a hostile world's—to start, and be silent with confusion; whilst thou ascendest the heights of unfading and celestial joy, and with loud and unrestrained acclaim, praisest Him, of whom it is justly written, "They looked unto him and were lightened, and their faces were not ashamed." And as with thee, such will be also the eventual fate of his whole church, the "worm Jacob," "the tossed with tempest and not comforted." The youthful king is a prediction of what awaits her. Crowns and royal robes lie ready for her, though at present, a beggar's garment scarcely covers her nakedness. Content thyself, until the day of thy investiture, with the glory of faith beforehand. The time is at hand, when it shall be said to her, "Cry out and shout, thou inhabitant of Zion, for great is the Holy One of Israel in the midst of thee!" "In that day shall the Lord defend the inhabitants of Jerusalem; and he that is feeble among them, at that day, shall be as David; and the house of David shall be as God, as the angel of the Lord before them." Zech. xii. 8.

VII.—THE SICK BED

"If thou hadst known, even thou, at least in this thy day, the things which belong unto thy peace!" Luke xix. 42. Such was our Lord's lamentation over the impenitent city of Jerusalem. Every thing that lives, has its time. A certain number of years and days of earthly existence is appointed unto every one. Short and transitory is its duration, even at its most extended period. Scripture, which is wont to measure and to estimate every circumstance, speaks of our earthly pilgrimage as a shadow, a dream, a vapor, "a tale that is told." It says, "Behold, thou hast made my days as an handbreadth; and mine age is as nothing before thee."

But however it may speak of the duration of this mortal life, it highly estimates its value. It calls the "fleeting shadow," the empty "nothing," and the transient "dream," an "accepted time," a "day of salvation," a "year of grace;" it even regards the short span as the prelude to eternity, and connects heaven and hell with the use or abuse of it. According to the Scriptures, our existence is given us for one sole object. In the brevity of the present state ought every thing to be calculated for an endless duration, and the foundation laid for immortality. He who does not subject every other end and aim, as of little moment, to that exalted one, which extends itself into eternity, wastes, in an unwarrantable manner, the valuable treasure of time, which God has vouchsafed to him. And oh, to how many amongst us may not the accusation apply, of having dreadfully trifled it away, even to the present hour! When they review the cargo, which, in their weather-beaten barque, they have brought over from their past existence to the present day, of what does it consist? Of mere worthless things and ballast—recollections, ideas, and property, by which they have gained nothing for eternity. What are you benefited, as regards eternity, by your having eaten and drunken, and cared for food and lodging? What does it avail your having brought up your children for this world, and made of them children of perdition? And what your having acquired for yourselves and them a handsome fortune? Of what advantage will "the unrighteous mammon" be to you at the last? Know ye not the words, which were addressed to the prosperous man in the Gospel, "Thou fool, this night thy soul shall be required of thee: then whose shall those things be which thou hast provided?" What avails that you have drunk occasionally of the cup of pleasure? "The world passeth away, and the lust thereof." Or what will it signify, that possibly you have obtained a wreath of honor, formed of the applause and admiration of the world? He, who pronounces the last and final decision, measures by a different scale than that with which the world measures. He causes the bright and shining light of his most sacred law to fall upon your days; and in this light—believe it or not—your life appears as a sinful life. What! say you. Yes, you stand as transgressors before his bar. As transgressors? Yes, nothing else, you who have not lived to God and his glory, but only in the curse-laden element of self-love and self-seeking. You turned your backs upon the eternal God; you sought yourselves, and not the hallowing of his name. You regarded the flesh-pots of Egypt as more precious than the treasures of the New Testament, and, though perhaps with an outwardly specious appearance, have lived as ye listed, without God in the world, and given up your reason to falsehood, your conscience to the vilest self-deception, your will to the dominion of selfishness, and your heart to the lusts of the flesh. There you now stand, and your souls are like a wilderness; you have no other peace than a church-yard repose: you bear in your bosoms no seed of eternal life, no witness of a Divine adoption, no hope of celestial glory. O ye unhappy, pitiable beings! And what do I see? There are some amongst you, whose hoary heads proclaim their advanced age; whose sentence of death is written on their foreheads; who already stand as isolated trees, because the forest of the companions of their youth has long ago fallen beneath the stroke of death around them; and who, in all manner of ways, by prosperity and adversity, have been, during their lifetime, so often warned, awakened, called away from the broad road, and

most powerfully reminded of the one thing needful
And in what state do I see them? Have they attained to a correct view of their situation? Do they
smite their hands together, and exclaim, " Oh, ye
lost years, ye misspent days of our life, do not accuse
us!". Are they lying weeping in the dust, and crying
for mercy? Alas, no! but just as they lived for
thirty, forty, or fifty years, so they live on. Every
thing is as it was. One has the cards in his hand,
instead of the Bible. Another is anxious for his
mammon, instead of a treasure in heaven. A third
overflows with idle talk, instead of ejaculations for
mercy. A fourth, for refreshment for the body, instead of that water which springeth up into everlasting life. And a fifth is full of the bitterest dis-
pleasure at the rapid flight of time, instead of weeping and self-accusation at the unjustifiable abuse he
has made of it. And, alas! all endeavoring, besides,
to add the little space for repentance, that still dawns
upon them, to the residue of their lost and by-gone
years, and to trifle it away as they did them. Oh,
horrible, horrible! Ye deluded mortals, what will
become of you? The axe is laid to your root, ye
unfruitful trees; the cloud of judgment rises ever
higher above your horizon, and there is now only
one step between you and the awful moment, when
the patience of the Almighty shall reach its limit,
and your eternal rejection be decided.

" If thou hadst known, even thou, at least in this
thy day, the things that belong unto thy peace!"
The words are serious; but did not you also hear
the kindly alluring voice, which sounds through

this thunder? Observe; it may still be known what belongs to your peace, and peace is to be found, even yet; for the mouth of truth affirms it. But what is peace? Peace is holy tranquillity, even in the aspect of lost years; peace is a silent sabbath of the heart at every occurrence; peace is a holy boldness before God and man; peace is a healed conscience, although fully aware of our guilt; peace is a feeling of victory, as opposed to the world, Satan, death, and judgment. Peace is greater than all other treasures, but no philosophy can bestow it; for how can the latter cleanse from sin? Not any works; for how are they able to justify? Descend into whatever mine, shake whatever tree, knock at whatever door in the world thou wilt, the poor world cannot afford it thee. Peace is but one; one only has peace; one only can give it. Know ye Him that says, " These things I have spoken unto you, that in me ye might have peace. In the world ye shall have tribulation: but be of good cheer; I have overcome the world." His name is "the Prince of peace." Come with me to Elsha's cottage. Elisha is about to weigh anchor, previous to his last voyage; and behold, in him, what is "the peace of God."

2 KINGS XIII. 14—17

" Now Elisha was fallen sick, of his sickness whereof he died. And Joash the king of Israel came down unto him, and wept over his face, and said, O my father, my father, the chariot of Israel, and the horsemen thereof! And Elisha said unto him, Take bow and arrows. And he took unto him bow and arrows. And he said to the king of Israel, Put thine hand upon the bow. And he put his hand upon it : and Elisha put his hands upon the king's hands. And he said, Open the window eastward. And he opened it. Then Elisha said, Shoot! And he shot. And he said, The arrow of the Lord's deliverance, and the arrow of deliverance from Syria : for thou shalt smite the Syrians in Aphek, till thou have consumed them."

THE day of our prophet's life is declining ; but, like the sun approaching the horizon, tranquil and solemn and beneficent, even whilst departing. He is probably well pleased at being now able to weigh anchor ; but a profound melancholy gets the better of us. How possible it is to connect ourselves most closely with such a man, and delightfully grow up with him, although we may never have seen him, and though he may have shaken the dust of the earth from his feet thousands of years ago! With respect to us, he seemed to have risen from the dead, and to have lived for us his life over again. We look at his gentle aspect, indeed, only in spirit ; but it has almost become reality to us ; we seem to hear the mild tones of his voice ; and now he is about to depart,—yes, really to die with respect to us, and our hearts are deeply affected.

Elisha, sick, mourned over by his sovereign, but continuing a prophet till his latest breath, are the three heads and subjects for our present consideration, during which, may the Spirit of grace assist and influence us!

I. The place of the closing and departing scene of our prophet's earthly pilgrimage is undoubtedly Jericho. Here stood Elisha's cottage ; here was the spot which he, above all others, called his home

THE SICK BED. 213

For our home is not where our cradle stood, but where the tenderest and most sacred engagments rendered us happy. There is our home, where we breathe the air of that love, which is born of God, and is therefore dipped in the fountain of immortality ; and where did Elisha breathe this heavenly atmosphere more purely and copiously than at Jericho, in the social circle of the "sons of the prophets ?"

On approaching his dwelling, on this occasion, alas ! we no longer find it as we have been wont to do. You remember how, at our former visits, we once found the brilliant cavalcade of Naaman the Syrian at Elisha's door. At another time, the sons of the prophets, in cheerful activity, busied with erecting new habitations and forming vineyards, because the old ones were no longer sufficient to contain the number of those, who daily resorted thither, for the purposes of religous instruction. Elisha, at that time, stood in the midst of them, as a strong and hearty man, encouraging and cheering them on by words of kindness. Alas, how silent is now the little colony, as if all who composed it had perished ! A gloomy veil seems spread over every thing, and the youths, we occasionally meet, mournfully hang down their heads, and look dejected. Nor is it without reason that they are so much cast down. Dark and lowering is the cloud which has gathered over their heads. Elisha, their unspeakably beloved and paternal teacher, is lying on a sick bed, and his state—they can no longer conceal it from themselves—is critical. It therefore seems to them, as if the sun of their lives were about to set; as if the bright and cheerful morning of their existence were approaching its close, in order to give place to a long and dreary night. Oh, how gladly would they also now prepare to depart, and say to the man of their hearts, " Where thou goest we will also go!" For the time, they know no sweeter thought than that they might be permitted to weigh anchor with their spiritual father, and, as it were, to steer across, in the same vessel with him, from the shores of earth, which have now lost all charms for them, to that heavenly land, where the sword of death no longer menaces the bonds of love, and the tears of parting flow no more. And I can well conceive how such might be their feelings. Oh, how much must the highly enlightened man, who was at the same time so cordial and pious, have been to them! It is said, indeed, that we ought not thus to cleave to any one; but he may well so speak, to whom a man has never been as an angel of God; as a strong support to the bending reed; as a lighthouse, on a distant coast, to the tempest-tossed mariner; and as the careful and attentive gardener to the isolated and languishing exotic. The high-sounding words, " He was but a man: of what avail can men be to me ?" is too frequently only a specious pharisaical mantle thrown around our shameful ingratitude, our heartlessness, and coldness. I, too, know that all my salvation is of the Lord; but yet I know men who, if they go home before me, will leave the earth more lonesome and desolate in my esteem, and will make heaven better known, and me more

ready to depart. And I esteem myself happy at
having found such individuals on my path through
life. The most precious gifts which earth, at God's
command, can present to us, are not horses, or
mules, or sounding metal, but dear and like-minded
individuals, divinely connected with us, and cordial
and intimate friends.

Come, let us enter the prophet's cottage. We
open the door of a quiet, modest chamber, and lo!
there lies the dear man of God, pale and sick on his
couch; and ah! it is but too evident, that we must
this time part with him entirely. Let us stand for
a few minutes at a distance, and yield ourselves up
to the silent train of thought, which steals through
our spirits.

Elisha sick! How many a sick person has he
healed, who recalled even the dead to life! He himself now lies, bound by a painful disease, on the verge
of the grave; but he experiences no miracle of
healing, or raising up from the arms of death. Nor
does he desire it, but joyfully expands his sails to
the wind, which is to bear him to the haven of Divine
repose. But suppose that he felt otherwise, it might
still have been asked, whether he, who was permitted to work miracles for others, ought not to have
had permission to work them for himself. The
men of God stood in the same relation to their
miraculous gifts, as we do to the spiritual talents
confided to us by the grace of God. They possessed them, as we do, only for the glory of God
and by no means for their own personal advantage.
Besides which, they never possessed them in such

a manner, as to be able to deal with them as they pleased; on the contrary, they were obliged, in every particular case, to receive them afresh from the Lord's gracious hand, and to act with them according to his behest.   Individually, they had to walk the same path of faith as other servants of God, and their superior official position did not prevent them from being humbled, like all their brethren, by the same painful consciousness of their inability and dependence; and by means of the same mysterious and obscure guidance, were exercised in faith on the sure word of prophecy.   They had also to learn the truth of the sentiment, "Blessed are they who have not seen, and yet have believed!"   Nor did they go beyond the words, "He must increase, but I must decrease."   Whilst at one time they were courageous shepherds, at another, they were like poor lambs.   If at one time they stood upon glittering heights, the communicators of Divine powers, at another, they lay, with other invalids, in God's hospital, being themselves in need of heavenly invigoration.

The room, in which our dying prophet lies, is outwardly not distinguished from any other.   Every thing is mute and quiet there.   No salutations from on high are heard, no celestial appearances are seen. The place where we stand, is certainly holy and awful.   We are not the only ones who surround the dying prophet's couch.   Angels of God stand with us, though invisible, crowding around us; yea, the Lord himself is there unseen.   The gates of paradise are thrown open.   Numbers of the just made perfect stand in readiness, exultingly to receive the home-returning soul of their brother. But all these are things seen only by the eye of the believing spirit, or at most but distantly surmised by the strongly affected heart. A thick, impenetrable veil lies over the whole, as far as the senses are concerned. The path of faith extends into the gloomy moment, when the heart ceases to beat, and the eyelids close; the coverings are then removed, and *sight* commences. The countenance of Him then shines upon us, who has said, "I will come again, and receive you unto myself; that where I am, there ye may be also." We no longer listen to his voice, in his written word, but from the breath of his own mouth. The gloomy garment of a sinful nature, which still veiled the Divine nature in us here below, falls forever from us, and amid the greetings of affection and the heavenly choirs, we feel ourselves borne aloft into the world of light and of eternal peace.

Elisha is obliged to tread the gloomy vale of death, whilst his master, the Tishbite, was privileged to take the direct road to heaven. Was Elisha, on this account, any less a favorite of God than Elijah? Certainly not. How consolatory, therefore, is the fact, that he is obliged to walk through the dark shades of death as we are! It follows, that this cannot be a bad or dangerous road, but must lead us as securely to our heavenly home, as the path of clouds on which Elijah soared. On this path, heavenly lights may also burn, and a friendly escort accompany the solitary wanderer

The body, indeed, is parted with; and who would not wish, with Paul, to be "clothed upon," rather than be "unclothed?" But in the surrender of our sinful flesh, the series of our sacrificial acts terminates and is completed—those sacrifices, which the wisdom of eternal love has once for all imposed on all the redeemed. And even as we see, together with the flesh, the last remains of the old Adamic nature become a prey to death, we do not offer up the former to destructive powers, but to the Lord, who in due time will reanimate it, and restore it to the spirit, spiritualized and glorified. And let no one be afraid of the intermediate period, as if he should be naked and without a tabernacle. "For we know," saith the apostle, "that if our earthly house of this tabernacle were dissolved, we have a building of God, an house not made with hands, eternal in the heavens," 2 Cor. v. 1.

Elisha knows that his day's work is finished, and eternity at hand. But he is not alarmed; for he in not like the Gentiles, "who have no hope." Superficial minds may indeed have asserted, that the idea of a future life was foreign to the pious of the Old Testament; and yet it was the believing view within the veil, that sustained them amidst the fatigues of their pilgrimage; that filled their hands with gifts and offerings to the Lord; that enabled them to deny themselves and every thing else for the Lord's sake. What reconciled them to Abel's death? Was it not the conviction of the sublime harmony, in which this jarring discord would terminate there? What did Enoch's translation pre-

sent to their minds? What but the blissful passage
home, which awaits all the servants of God? What
did they read in the beaming countenance and
emphatic words of the dying patriarch, "Lord, I
have waited for thy salvation!" Could it be any
thing else than his conviction, that he was going to
the Father? What did the significant words, which
the Lord was wont, in later periods, to write upon
the tombs of the heroes of his kingdom, "the God
of Abraham, of Isaac, and of Jacob," announce to
them? Did not this Divine self-appellation compel
them to the inference, that although these patriarchs
had left the world, they could not be dead, but must
be alive? "God," says the Lord Jesus, in reference to this very point, and explaining the mystery
of the above-mentioned title of Jehovah, " is not the
God of the dead, but of the living." God would
never call himself the God of corrupting dust, much
less of a thing which did not exist ; it is, on the
contrary, beyond a doubt, that he, to whom the
eternal God describes himself as belonging, really
exists and lives to God, even as God lives to him.
This inference cannot be refuted. In other respects, what the apostle says continues true, "that
the way into the holiest of all was not yet made
manifest, while as the first tabernacle was yet
standing," Heb. ix. 8. But the reference here is
not to the sanctuary of heaven itself, as if that had
continued concealed. The ancients were well acquainted with it ; and how should Elisha be ignorant of it, who, at the ascension of his great predecessor, saw the opened portals of the eternal home

with his bodily eyes! In the passage above mentioned, the reference is solely to the way into the
sanctuary, as being opened and prepared by the
blood of the Lamb, to the free access of the sinner
to the eternal tabernacle in the robe of righteousness of the Divine Surety; and certainly, upon
this point, a veil rested, more or less obscuring to
the vision of the Old Testament saints. But even
then, individuals of the chosen race saw more profoundly and acutely than the people in general.
To David, for instance, the Gospel was not concealed by the law. The Lord taught him "the
hidden wisdom," and the king knew what he was
desiring when he prayed, "Purge me with hyssop,
and I shall be clean; wash me, and I shall be
whiter than snow." Who will doubt for a moment, that this light shone also upon Elisha? His
entire history reflects nothing but New Testament
peace; on his forehead beamed, like the starlight,
the reflection of an uninterrupted desire after a
better world, and his walk and conversation was
in heaven.

II. Silent, and plunged in the contemplation of
heavenly imagery, lies the prophet on his couch,
when, unexpectedly, a splendid chariot drives up to
his little cottage, and immediately afterwards, a
young man enters his room, who at the sight of the
sick man, throws himself upon him with many tears,
and, sobbing, breaks out into the lamentation, "O
my father, my father! the chariot of Israel, and the
horsemen thereof."

Who is this deeply affected and sorrowing individual? It is no less a person than the king of Israel, Joash, the deceased Jehu's grandson. When the news of Elisha's sickness reached his ears also, it affected him profoundly and strangely, and he could not resist the heartfelt impulse to hasten in person to the venerable man of God, to testify to him his esteem and affection before he died. You will have perceived, that he salutes him with the very same words, which once Elisha uttered, when his master left him in the desert, and ascended into the clouds. By this expression, the king intends to say, " O thou strength of Israel's host, its citadel and fortress, leave us not! O man of our confidence, abide, abide with us !" A beautiful testimony! It must have occasioned a pleasing surprise to Elisha, not on account of the honor thus done him—for that he had no desire—but on account of the gratifying sentiment which the king therein expressed, and which seemed to the prophet to contain a renewed pledge that better times were in reality about to dawn upon Israel. Besides this, the king's words translated him in a lively manner into that frame of mind, in which he once gazed after the ascending Elijah; the homesickness, which then seized him, again burnt brightly in his heart; but it was a feeling of a more cheerful nature, for he was aware that it would shortly be satisfied in the most blissful manner.

But it is true also, that king Joash was at that time hard pressed. The Syrians threatened him with another attack, and a large share of his excitement and emotion might be placed to the account of that circumstance. Nevertheless, it is very gratifying to observe, that he was able to estimate how valuable such a man as Elisha was to the country ; and that he perceived, that especially in seasons of distress and danger, the strongest pillars, walls, and bulwarks of a state are not expert politicians and wary diplomatists, but men possessed of the soaring wings of faith and prayer, and who are at home in the house of God. Alas, that in the present day, princes so seldom share the views of king Joash! Alas, that many of them are so deluded, that they seem to consider the possession of such men, so far from being a propitious circumstance, to be rather the contrary ; and make a point, as much as possible, of ridding the country of them. Their intention is, to remove the light and the salt from their dominions, and to hew off from the body-politic the only hands which, according to the promise, were able to open upon them the sluices of heavenly blessings. And when these potentates even take measures to extirpate vital religion and Bible-faith from the hearts and cottages of their subjects, there is nothing more certain, than that they are thereby sawing off the main support of their own thrones, and are placing their government, as well as the welfare of the whole country, on powder mines, which will sooner or later explode and blow up both into the air. In what are called natural rights, no sure basis can be found for any of the sacred ordinances and institutions of human society, nor any guarantee for their continuance. Natural rights do not protect thy property, for they are unable to prove that rich and poor ought to be together. They are not in a condition to prove the unjustifiableness of the Jacobin watchword, "Liberty and equality." The victorious weapon against communism is only to be found in the armory of the Divine word. Natural rights are unable to establish the duty of filial obedience towards parents, as such; their moral declamations are silenced by the simple and frivolous objection, that parents did not give life to their children with the intention of doing good to them, and therefore have no claim to their gratitude, nor even to their submissive obedience. What are called "the rights of man" can have nothing tenable to object to the war-cry of the present day, "Emancipation!" even within the limits of the family circle. The connection of filial subjection finds its guarantee and support in the word of God alone; for the latter teaches us to honor our parents as the representatives of the living God. Natural rights know nothing of the sacred nature of the marriage union, but are only acquainted with a contract betwixt man and wife, dissoluble every moment; nay, even virtually dissolved, as soon as in any way infringed upon by one of the parties, and then no longer binding upon the other. They have no conception of the marriage state, as a Divinely connected alliance, in which the union of Christ with his church is vitally reflected, that which is natural rendered subject to the spirit, and Divinely glorified, and in which the parties thus connected, mutually educate themselves and their children, the Lord's gift, for heaven, and in which the kingdom of God ought to be actually represented in miniature. Natural rights never elevate themselves to this superior mode of contemplating matrimony; they banish it for ever into a lower sphere. Their rules against adultery are formed of mouldering materials; and their panegyrics on chastity are without a basis, and soon betray themselves to be phrases without nerve or stamina. Natural rights do not sustain the loyalty of the people towards hereditary monarchs; but even as in their view of the relation of subjects to their sovereign, they do not go beyond the cold idea of a special agreement, they would be unable to produce any thing, which shall stand the test against the lawfulness of revolutions, when, according to the decision of the majority of the people, the monarch failed in punctually fulfilling his duties. They are ignorant of a sovereign " by the grace of God," and national piety is to them an empty name. The latter takes its rise and derives its support solely in real religion, which teaches as to recognize, in the dynasty, a Divine institution ; in " the powers that be," a vicegerent of God, who bears the sword in his name.

Thus are social and civil order and the state exclusively borne and maintained by the word of God ; and the overthrow of all human and Divine order is at hand, so soon as this sacred ground departs from under the feet of the nations. Hence those princes, who mean well towards themselves and their subjects, instead of persecuting and undermining the faith of the Gospel, ought much rather to promote it in every possible way. Time will show, that every thing which bears the name of fidelity, obedience, piety, and morality, will, in the long run, be maintained only where social, civil, and political institutions are regarded in the light in which they are exhibited in the word of God, and where, in human legislation, the echo of the Divine is heard, and obedience rendered for the Lord's sake. Hear what the Scriptures say : "Submit yourselves to every ordinance of man for the Lords sake : whether it be to the king as supreme ; or unto governors, as unto them that are sent by him for the punishment of evil-doers, and for the praise of them that do well." Paul says, "Let every soul be subject unto the higher powers. For there is no power but of God ; the powers that be are ordained of God. Whosoever, therefore, resisteth the power, resisteth the ordinance of God ; and they that resist shall receive to themselves damnation." "Mercy and truth," says Solomon, "preserve the king, and his throne is upholden by mercy." And the Psalmist says, "Surely his salvation is nigh them that fear him ; that glory may dwell in our land. Mercy and truth are met together ; righteousness and peace have kissed each other. Truth shall spring out of the earth ; and righteousness shall look down from heaven."

But that which caused king Joash to shed tears, and forced from him the lamentation, was not only his anxiety at the loss of the prophet, but at the same time, a lively feeling of penitence respecting the conduct he had hitherto observed towards him.

He deeply felt, that he ought to have honored the man and his word in a very different manner than had been the case. Like the far greater number of the people, he had not duly appreciated the Divine and gracious gift, which the country had received in the seer ; and hence he now felt the bitterest qualms of conscience on that account. Ah, death is a strict investigator ! How often do we meet with such instances of a too long delayed repentance ! How often do we hear the painful exclamation, "Oh that I had more clearly perceived what the Lord had vouchsafed to me in this or that individual !" Let us therefore learn, at length, the lesson with such experience is calculated to teach. Let us spare ourselves the bitter conciousness of having shamefully neglected the blessing when it was so near us. Let us this day enter upon the path, of which we might have eventually to lament, and say, "Oh that I had taken it, when such impressive admonitions and directions were given to me respecting it !" and let us, this very day, begin that course of life, of which it may so soon be said, "Oh what a different life would I begin, if it would please God once more to lead me back to the point from which I started at such and such a time !" But God may possibly not regard our wishes ; the time allotted to us may have expired, and repentance and good resolutions have come too late. But no ; true repentance is always in good time. God is great in his long-suffering and tender mercy ! Even Joash's tears found favor in his sight.

III. Elisha soon fathoms the heart of his sovereign. As the representative of Jehovah's graciousness and kindness upon earth, he is very far from seeking to drive the sting still deeper, which had wounded the king, even unto blood. He turns to the Lord with a sigh, not that he would put Joash to shame, but manifest to him the richness of his tender mercy, for the purpose of leading him by his goodness to repentance. And the Lord listens to the voice of his servant, who was as far from cherishing within him any feeling of aversion for the slights and mortifications he might perhaps have received from him, as he was from being in any way dazzled by the honor of his royal visit, or from suffering the consciousness of that, which here above all things might tend to the benefit and welfare of the man, as well as to the glory of God, to be obscured. The prophet is Divinely commissioned to promise victory to the deeply affected king. No sooner does he receive the heavenly message for Joash, than he feels fresh vitality streaming into his own veins. Renovated, and as if new born, he suddenly raises himself up on his couch, and joy beams from every feature. You inquire what it is that thus animates and cheers him ? First and principally, the desired and Divine intelligence, that the heathen shall not succeed in their attacks upon Israel. You observe that the prophet is here made known to us in a new point of view of his rich intellectual life. We here meet with his patriotism. When the question concerns the love of our native land, and ardent attachment to the country of our fathers, let the inquiry be made of Israel's worthies, and especially of the ancient prophets. In them it meets us in real manifestation; there it received a Divine unction, and expanded itself to a flower, which finds its place even in the sanctuary of God, and amongst the imperishable plants of the Holy Spirit. It is truly affecting to observe with what tenderness those men of God embrace and bear upon their hearts their fellow-countrymen and native land, even when they find in it scarcely any thing but spiritual death, decay, and moral degradation, and experience from their countrymen nothing but bitterness, hatred, and persecution. That which binds them, even under such circumstances, so indissolubly to their homes, is not a blind, fleshly instinct, nor that low ambition and jealousy, into which the patriotism of mankind so often resolves itself; on the contrary, it is the footstep of Divine compassion, the traces of which they perceive throughout their country; the numberless monuments of Jehovah's faithfulness and favor, which are everywhere scattered through it; the rich and stupendous history of their nation; the graves of all the venerable men of God and highly favored patriarchs between which they walk; and especially, the multitude of incomparable promises and encouragements, which cheeringly pointing to the remotest ages, expand themselves, like a brilliant starry sky, over their countrymen and their homes. All this maintains within them a fire of attachment to their native soil, which many waters cannot quench, and which, even in the days of extreme spiritual desolation, does not suffer them to grow faint in prayer, or weary of hoping. "It is still the Lord's inheritance in which we dwell," which is their inward feeling; and it is from this conviction, that the plant of their indestructible, Divinely irradiated patriotism springs up and flourishes.

Elisha clothes his message to Joash, in order to make it the more impressive, in a prophetic act. "Take," says he, "bow and arrows." The king takes them. "Put thine hand upon the bow." Joash does so. The prophet intimating to the monarch, that another would aim with and for him, lays his hands on those of Joash, and says, "Open the window eastward;" which was the direction from whence the hostile Syrians would come. Joash opens the window. "Shoot!" says Elisha, and the king shoots. The sick and aged seer then exclaims with a joyful and elevated voice, "The arrow of the Lord's deliverance, and the arrow of deliverance from Syria: for thou shalt smite the Syrians in Aphek, till thou have consumed them!"

What gladsome effects speedily followed these words! By them the Lord exalted Elisha as a rain bow, a friendly star, yea, as a sun, which illuminates a whole district, in the thunder-cloud aloft, which hovered menacingly over Israel. The fact that the son of Shaphat was permitted to depart with such a prophecy in favor of Israel, spread, even over his dying hours, a degree of glory, which, though of a different kind, and less obvious to the eye of sense, yielded nothing in splendor to that, in whose brilliant fire Elijah was translated. How entirely did it correspond with Elisha's character

and vocation, that he should bless even that which
is temporal with a message of deliverance. The
flaming cloudy chariot, the glowing steeds with
thundering hoofs, would not have been a suitable
escort for him; they were better adapted for the
departure of the zealous Tishbite.

Elisha's words are fresh and powerful. They
are like arrows shot from the tight bow-string of a
perfect inward confidence and certainty. They
resemble a general's word of command. And
when we hear him with such confidence exclaim,
"The arrow of the Lord's deliverance, and the
arrow of deliverance from Syria; for thou shalt
smite the Syrians in Aphek, till thou have consumed them!" we almost suppose, that it is Jehovah himself who is speaking. Oh what firmness
does the certain knowledge inspire that it is God's
cause for which we are striving—a disclosure from
him which we are making—his words which we
are uttering,—and how successfully does it operate on what is commenced, undertaken, and
spoken in this conviction! Almost indescribable
is the power he exercises, to whom it is given to
preach the word of truth, with the full and vital
persuasion that it is indeed the word of God. Such
a man wields a royal sceptre; the spirits are subject to him; a two-edged sword goeth out of his
mouth; and the ground he occupies becomes a
battle-field, yea a battle-field after a victory. He
works wonders before we are aware. In one place,
spiritual restraints are imposed; in another, darts
and hooks are cast into the heart; in a third in-

stance, a leviathan is bound in chains of adamant; in a fourth, the strength of the wicked is broken, the audacious confused and ashamed, the adversaries disarmed, blasphemers silenced, and the licentious forced back, at least, within the bounds of external order. It is true indeed, that such an one will gather round Zion's banners and really convert only those, whom omnipotent grace converts and gains over by his means; but effects of the kind described above, will everywhere and always accompany his word.

Do you object, and say that we do not always see such results as these, where the word of God is preached? I beg you first of all to reflect, that in the present age, which is so much inclined to scepticism, the word of God, where it again resounds in the church, is not always preached with the complete unmingled conviction, that it is indeed, to the very tittle, a word from God; in which case, the word preached is only like Elisha's staff in Gehazi's hand. And then observe, that very many do not give the word in its full harmony, and according to its undiminished contents; but weaken, empty, and unnerve it, from the fear of man; and then it cannot fail that a secret condemnation steals into their conscience, and robs even the most reprobate of their hearers of that elevating and imposing consciousness that the words he hears are uttered in the name of God. But when this consciousness supports the word and the testimony, the latter never fails of its weight and influence; and if it does not convert, it binds or promotes the ripening for judgment; and even this occurs under God's government, and in accordance with his good pleasure.

The prophet himself was ignorant in what manner the Syrians would be consumed at Aphèk, nor did he trouble himself on that account. After having received the assurance, he leaves the mode of fulfilment to the wisdom of Him, who knows on all occasions how to fulfil his word. Let us take an example from it, and lay aside our cares, as soon as we have the promise of help. Mark, the latter forces its way through mountains of hindrances and obstacles; for the honor of God depends upon its being realized and found true. Take thy bow, open the window, and shoot. In the Lord's name, I lay my hands on thine, and say, The arrow of the Lord against Babylon! The time shall come when thou shalt exultingly exclaim, "Babylon, Babylon is fallen!" Think not how it may take place; but, strong in faith, triumph beforehand. It is true that the system of the seven hills celebrates fresh victories in our days; but dost thou not remark in its exultations, something forced, and that it is the struggle of despair, for which it prepares itself, whilst suspecting the mines beneath its feet? And though it may fight courageously, yet the Almighty's sword is sharp, and his lightnings powerful, to rend the green tree as well as the dry. Lift up thy head and banish care.

Bend the bow, and shoot! The arrow of deliverance from the libertines and antichristian church! thou shalt see them become thy footstool: for thus saith the Lord, " Why do the heathen rage, and the people imagine a vain thing ?   He that sitteth in the heavens shall laugh ; he shall speak unto them in his wrath."   It is true they have a proud tongue, and foam out blasphemy, and speak loftily in the present day.   But do you not already see them, as a warning example, shivering as from the icy touch of death, on the naked glacier summits of their comfortless wisdom ?   Do you not see them tottering and losing their balance on the bloody spikes of their atheistical theories ?   Do you not see them increasingly falling upon the swords of their own absurdities ?   But even were this not the case, and though they stood firmly and powerfully in strong positions, the hammer of the Lord has an awful weight, and dashes in pieces brazen shields like earthen vessels ! The hour, when the fact shall prove it, is no longer distant.   Therefore be of good cheer and undismayed, however much they may rage.

Draw the bow, aim, and shoot !   The arrow of deliverance from the world, sin, death, and the devil ! Thou shalt clap thy hands rejoicing over them, and exclaim, " The destroyers have fled from the battle, I have gained the victory !"   Though it scarcely seems possible, yet the promise has been made to thee.   Though the strong may wave their banners over thee, yet their strength is broken.   However the world may threaten thee with its snares, sin tear and shake thee, the king of terrors alarm thee, the devil with his fiery darts still assail thee ; eventually a mighty voice from on high shall exclaim, " Let loose those whom ye have unjustly bound !"

and thou shalt rejoin with unspeakably triumphant joy, "The snare is broken, and I am free!" A blow will at length be given, which thou thinkest is made at thee; thou diest, yet in reality not thou; thou livest; those powers of darkness alone have died within thee.

Therefore set thy foot firmly on the rock of the Divine promises, give the Lord the glory by "quietness and confidence," and say, in storm and tempest, as well as in sunshine, "The Lord is my light and my salvation; whom shall I fear?"

VIII.—"SMITE SEVEN TIMES!"

Know ye the history of Jabez? You may read it in 1 Chron. iv. 9, 10. "Jabez was more honorable than his brethren: and his mother called his name Jabez, saying, Because I bare him with sorrow. And Jabez called on the God of Israel, saying, Oh that thou wouldest bless me indeed, and enlarge my coast, and that thine hand might be with me, and that thou wouldest keep me from evil, that it may not grieve me! And God granted that which he requested."

The narrative is short and pithy; but important and well worthy of consideration. The signification of this brief memoir of one of Judah's descendants is this, that it places beyond a doubt the possibility of a perfect deliverance, even during the period of our earthly pilgrimage, from all inward oppression, care, and sorrow; and at the same time, points out the way in which, whilst here below, we may attain to a truly peaceful and joyful state.

Let us endeavor to become a little better acquainted with the subject of our short narrative. Whilst contemplating the fundamental lineaments of his state of mind, many amongst us will think he beholds in it his own image and effigy. At first, however, we are only told what he afterwards became. "Jabez," it is said, "was more honorable than his brethren." He was not so originally. The narrative gives no clear hints of his previous condition. His life was enveloped in darkness, and his soul heavily encumbered from childhood up. He was known only as a timid, dejected, sorrowful mortal, who crept along in a thoughtful mood, and of whom every one was conscious, that some secret burden lay upon his heart. But whence proceeded this gloom, which lay extended, like a sepulchral shade, over his whole appearance? The narrative gives us some explanation of the matter. It tells us, that his mother had borne him with sorrow. The occasion of the mother's grief is not stated. Who can tell, whether it arose from anxiety respecting the salvation of her offspring, or from trials and melancholy forebodings, of the cause and object of which she herself could give no account? Be it as it may, the dejection of the mother imparted itself to the child. Do not, however, accuse God on that account, lest you should be compelled bitterly to repent of your hasty judgment. The parent brought forth; but in her case, the saying of our Lord was not realized, "A woman when she is in travail hath sorrow, because her hour is come; but as soon as she is delivered of the child, she remembereth no more the anguish, for joy that a man is born into the world." She could not even rejoice over him, when, as a suckling, he lay upon her bosom. She beheld him with feelings of melancholy, and with gloomy anticipation called him "Jabez," or, "the child of sorrow." And this name became, in the sequel, a new source of secret grief to the poor boy; for it was the custom in Israel, to give children significant names, and not unfrequently such as implied the expectations cherished respecting them. This naming of children often took place also by Divine command, in such a manner that the man's future fate and entire course of life were really intimated in the name. Contemplated from this point of view, the name of Jabez was not formed to cheer the soul of him who bore it, or to fill it with pleasing thoughts and joyful hopes. The name "Abraham," the father of many nations, had much in it that was encouraging; for it reminded him of the mighty promises given to the son of Terah, and could irradiate, as with a sunbeam, the darkest hours of his life. The name "Enoch" was doubtless a cause of heartfelt pleasure to the patriarch who bore it, for it signified a devoted one, and expressed the blissful relation in which he stood to his covenant God, and the latter to him. But no friendly meaning could be drawn from the name of Jabez, whichever way he turned it. Jabez signifies a man who is born to sorrow, who diffuses only grief around him; and hence he would naturally think, I not only bear the name, but the reality; I only know and cause distress; I am born to sorrow and suffering; what will become of me in future! Thus he seems to have spent his days without any real joy or peace, filled with care, as if, wherever he went, he only breathed the sultriness of an approaching thunder-storm.

O Jabez, thou hast brethren and sisters in abundance! They are to be found, far as sin has scattered the seeds of destruction, and the black wings of death extend their shade. The cheerful exterior of humanity is deceptive. There is much secret sorrow, and concealed and unconfessed depression upon earth. Profound sorrow is often felt, where it might least be expected. I will not speak of individual and particular distress, although I know and could say enough respecting it. To one, his father says with sorrow, he fears he shall never make any thing of him; and this expression haunts him as if it were a prophecy. Another is unable to obtain his dying mother's blessing, having aided in bringing her with sorrow to the grave. How gladly would he again, a thousand times, dig up her corpse with his hands, could his earnest entreaties still wring from her one sound of pardon! A third is descended from a family on which, to judge from its history, the curse appears to rest; and this terrible idea pursues the man like a fearful apparition, which robs him of every joy. A fourth is unable to rid his memory of the imagery of an old and evil-boding dream. He says indeed, "I am not superstitious," and yet the dream tortures and torments him. A fifth is burdened with the secret of a heinous crime, and yet wishes to be thought that he does not believe in a future judgment; but his peace is gone; and I behold him a vagabond and a fugitive like Cain. A sixth has the misfortune of being unable to obtain the confidence of any one. He stands in the wide world like an outlaw; and what does it avail him, that he is in want of nought beside ! He is miserable in the midst of his possessions. A seventh supposes that, in his youth, he has committed the sin against the Holy Ghost. And perhaps he says, "I do not believe in the Bible;" and yet it hovers over him like an angel with a flaming sword, and he hears, in every period of calm reflection, its sentence of condemnation, and experiences that God's word, even where disbelieved, is "not bound." An eighth acts the part of a stage-player, his life long; a disguised hypocrite, whose real self is never openly exhibited. His conscience reproaches him with it, and reproves him for being a detestable character. He is unhappy under its accusations, and yet continues to play the impious game to this hour. A ninth—— but these may suffice.

It was not my intention to have spoken of the particular distress of heart of different individuals, but of that universal secret unhappiness, which, without manifesting itself outwardly, reposes, like a mighty and indestructible shadow, on the inmost centre of the soul. I intended to have addressed you, who would not hesitate for yourselves individually, to subscribe to the confessions, that to the honor of the Gospel, which he despised, a man was obliged to make, who, in the common acceptation of the word, was one of the happiest of those who ever dwelt upon earth. He was a great genius, possessed of wealth, fame, honor, the favor of the great, health and every thing else of which the children of this world form the bliss of their imaginary heaven. I refer to Goethe; who confessed, when

nearly eighty years of age, that he could not remember being in a really happy state of mind, even
only for a few weeks together ; and that when he
wished to feel comfortable, he was obliged to veil
his self-consciousness ; for these are nearly his own
words : " If thou art desirous of being happy and
joyful, do not look into thine own bosom." And
again : " If you become acquainted with those who
resemble you, you will immediately withdraw from
them." Let those also, whom I have now in view,
open to us the secret ground of their hearts, like
the individual above mentioned, and we shall certainly miss, even here, the paradise, which their exterior would so often pretend to be within. Alas!
we continually become more clearly convinced,
how extremely vain and worthless is every thing
which the world calls fair and splendid ! Does
not this life unceasingly appear a concatenation of
delusions ? Beauteous hills and enchanting valleys
in the distance ; but when we hasten towards them,
we find them merely aerial forms, whilst nothing
satisfactory lies behind. Oh, how full of shadows
and phantasms is this world ! And when we think
we have really planted a little Eden for ourselves,
before we are aware, the mildew or the hoar frost
falls upon it, and ere the evening comes, we see
the fair and scarce unfolded flower decay. Appalling is the instability of every thing earthly. All
around us shakes and totters. How is it possible
to be happy with such an insecure possession ?
And ere we are aware, we totter ourselves. Age
arrives, and we become conscious how the powers

of the soul gradually sink with those of the body, and then even our personality and ability belong to the glory, of which the prophet sang, " All flesh is grass, and all the goodliness thereof is as the flower of the field." We see ourselves threatened with the loss of ourselves. Oh say, who can be happy in the midst of such experience? And who is it that lies in wait for us in the distance? Who is that fearful and gloomy being? Oh, death, death, how dreadful, how bitter thou art! Sooner or later, the destroyer, the king of terrors, will also enter our abode, and every thing we possessed will depart, and we also. Dark as midnight is the wing of death, which is already unfolding itself over our heads! How can we perceive it, and remain unmoved! And to all this wretchedness, is still to be attached the gnawing worm in the heart's inmost recesses. *You* do not wish to know his name; but we know it. The gloomy consciousness of guilt is the worm; it is the powerfully suppressed, but yet indestructible feeling of having lost a life, the effect of an evil prediction, which the conscience pronounces over us in horrible, enigmatical sounds; a brief, hollow, concealed feeling of the curse. It is true, as often as we see your exterior, you generally seem cheerful, although you do not understand how to close the shutters in such a manner, as to prevent our occasionally casting a transient look into your inward state. Ah, could we but listen to you between your chamber walls, we should have still further evidence! And could you but be induced to give us a frank unbosoming, with respect to your inmost thoughts and feelings, O Jabez, in what numberless counterparts should we see thee standing before us!

Yes, there is much secret unhappiness on earth, but none which may not be thoroughly overcome. What, really none? Such is the case. And can I, too, be freed from my misery? Yes, thou; even thou! But the paths, which thou art now traversing, will never lead thee thither. Mark, the momentary stupor, which thou takest home with thee from thy social meetings, nightly revels, and visits to the theatre, is soon followed by a so much the deeper immersion into joyless shades of gloomy apprehension, which bring night into thy heart. Oh, look at Jabez! The happy man at length reached the ground of his mysterious sorrow, and discovered its source—not, indeed, in his maternal inheritance; not in the signification of his melancholy name; nor in the imperfection of earthly things; but in this, that he was without God, and without hope in the world. And from this source it is, ye disturbed souls amongst us, that the shadows rise, which rest upon your existence; and this it is, which explains the whole mystery of your inward discomfort and distress. After years of depression, and probably after a thousand unsuccessful attempts at tranquillizing himself, Jabez arose; and whither did he go? Look, with one effort he attains his object! Behold him lying in the dust before the God of Israel, and pouring out his poor heart before him, which has so long and silently concealed its gnawing pain. " Oh that thou wouldest bless me indeed," is his prayer, "and enlarge my coast,"—this he only requests as a sign that the Lord is gracious to him,—"and that thine hand might be with me, and that thou wouldest keep me from evil, that it may not grieve me!" he refers to the evil which his name foreboded. "Then"—well, what then? You perceive he is desirous of saying more; but tears choke his utterance, and, overcome with melancholy, he feels compelled to break off in the midst of his speech. But the Lord knew how to complete this fragmentary prayer. He hears the inward distress of a contrite heart, crying to him for grace, pardon, mercy, and the salutation of peace from on high. He hears— and what do the Scriptures inform us is the result? We read that "God granted him that which he requested." And when Jabez arose from the dust, he felt as if new born, "more honorable than his brethren:" a happy man of God, filled with peace and joy.

It is no delusive idea, that on this side eternity, there is a kingdom of peace, where fountains spring, whose waters forever quench the thirst of the soul. It is not a fable, that in this desert pilgrimage, there flourishes a "tree of life," whose leaves are "for the healing of the nations." It is no deception, that the sinner, even here below, may attain to treasures of mercy, which heighten the present state to an outer court of heaven. But which is the way to it? The way is to take refuge with the God of Israel. If you wish to become more closely acquainted with the way, listen to the narrative which we shall now consider.

2 KINGS XIII. 18, 19

" And he (Elisha) said, Take the arrows. And he took them, And
he said unto the king of Israel, Smite upon the ground. And he
smote thrice, and stayed. And the man of God was wroth with
him, and said, Thou shouldest have smitten five or six times; then
hadst thou smitten Syria till thou hadst consumed it: whereas
now thou shalt smite Syria but thrice."

THE scene, which is here presented to us, is enigmatical, but evidently it is not unmeaning. Certainly, it might be thought strange, that I should venture to introduce this little event on the present occasion, when intending to prepare ourselves for the
reception of the Lord's supper. But suspend your
judgment, until we have investigated the meaning
of this singular scene. Three things are recomend-
ed in it, not only to the king of Israel, but to us in
particular, who intend approaching the table of the
Lord.

First, Reason taken captive under the obedience
of faith.

Secondly, The giving up of a false moderation in
our pretensions and desires.

Thirdly, An unconditional and joyful confidence
as to the granting of our petitions.

May the Lord be pleased, during our present
meditation on these topics, to implant these three
noble and spiritual virtues in our hearts, by his
Holy Spirit?

I. The little narrative, which includes in it the
Divine call to these three essential things, places us
again by the side of the sick bed of Elisha. There

lies the aged seer, joyful as a hero going to receive his crown. Before him, with a beaming countenance, stands king Joash, with the bow still in his hand. He has just received the extremely desirable communication, that he should smite the Syrians at Aphek, till they were destroyed. But the Syrians at Aphek did not constitute the entire Syrian host; they formed only one of its divisions. The Lord, however, had still further triumphs in reserve for the Israelites, over these their hereditary and arch enemies; and to this, the second prophetic act refers, which is brought before us in our text.

Whilst Joash is revelling in the anticipation of the exultation of victory, and proudly thinking to himself, "Yes, we will smite them; the arrows of my brave soldiers will overthrow them," Elisha, with solemn gravity, says to him, "Take the arrows." The king takes them. "Smite upon the ground!" continues Elisha. Joash is surprised, as if he thought this ceremony less worthy of him than the martial drawing of the bow. He reflects a few moments, as though he had been requested to do something of a childish nature; and then, because the prophet had enjoined it, he smites upon the ground, but only thrice, and in rapid succession, in order to be rid of the strange transaction as soon as possible; and "stayed," continues the narrative, as though it would say, he resumed his posture, again assumed his kingly bearing, in order that if he had at all infringed upon it, hastily to compensate for it. Elisha saw and observed the whole, and it is said, "The man of God was wroth with

him, and said, Thou shouldest have smitten five or
six times ; then hadst thou smitten Syria till thou
hadst consumed it : whereas now thou shalt smite
Syria but thrice."

However strange and enigmatical this trait appears at first sight, yet we well understand its
meaning. It is deep and rich in references. Come,
let us try to discover them.

The symbolical act of shooting with the bow,
still afforded Joash room for the idea, " I and God
will soon make an end of the enemy." That of
smiting on the ground, left no place for egotism,
but necessarily induced the thought, that God alone
would do it in a wonderful manner ; since smiting
on the ground had never yet vanquished an army.
But the idea, " God and I," pleases us more than
that of "God alone." The Lord, however, does
not suffer it in his people, but always ably cuts off
the latter part of the expression. The act of shooting with the bow showed, generally, the promised
victory through a human medium, and made the
whole affair the more plausible to reason.

The second symbol required a belief in miracles.
Joash might suppose that, although he smote the
earth, the uncircumcised would not suffer in consequence of his doing so. And yet such shall certainly be the case, if it please God that these strokes
shall overthrow them. If it be the will of God
that as many wreaths of victory shall shoot forth
from the earth, as often as thou smitest it with thy
hand, they shoot forth accordingly. Joash ought
not to forget, that he has to do with a man of God,

and that what he enjoins upon him is Divinely commanded. He ought to feel assured, that God does not command any thing that is empty, impotent, or unwise ; and though it may seem to be so, yet "the foolishness of God is wiser than men ;" yea, than the wisdom of all men. But Joash did not think of all this, nor take it to heart. He only saw, in the prophetic act, something strange, which would not produce any great result. Strokes, thought he, on the heads of the Syrians, might gain us battles ; but strokes on the ground ! O Joash, how little dost thou yet understand the mighty God in the mysteriousness of his procedure ! How often has he given to one and another of his servants, things to perform, which, in themselves, were powerless and trifling ; but he said, " Accomplish it !" and the promise of a blissful result, which he had connected with it, never failed. The more evident the impotency of the means recommended by the Lord, so much the more unequivocally did it become apparent that the effect was miraculous. But as the result always occurred, only in consequence of the performance of the act prescribed, a doubt could never arise, whether it was a mere accident, or really, an immediate interposition of the living God. There was, at the same time, something consolatory and highly gratifying to the feelings, in the fact of the Lord's condescending so far to sinners, as to let them participate, to a certain degree, in his acts. The blood of lambs would have been unable to have afforded protection from the destroying angel ; but after

God had said, "He that sprinkles his door-posts therewith shall remain untouched," the Israelites encountered all the objections of reason with the simple conviction, "The Lord knows what he hath said," obeyed, and continued secure. The foaming sea is not afraid of a staff; but after Jehovah had said to Moses, "Stretch out thy rod over the sea," Moses did well to overturn every thing which would have warned him against such a seemingly useless act, with the idea of God's omnipotence; he lifted up his staff like a general, and threatened with it, as though he would command the foaming billows, and he did command them, for the waters divided; at the word of Moses, the flood foamed up on heaps, the waves subsided in the sea, and the children of Israel went through between them, dry-shod. A branch, hewn off from the tree, cannot sweeten any bitter spring; but when, in the desert, the Lord gave the word, the waters of Marah were healed by a piece of wood; and at such a time, it was proper, that those who were perishing with thirst, should refrain from useless sophistry, and—with the consideration, that the ability which was wanting in the wood, God could easily infuse—submit, in good faith, to the Divine direction, and their faith was not put to shame. Who ever heard that the brazen image of a serpent, by being merely looked upon, rendered the bites of poisonous adders innoxious? Nevertheless, after the dreadful assault, which the children of Israel sustained on their way to the Red Sea, Jehovah said to his servant Moses,

"Make thee a fiery serpent, and set it upon a pole, that every one that is bitten, when he looketh upon it, shall live." It was no easy thing to enter seriously into the matter; but notwithstanding all scepticism, the simple idea, that God had enjoined it, again prevailed; and all who were obedient to the Divine injunction, were immediately healed of their wounds. Oh, give God the glory, whatever he prescribes, however strange it may seem; and taking reason captive under the obedience of faith, do as he says! The result will be beneficial; and on reflection, we shall afterwards find, that even the thing prescribed was not so very arbitrarily selected, but had its own depth and meaning. What a depth was there in the sprinkled blood of the lambs in Egypt, as a type of the blood of Jesus; the rod of Moses, as the symbol of the sceptre of Divine power and strength, which the Lord, in their first-born Brother, intended placing in the hands of men; and finally the brazen serpent! What an abundance of the most mysterious references did it include! And what shall I say of the holy communion? It is an outward, and visible sign; but a sign in which the nature and character of the entire Christian religion is represented; and in which all the rays of the Gospel sun are concentrated as in a focus. What is a morsel of bread and a sip of wine, when weighed in the balance of natural estimation? Little or nothing. But to the sacrament, the word of God is attached, which always imparts significance to that which was devoid of it, and gives weight and value to that which is in itself trifling. The Lord said, "This is my body; this is my blood; this is the new testament in my blood:" and by the mouth of the apostle, "This bread and this cup is the communion of the body and blood of Jesus Christ." The Lord hath enjoined us to eat of that bread and drink of that cup; promising that, in doing so, he would spiritually bless us, and nourish, strengthen, and refresh our inward man. Let it suffice us that he has promised it. Let us not regard the meanness of the outward elements, but give his word the glory. Approach, therefore, filially and expectingly. The Lord would cease to be what he is, were he to put our faith to shame, and suffer us to depart empty from his table.

II. To the unbelieving contempt with which king Joash almost rejected the symbolical act assigned him, was joined, as would appear, a certain false moderation in his wishes and desires. If, thought he, each stroke is to portend something good to me, three will certainly be enough. But what was the consequence? "Thou shouldest have smitten five or six times," said Elisha, "then hadst thou smitten Syria, till thou hadst consumed it; whereas now thou shalt smite Syria but thrice." How thoroughly did Elisha divine the character of his prince from the nature of his strokes; how minutely did he perceive and investigate the most secret emotions of his heart! Thou thinkest—is his meaning—that if God would assist in some degree, that thou wouldest take care of the rest

Thou wouldest not willingly be too troublesome to him. Thou hast still much strength in thy hand, and dost not perceive that God must do every thing, and he alone! For if Joash had only weighed all the sufficiency and ability of man, that impotent worm, in the true balances, and had become thereby thoroughly healed of every species of self-confidence, he would have smitten the ground again and again both firmly and energetically, and not have ceased, till Elisha had given him a hint that it was enough.

O brethren, do not smite thrice, but six or seven times! "Open thy mouth wide, and I will fill it," saith the Lord. It is not sufficient, for your salvation, to receive only a little comfort or refreshment amidst the fatigues of this life; you have more important and more deeply rooted necessities, which require to be satisfied. Be fully conscious of them, and let their thorough and entire satisfaction be the gift, which you claim at the throne of grace. Reflect, that you are not merely oppressed, but also that you are sinners; and that you do not merely labor under this or that temporal burden, but under the incomparably heavier load of the curse and condemnation of God. Consider, that you must arm yourselves not simply against death, with the consolation of being immortal, but, above all, against the terrors of a future judgment, with a well-grounded hope of passing safely through them; and that you have not merely to look about you for a staff, with which you may pass through the world, but with which you may, at the same time, pass uninjured through the camp of the prince of darkness and his angels, and by the verge of the pit of destruction, into eternal life. Away, therefore, with that false modesty with respect to heavenly blessings, which springs only from blindness, or self-righteousness ! Elevate your desires. Ask for the forgiveness of all your sins in the blood of the Lamb. Ask for the bridal attire of the righteousness of Christ, the fiery baptism of the Holy Spirit, the assurance of your state of grace, the letter and seal of your adoption. Ask for the peace, which passeth understanding ; the courage, which is so far from turning pale at the approach of death, that it inscribes upon its shield, "I have a desire to depart, and to be with Christ." Ask for the assurance of faith, which sends through heaven, and earth, and hell, the bold inquiry, "Who is he that condemneth? See, such are the blessings, such the gifts. Apply to the Lord for them all— not merely for one or another of them. Smite not twice nor thrice; but six or seven times. You are very destitute and very wretched ; farthings and pence will not avail you ; a whole treasury must unfold itself to you, in order that you may be raised up from the dust of your poverty. Nor imagine for a moment, that you are able to share with God, in the mighty work of your restoration. The Lord alone must do it ; he must begin, continue, and complete ; invite to repentance, forgive, justify, sanctify, preserve, and tread down the adversary under your feet. The Lord must do all. We are insufficient, in our own strength, for any thing that is good. Therefore renounce all improper timidity, and smite seven times, my brethren!

III. And then confide! confide! When the Lord, by the seer, told Joash to smite upon the ground, it was as if he had unfolded a whole parchment before him, on which the king might write whatever he wished and which the Lord would consider as a valid letter of credit upon himself. The Almighty laid in the buddle of arrows, in Joash's hand, as it were a divining rod; but Joash did not understand the advantage thus given him. He knew too little of God. He thought, according to his narrow-minded ideas, that he must not venture to approach him in such a manner; and it happened to him according to the measure of his faith. He smote the Syrians thrice, but did not destroy them, and merely inflicted wounds, which were afterwards healed. Act differently to the king of Israel, my friends. Hear what the Most Merciful in heaven has said: "Though your sins be as scarlet, they shall be as white as snow; though they be red like crimson, they shall be as wool." "Oh that thou hadst hearkened to my commandments! then had thy peace been as a river, and thy righteousness as the waves of the sea." "They shall not hunger nor thirst; neither shall the heat nor sun smite them; for he that hath mercy on them shall lead them; even by the springs of water shall he guide them." "Ho, every one that thirsteth, come ye to the waters, and he that hath no money; come ye, buy and eat; yea, come buy wine and milk without money and without price." "As one whom his mother comforteth, so will I comfort you." "I am come that they might have life, and that they might have it more abundantly." Oh, he has opened his entire treasury to his people, and placed it at their disposal! He will give all things to them that ask him—not in the way of rewarding the worthy, but that he may show the riches of his mercy to the unworthy and to sinners, and glorify his free grace in them. He has laid all things, in the most unlimited sense of the word, at his threshold, for all the poor Lazarus fraternity, who are not ashamed of the beggar's badge. Or know ye not the proclamation of the King of kings to his people? "Whatsoever ye shall ask in my name, I will do it, that the Father may be glorified in the Son!" Thus Joash's bundle of arrows, and more than they, are placed in your hands; therefore do not hesitate nor consider long, but smite on the ground boldly, powerfully, and firmly. Believe and trust.

In the holy sacrament, all the treasures of Divine compassion are symbolically offered to us. But we also find them essentially there. How many might blissfully take them home with them from the Lord's table, which was instituted in order that, in the pledges of the consecrated bread and wine, the Divine title to all those jewels might be placed in the hands of hungry and thirsty sinners! And if you are anywhere permitted to resign yourselves to the hope of finding the Lord at home, where would it be more likely than at the institution, which appears, not without a profound meaning, in the form of a feast; which assures you of the presence of its Master? Oh that he himself would teach you to take reason captive under the obedience of faith; that he would urge and impel you to renounce all false moderation in your petitions and desires, as regards the fulness of his grace; and, on the contrary, that he would fill you with a joyful and implicit confidence in the riches of his mercy, and the liberality of his love! Would you but approach his sacred table in this manner, he would not fail, my friends, to meet you benignly, to fill you completely from his fulness, and enable you to join in the exultations of the comforted daughter of Zion, "I will greatly rejoice in the Lord, my soul shall be joyful in my God; for he hath clothed me with the garments of salvation, he hath covered me with the robe of righteousness."

IX.—THE DEATH OF ELISHA

"O DEATH, where is thy sting?" exclaims the apostle, 1 Cor. xv. 55, speaking in the name of all who have been bought with the blood of the Lamb, and in the words of the Old Testament evangelist, the prophet Isaiah.

"O death!" says he at the commencement, turning himself to that destroying, ghastly monster, which sin brought forth at "the tree of knowledge," under the overshadowing of the Divine wrath. Men are usually wont to shrink back, with horror, at the sight of that gloomy and terrific being; and even the slightest remembrance of him falls, like an embittering drop of wormwood, into our cup of joy. Paul, on the contrary, purposely seeks out the hideous spectre; nay, he even cites it before his bar, as a conqueror his vanquished and disarmed foe, as a judge the captured and fettered delinquent.

"O death!" cries he, adjuring him as though he were a real personage. And does not the sable king of terrors traverse the creation as if he really were so? Does not, in him, a disguised executioner, with an insatiable sword, pass through the ranks of the living? Does he not sit, as in gloomy majesty,

on a throne, which, piled up of crowned and un-
crowned skulls, incessantly casts forth destroying
lightning. Where is there a hero like him, whose
slain cover the circle of the earth? Who among
the strong can be compared to him, who can point
in every place to the trophies of his victories, and
the memorials of his triumphs? There they stand,
stone upon stone, and hillock upon hillock; and not
a single day appears, in which new ones are not
raised, and thousands of victims fall beneath his
murderous sword.

And yet the apostle meets him with the inquiry,
"O Death, where is thy sting?" Strange question!
Will death be at a loss for a reply? Oh, where does
not the sting of this monster and his poisoned and
murderous dagger meet us? "There," might the
king of terrors reply, "there is my sting, where from
gloomy sepulchres the effluvia of corruption strike
the sense; where the proud lord of the soil feeds
the worms with his flesh; where the mere remembrance of my majesty makes you shudder; where
the thought of my approaching visit clothes the firmament of your life with dark clouds; where the
hands are wrung over beloved corpses, but wrung
in vain; where fresh-closed graves are watered
with a flood of tears, but the graves are not softened
thereby nor moved to compassion; where I un-
sparingly snatch the darling child from its affectionate mother, and the beloved wife from the bleeding
heart of the sobbing husband; and where bereaved
widows pine away in grief and sorrow; where you
hear the last gasp of the dying, and the despairing

and agonizing shrieks of those, who are violently carried away, who offer all they have, and even the insignia of royalty for their lives, but vainly await their acceptance; there, where I thus destroy the edifices of happiness, burst the bonds of affection, transmute the saloons of pleasure into caverns of sorrow, and fill the heart with the terrors of hell, and hell with new victims—there pierces my sting; there slays my sword; there are my horrors; there my terrors are displayed."

Thus might death, the prince of terrors, speak. Nevertheless the apostle mocks at him, and abides by his question, "Where is thy sting?" This is something unheard of. From whence does Paul derive his courage? What justifies his triumphant shout over this last enemy? We shall this day hear what it is. The most abundant justification exists. "Thanks be to God, which giveth us the victory through our Lord Jesus Christ!" Death is swallowed up in victory; life is brought to light.

2 KINGS XIII. 20.

" And Elisha died."

WE have now, my friends, arrived at the prophet's dying hour. The Scriptures do not attach much importance, as regards the children of God, to what we call their death. Even as we ourselves, at the birth of a butterfly, do not linger at the ruined chrysalis, but direct our whole attention to the beauteous creature then coming forth to the light; so the view of the Scriptures, at the last moment of a departing saint, rests only on the soul now making progress toward completion, whilst it leaves unnoticed, as something trivial, the pallid corpse. Happy are all they, who have attained to the same method of contemplating the subject! May our present meditation pave the way ' it in at least a few instances!

We drop at present the thread of our narrative, and return to the sick bed of the man of God. We will see him die; we will see if he dies like us, and ask him whither he is going. In the solemn stillness of his chamber, we will inquire if another world exists; if it be open to sinners; and particularly, whether we may comfort ourselves with the prospect of it.

I. We have reached the spot. There lies Elisha; his eyes already half closed. A small number of the sons of the prophets stand weeping, and inexpressibly dejected, around his bed, watching the last heavings of his breast. Oh that we could comfort these deeply smitten mourners! but we ourselves feel too much pained and oppressed. O death, how terrible thou art! Are not the noblest safe from thy murderous scythe? and is there no Divine barrier drawn around such a man as Elisha, on which the inscription flashes upon thee, "Hitherto, and no further?" We ask; but the dark angel heeds us not, and continues his fearful operation in awful silence; more deeply extinguishing the light of the eyes, and plunging the earthly consciousness of the departing saint in nigh and darkness.   Ah, he threatens to bury our hopes also in similar obscurity.

Is there any exit from these shades, any escape from such ruin?   Is this appalling dissolution really only a gloomy phantom, and the process of dying, notwithstanding the appearance to the contrary, in reality only an outlet to a life of glorification? Does not my being cease with my last breath, and is the world beyond my grave not walled up? Beyond the limits of this visible creation, is there an invisible one, open to receive my spirit, on escaping from the catastrophe of death?   Oh, a longing for such a world beats in every heart, although frequently only manifest, when the ground begins to recede from beneath the individual's feet. Who wishes to die, much less to be annihilated? Dreadful thought, that death should be the close of all: and is it not?   Oh, how can it be imagined?   A presentiment tells us that there is a future state.   There must be a haven for those, who are tossed about on the stormy sea of life; a state of retribution for the innocently oppressed and slighted; a garner for that which is truly great, holy, and noble under the sun!   Yes, presentiments say so, but what are they but an expiring taper; whilst the exhibition of death is like a storm, before which the taper cannot stand.   What is presentiment, but a harmless singing bird in a gloomy thicket; whilst the spectacle of corruption is a monster, which swallows up the bird.   Oh, the horrors of actual dying! the rattling in the throat —the vanishing of the senses—the gasping the last

breath—the cold, stiff, silent repose in the coffin—
the commencement of corruption—the interment
in the lonely and gloomy grave—the cold moist
clods that cover it, and the grassy hillock with its
withering garlands, and with the gradually dimin-
ishing dew of tears! Were there only some ad-
mixture of light, an audible clapping of the pinions
of the departing spirit, or the visible entrance of
an escorting angel, or even only a preternatural
light glancing through the darkness! But nothing
appears to counterbalance the melancholy idea
of annihilation—all is sombre, deeply veiled, and
mute! And yet!—But no, it is not presentiment,
which produces this hope of a future existence in
the face of the horrifying images described above;
and just as little is reason able to do so, although it
has attempted it. Reason has sought, for centuries, a certain and well-founded consolation with
reference to immortality. It has planted the ladders of philosophic logic to find the other world;
afterwards soared about in the balloon of bold
speculation; inquired of persons who have been
entranced, magnetized, and in a state of somnam-
bulism; and what has it discovered? It speaks,
indeed, also of an elysium, of higher regions, and
the like; but these are modes of speech, poetical
expressions—that is, poesy, in the reality of which
it does not itself believe; but it never yet saw
any thing clearly, or arrived at any incontestably
safe and certain conclusion. That conviction,
which rises above the horrors of death and the

ashes of the tomb, is only found on the radiant heights of revelation.

We may derive it from the garden of Joseph, and carry it away with us, especially, from the mount of ascension. Let us approach nearer to the sacred spot. See, there stands, surrounded by his dear disciples, the Man, who through the whole of his life appeared like one who was ever ready to ascend, and was only held fast to earth, to which he did not belong, by the bonds of some great object he had in view. He, whose entire miraculous manifestation bore upon its front a mighty proof of the existence of another world; of whom one felt persuaded, that he proceeded from another world, and must return to it; who also referred, times without number, to his "Father's house," from whence he had descended, but reserved for the sequel, the actual proof of its real existence. There he stands, only present, as respects the body, for a few moments longer upon the earth. He is preparing to conclude and crown his temporal labors with that proof. But first of all, he gives his disciples a sublime and majestic parting address. "All power is given unto me," says he, "in heaven and in earth." "Lo, I am with you alway, even unto the end of the world." Nay, he even gives the whole world over to them, with the commission to take possession of it in his name, and for him. He then lifts up his hands; blesses his faithful followers at parting; and whilst the latter are wholly absorbed in the contemplation of his benignity, and think they had never before seen such a heaven of love and grace beam from his looks, they feel themselves pervaded by his benediction, as by a stream of peace from paradise. He rises in silent majesty from the earth, soaring in a posture of blessing, upwards from the circle of his followers; ascends higher and higher, visibly, bodily, and occupying space, towards heaven; and the disciples stand and look after him with adoring wonder, till a cloud intervenes betwixt him and them, and veils from their view, the most sublime and promise-laden spectacle.

What say you to this event? The question concerning another world is now decided, not, indeed, by any philosophical proof, but by something in power and convincing influence far exceeding all rational syllogisms—by a fact. What need is there of further testimony? Another state exists. We visibly behold one enter it. It is a locality beyond the ether, a real space-occupying world; for the Lord ascended thither in his bodily form. And it must be a blissful world. "God is gone up with a shout," says the Psalmist, "even the Lord, with the sound of a trumpet." Oh, let us congratulate one another upon this tangible seal to our hope of immortality! We creatures of sense require such a sensible proof of the existence of a heavenly kingdom.

"But"—what! can there still be a "but" in the face of such a fact? However, I understand what is meant. He that cannot believe a narrative for which, like that of the ascension, the disciples submitted to be stoned and crucified; a narrative which, if it still needed confirmation, received it so abundantly in the outpouring of the Holy Spirit, and in the establishment, guidance, and government of the Christian church ; a narrative, which is not presented to us as an isolated wonder, but as an indispensable link in the whole connection of the life of Jesus ; which took place in consequence of the most express and indubitable predictions, and can so little surprise the reflecting mind, that, on the contrary, it must have been felt as strange in the highest degree, had it not occurred ;—for ought not He, who came down from heaven, to return thither ? and did not a coronation and triumph, at the close of his career, such as he received, belong to him, who had so completely accomplished the mighty work committed to him by the Father ? He, I say, who is unwilling to believe a narrative like that of the glorious ascension of the Son of God, ought to deny all history in general ; for where is there a fact in profane history, more powerfully confirmed, and by its widely extending results and events more exalted above the shadow of a doubt, than the Gospel fact in question ? The just man believes, and lives by his faith.

We return, from the Mount of Olives, to the chamber of Elisha. Oh, how are the shadows dispersed, the horrors expelled ! Now close, ye dear eyes ; and cease to beat, thou faithful heart ! In order that the butterfly may rest on the flowers of paradise, the chrysalis must be rent ; and the buds must burst, that the rose may expand in all its beauty. Place not the inverted torch, but the upward flickering flame, as a symbol at the death-bed of our friend ; and instead of the cypress wreath, let a garland of evergreen bloom on his pallid temples.

II. A future world exists. This is the first conviction we bring down with us, from the summit of the Mount of Olives, into the vale of death. But is heaven open to sinners ? Hallelujah, it is so ! This is our second truth. " The breaker is come up !" is the exulting exclamation of the prophetic seers. And so it was. " They have broken up, and have passed through," they joyfully cry out. Those break through, who belong to Christ. Heaven is therefore open ! What bars and barriers closed it once ! Three cherubim, instead of one, kept watch at its gate, with swords that turned every way : Divine justice, Divine holiness, and Divine truth. They have retired. The door is open. To whom ? To the eye ? yes, to that also. We look into the other world, and what a sight ! Jesus, our first-born Brother, in infinite glory on the throne, the reins of the world's government in his pierced hands. He, the breaker of the seals, the accomplisher of his Father's counsels, the supporting, governing, and nurturing King of his church.

But heaven is open not only to the eye, but also to the heart that finds on Jesus' breast, a comfortable landing-place for his sighs, and in Jesus' paternal lap, a lovely discharging place for all his cares. Paradise is also open to thy feet. Direct thine ear upwards. That is not merely the music of angelic choirs, which sounds down to thee. Hark the theme, "The Lamb that was slain is worthy!" Hear, hear! "Thou hast bought us with thy blood. Hallelujah to the Lamb!" Dost thou perceive? They are human voices; and if thou listenest attentively, thou wilt clearly hear the voices of the crucified thief, of the publican, of Manasseh, Rahab, Magdalen, and thousands of their brethren and sisters and thine. Heaven is open to sinners, transgressors, and those who are deserving of hell. And is it really so? The miracle on the Mount of Olives renders this also sure and certain.

What should be our exclamation from the vale of death, on seeing Jesus ascend on high? "Oh, that thou wert one of us, and our Mediator!" would be our ejaculation, "then should we possess the right of entrance into paradise. Oh, that thou wouldest be to us, as a general to his host, for the keys of the city of God would be given to the latter, on thy receiving them! Oh, that thou wert our head, as Adam once was; then would thy members be included in thy happy lot!" Such would naturally be the language of our heaving breasts; and, lo, what we wish and long for really exists. For who stood in our place, and undertook to rectify our cause before the Lord? Who took upon him our debts, in order to pay them; our obligations, in order to fulfil them? Who said, "I must restore that which I took not away?" "I sanctify myself for their sakes, that they also might be sanctified through the truth?" "Jesus," is our reply. But, as in this quality of Mediator, Surety, Intercessor, Head, and Second Adam of all those who take refuge with him and believe on him, he soars aloft from the Mount of Olives to his eternal home, to be crowned, and to take possession of the treasures of celestial glory—the apostles do not hesitate, with all confidence and boldness of heart, to exclaim, "Ye are ascended with him to heavenly places, your citizenship is in heaven."

Can you imagine to yourselves a surer foundation than that, on which our hopes of immortality are founded? They do not rest on scientific inferences, nor demonstrations, which may well shun the light —no; but upon well-known facts, real histories, which are not shaken by the billows of impending distress, and present a brazen front to the terrors of apparently contradicting experience. Elisha was also acquainted with this immovable, adamantine, blood-besprinkled basis, which firmly holds the anchor of our hopes, whatever may roll over it. He saw its glimmer through the sacrifices of the temple, as well as from the prophetic sayings of the Divine interpreters. He knew the Lamb that was slain from before the foundation of the world; and it is on the blood of this Lamb, though dying, he so gently and peacefully reposes.

He begins to respire with greater difficulty, and his pulse becomes weaker. We are no longer terrified at the sight. Depart, Elisha! we shall follow. The hour must come. Our life is a pilgrimage; our growing old, a hastening to our home. We gladly go forward, and stretch the sail to the im-

pelling wind, because we know whither we are
hastening. Oh, how fair is the promised land,
where youth fades not, where spring forever blooms,
whose joy is unmingled with bitterness, where light
is without shade! Depart, Elisha! we will joyfully
follow. If Christ be our life, death can only be our
gain.

His face becomes more pallid; but no darkness
clouds his brow, no convulsive doubt distorts his
features. The most profound repose is expressed
in his whole countenance. Hark, hark! "I depart
in safety," he exclaims, with quivering lips. Yes,
as long as the obedience of the Surety retains its
value in the sight of God, or that for the sake of
Divine justice, it is not permitted that the adversary
should devour a saint; and as long as the promise
stands fast, "The mountains shall depart, and the
hills be removed; but my kindness shall not depart
from thee; neither shall the covenant of my peace
be removed"—so long shall there be nothing more
sure, than that the members of Christ, whatever
may occur, shall attain the object of their heavenly
calling: no pit, into which they fall, reaches down
to hell; no snare, in which they are entangled, that
is not burst asunder; no sea foams around them,
which must not yield them a passage. Proceed
with a firm step, my brethren; we shall force a
passage. As true as the Forerunner, preparing the
way, preceded us; so true it is, that we shall never
stick fast in any valley of temptation, in any narrow pass, nor ever perish in the desert from hunger
and sorrow. And on our arrival, the just made

perfect, with palms in their hands, will be found standing upon the ever-verdant shore awaiting us!

The prophet is "fallen asleep." Then let him sleep! He is not lost to us. We are members of the same body, an intimately and eternally united procession of pilgrims. Our love remains,—it has been immersed in the spring of immortality; it passes over the grave, and embraces its objects, who have entered into their glory, only the more closely and firmly. And in the degree in which the number of our beloved friends increases there, our longing to be joined with them, and the feeling of our being strangers on the earth, increases also in intensity. The roots, which we have struck on this side of the grave, become ever looser, and ever freer do we hover above the heights of the earth, ever more powerfully are we attracted upwards and heavenwards by the glimmering lamps of our home, the benignant stars; and the more fully is formed within us the image of those peaceful pilgrims to Jerusalem, of whom the Psalmist sings, that they go forth weeping, bearing precious seed; but return with rejoicing, bringing their sheaves with them. Oh desirable state, to have left the world, before the world leaves us! Oh glorious freedom, to be beforehand with the angel of death, in the matter of weighing anchor, and to have outstripped him with the wings of an ardent longing to be at home!

Elisha has finished his course. He has entered into his rest; he is at home. The sons of the prophets stand round his bed, immersed in profound

grief. Nor do their tears flow without reason.
The Zion of God regrets the loss of such a man.
For here was more than a "schoolmaster," one
that was greater than a taskmaster, more estimable
than a teacher of the law. There are still those
to be found, such as I have described above; and
when one of them departs, another soon succeeds to fill up the vacancy. But here was an
evangelist, a preacher of grace, a herald of the
loving-kindness and tender mercy of our 'God;
and there never is a superfluity of such men upon
earth. And how much had Elisha been to the
church of God in other respects! What miraculous
deliverances did he accomplish! What a host did
he prove in the Almighty's hands, in the way of Israel's adversaries! What a barrier did the Lord
throw up, in this single individual, against the
infernal waves of idolatry amongst the lofty and
the low! Well might king Joash throw himself
weeping over the dying man, and break out into
the lamentation, "My father, my father, the chariots of Israel, and the horsemen thereof!" Israel's
crown was gone; a conductor, to speak humanly,
had fallen from the people's roof; a walking spring
of consolation was dried up, and a vine hewn
down, than which none in Canaan had ever borne
sweeter grapes.

How peacefully does the noble corpse lie there,
as if he were not dead, but slumbered only, and
dreamed paradisiacal dreams! Here death no
longer presents a terrific or horrifying appearance. It is evident, that his going home has been

arranged with paternal care ; it is not a dying and being torn away, against one's will, from the land of the living. The appearance of the chamber of death is that of poverty. How devoid of state does the dear man of God lie upon his couch ! Here we see nothing of pomp or display. No golden candelebra illumine the gloomy chamber ; no splendid insignia of high dignities or offices glitter upon the pall ; no crown, no star of nobility, no wreath of honor reminds us that any thing more than a common corpse reposes here. But something else, which far outshines all this, gives, nevertheless, an intimation of it. Oh, he who has an eye for it, discovers here a funereal state which kings and princes seldom enjoy. Children of God stand and water the pale forehead of the corpse with the tears of ardent affection and sorrow ; and this is more than if a diadem of gold and pearls encircled it. Friendly angels, who accompanied the holy man during his life, and bore him on their hands, surround, in the character of silent and affectionate watchers, the solemn couch ; and whenever did nobler shield-bearers and attendants than these stand round a prince's corpse, when lying in state ? The gratitude of innumerable souls, who are eternally indebted to him, weave tender invisible wreaths for the dear departed man of God, from flowers which never fade. And that which completes the whole, is the wondrous reflection of profound and Divine peace, which the richly favored soul, on departing, leaves

behind, as its last significant trace in the pale fea
tures of its cast-off tenement.

No, no ; the open door of eternity has not been
dreadful to our friend. He saw it beaming with
bright and lovely festal lights. It seemed to him a
triumphal arch, under which he was to pass, after
surmounting the struggles of the present life, in
order to receive the crown of righteousness. He
read, as the inscription over it, the words, " They
that sow in tears shall reap in joy." But if a person, under the Old Testament, no longer felt any
reason why he should shrink back at the gates of
death, how much less, my brethren in the Lord,
ought we to be afraid of them, who see them
beaming in the full splendor of New Testament
illumination and glory, and read upon them passages, such as the ears of the saints of old never
heard ! No cloud any longer shades their entrance. No terrific form meets us near them.
The King of kings, according to his promise, " I
will come again," receives us at the threshold of
eternity, with the open arms of his love. The
holy angels crowd to the gate, in order, with the
music of their harps, and joyful and affectionate
greetings, to welcome and introduce the new citizens of the kingdom. Thousands of the most
blessed promises are the tapers, which enlighten
the antechamber with solar radiance. Over the
glittering portal stands the inscription, " Enter, ye
blessed of my Father, and inherit the kingdom prepared for you from the foundation of the world !'
Immediately adjoining it are the amazing words,

"The glory which thou gavest me, I have given them." Inside the gate, a seraph sent from God, beckons to us, holding in his hand a wedding garment, pure as the light, a palm-branch of triumph, an unfading crown of glory, and the golden key to a mansion of peace in the Jerusalem above. All for the new comer! The golden harp of heaven glimmers in the distance. And, oh, what harmony salutes our ears from the background! It is the echo of the eternal hallelujahs, the rapturous sound of the mighty song of the perfected church; the hymn, whose never-ceasing chorus is, "The Lamb that was slain," and which is responded to by the eternal acclamation, "Thou hast made us kings and priests unto God by thy blood."

Lo, such is the gate of eternity for the members of Christ's kingdom. It is a triumphal arch. We ought to rejoice aloud, whenever we think we see it about to open. But how seldom in Zion is the last journey commenced with rejoicing! The reason lies in the weakness of our faith, and our legality and self-righteousness. We refuse to rely solely on the blood of Christ; and yet all the glory must be given to his blood. Hence it so frequently happens, that we have to pass through a variety of painful processes, before we bid adieu to things temporal. The last remains of self must be put away; the false ground depart from under our feet. It is then that the various ladders we have endeavored to plant, in our own strength, heavenward, are broken by the hand of God; then follow bitter castings down from imaginary states of holi-

ness, subsequent strippings to the bone and mar-
row; developments of the depths of corruptions
within us, which make us shudder; the demolition
of our most specious works, and the like. "Nothingness" is the final cry; and conflict, storm, and
darkness, are experienced before the anchor is
weighed. Many are thrown, by the breakers, on
the opposite shore; others, after their humiliation,
are again raised up in Christ, and depart rejoicing.
But, however a child of God may remove, timidly,
or heroically and exultingly, he has no need to be
anxious. "Father, I will," says the Prince and
Surety of sinners, bought with his blood, "that
they also, whom thou hast given me, be with me
where I am; that they may behold my glory,
which thou hast given me: for thou lovedst me
before the foundation of the world."

X.—THE MIRACLE AFTER DEATH

WE meet in the epistle of Jude, with the follow-ng passage (v. 9:) " Yet Michael the archangel, when contending with the devil he disputed about the body of Moses, durst not bring against him a railing accusation, but said, The Lord rebuke thee." The apostle here touches upon a circumstance, of which no mention is made in any other part of Scripture. Whether Jude was indebted for it to an ancient tradition, or to an immediate Divine revelation, does not affect the credibility of the re-markable occurrence, since it is already placed be-yond a doubt, by its being found in an apostolic epistle.

The practical application, which the apostle makes of the wondrous event to which he alludes, will at present less concern us, than the fact itself. What kind of a contest is that which he mentions, between whom, and especially what was the cause of it ?

Michael and the devil are introduced as the act-ing personages. The former is not entirely un-known to us, since he is several times mentioned in Scripture. Many have supposed him to be the

Son of God, but without reason. He is one of the created angels, but, as his name implies, arch, or prince, and superior angel, belonging, with reference to his gifts, position, and dignity, to a higher order of those celestial beings, as Satan also did, before his horrible fall. His name, being interpreted, means, " Who is like God?" Such an exclamation forms, probably, the fundamental principle in the angel's soul, and an adoring, loving admiration of the glory of God his chief feeling. His name is, therefore, the expression of his inmost, deepest, and most essential being.

The other person, in our warlike representation, is the devil, the head of the fallen spirits, the archenemy of all Divine order; a murderer, liar, and destroyer from the beginning ; the same who, in the devil-denying enlightenment of modern times, has woven a net, which catches the little birds of itself, without his assistance, and, after he has deceived the people into the idea that the march of intellect had long since carried him along with mandrakes and apparitions, as a phantom, to the grave, has established his dominion over the world in a degree and to an extent, which cannot fail to cause surprise and horror to all whose eyes are opened.

The scene, brought before us, represents therefore a remarkable meeting—a coming into contact of the opposite poles of the spiritual world—a war between the representatives of the kingdom of light and that of darkness. Where was there ever a more stupendous combat than this heard of!

We, however, are glad of the conflict. We see,

by it, that we do not take the field against Satan alone. The angels of the Lord have declared eternal war against him : nor is it for themselves they wage it ; they are the body-guard of Israel's host, the shield-bearers of the children of God. The arena of this sublime contest is a grave, and that, too, of one of whom the Scriptures bear the honorable testimony, that a prophet like unto him, has not since risen up in Israel. The quarrel of the two princes arose about the body of Moses. You know that Moses did not enter the promised land, however gladly he would have accompanied his people thither. "I pray thee, let me go over," are his words, "and see the good land, and the goodly mountains!" But the Lord said, "Let it suffice thee, speak no more of this matter." Because of a few words, which had escaped him, as he himself informs us, this ardent wish of his heart remained unfulfilled. At the rock in the desert, he had been carried away, for a few moments, by the unbelief of the obstinate people, and had uttered the vexatious and distrust-exciting words, "Must we fetch you water out of this rock ?" But in those Old Testament days, when it was intended, above all things, that the holiness and inviolableness of the Divine law in all its splendor should be manifested, the Lord could not permit even this mere momentary fit of a murmuring disposition, to pass unpunished in his servant, although, in other respects, so faithful, and in him so much the less, since he was the representative of the holiness of the law. Hence the sen-

thou shalt not go thither unto the land which I give the children of Israel."

Moses died on Mount Nebo. He died blissfully, in the salutation of the Divine favor and love. Great honor was also done to his corpse. The Lord himself buried it, but privately ; no man ever knew the place of its repose. But the fact, that God himself condescended to inter it, evidently intimated, that he had some particular object in view with this corpse ; and we possibly do not err if we conclude, that he intended to raise it up from the dead, even before the last great day.

But what was the cause of the quarrel at the grave of Moses? Some have supposed that Satan wished to disinter the body of Israel's leader, in order to restore it to the Jews, as an incentive to the practice of idolatrous adoration ; and that the archangel opposed his intention. But this idea is devoid of all foundation ; the more so, since we do not find a single instance, in the history of the children of Abraham, of their idolatrously honoring or adoring the body of any deceased individual. Others have viewed the whole transaction allegorically, and have thought they discovered in it, a reference to the annulling of the legal economy by the covenant of grace, in the blood of the Lamb, against which, Satan, acting for the interests of his kingdom, remonstrated. But this view of the subject is perfectly arbitrary, and could only be regarded, at most, as an ingenious application of the fact. No, an historical fact is here stated to us. The period of time in which it occurred was, doubtless, that in which the Lord prepared to raise the body of Moses, and glorify it. We cannot with certainty affirm whether this period ought to be fixed before or after our Lord's resurrection; but the assertion of the apostle, that "Christ is become the first fruits of them that slept," leads, if not compels, us to place the resurrection of Moses after that of Christ. We read also, that in consequence of the latter, many bodies of departed saints, not merely in the neighborhood of Jerusalem, but also in the promised land generally, rose from their graves, reanimated and glorified; and amongst these was most probably Moses, the prophet, with whom God once conversed as a man with his friend. Therefore, that could not have been the resurrection body, in which he previously appeared on the holy mount, with Elias, at our Lord's transfiguration.

Be this as it may, God intended to glorify the body of Moses; on which Satan stepped in, and entered his protest against it. " No," said he, " such honor does not belong to the corpse of Moses. Moses, in consequence of his being denied an entrance into the promised land, was marked out as a sinner and transgressor before the whole people; he therefore belongs to me, and I raise legitimate objections to the distinction and glory intended him." Such was the language of Satan, "the accuser of the brethren," as the Revelation calls him, whose envy and malice refused to allow this glorification to Moses, the shield and standard-bearer of the kingdom of God. He was opposed by Michael, the archangel, who, according to 1 Thess. iv. 16, appears chiefly to be employed where the dead are raised, and who begins to contend with the prince of darkness in favor of Moses. We are not, indeed, informed in what manner he conducted the cause of the deceased; it may, however, be imagined. He did not stand in the breach for him, either with Moses' virtues or his faithfulness, although no one was more faithful in the house of the Lord than he. He could not have gained his end with these weapons; on the contrary, could he have brought forward nothing better in the prophet's defence, he would have been obliged to have left the field to Satan, who, this time, fought with the holiness of the law; and to have yielded up to him the right of possessing, not only the body, but also the soul of Moses. Michael assails the accuser with the weapon of the mediation of the Son of God; he casts into the scale of his client, the sacrifice of the Lamb; he places the blood-bought righteousness of the great High Priest as a wall and rampart around him, and says, well knowing that he himself could not mediate for Moses, "The Lord"—that is Christ, the thorn-crowned Surety— "rebuke thee!" And certainly, Satan could do nothing further, when opposed by the propitiation and the priestly intercession of Christ. He was obliged to be mute, and again roll up his accusations. The Almighty then pronounced his creating fiat over the grave of Moses; corruption fled, and that which had been sown in dishonor and weakness, rose again in power and glory.

Christ's redeemed are God's property, both as to

body and soul. Living or dead, they repose on the bosom of his love. Nor does he forget their mouldering remains in the tomb. They are holy to the Lord, and continue so eternally. We find these consolatory and animating truths exhibited in the narrative, with the consideration of which we shall conclude the series of our meditations upon the life of the prophet Elisha. The scene we are approaching, impresses the accrediting seal upon the prophetic mission of our seer. May it impress a similar one upon our belief in the living God, whose mercy is everlasting unto all who trust in him!

2 KINGS XIII. 20, 21.

"And Elisha died, and they buried him. And the bands of the Moabites invaded the land at the coming in of the year. And it came to pass, as they were burying a man, that, behold, they spied a band of men; and they cast the man into the sepulchre of Elisha: and when the man was let down, and touched the bones of Elisha, he revived, and stood up on his feet."

A MYSTERIOUS event is here brought before us; the last, if I may so speak, of Elisha's life. I grieve to utter the word "last," as though it were no ideal, but a real taking leave of the man of God, after having conversed with him for so long a period. How intimately we have become acquainted with him! The love that is from God, passes over thousands of years, and embraces the remotest object as if it were present, and that which it has never seen as if it were walking bodily before our eyes. The communion of saints knows neither time nor space. Having once entered into it by the birth from above, we dwell and walk, even during the present state of existence, in the assembly of all Jehovah's favorites, who, from the beginning of the world, have found their home in heaven, and hold converse with Abraham, David, Peter, Paul, and John, and whatever may be the names of all the just made perfect, only, indeed, in spirit, but not the less cordially and confidentially, as with a brother, whom we still look upon with affection here below.

To-day, we are to make a pilgrimage to Elisha's grave, in order there to witness a stupendous miracle. The latter, and its object and intention, will form the subject of this our closing meditation, to which, may the Lord graciously add his blessing!

I. We proceed in the direction of Jericho. The burial-ground of the peaceful colony of the brethren on the banks of the Jordan, with which we are already so well acquainted, is the scene of the occurrence we are this day to contemplate. There rests Elisha. Yes, the sons of the prophets could not let themselves be deprived of the honor, that the last resting-place of their ardently beloved master should be in the midst of them. They had carried him out about a year before, accompanied by a small number of people, who followed in silence. Tears of affection fell upon the way by which they went; these were the roses and lilies which they strewed. Many painful sighs and ejaculations burst forth; these were their requiem— their funeral hymn. One said, "I am burying my spiritual father, by whom I was begotten again unto eternal life !"   A second, " I am burying the man, who was to me a beacon on the rocky sea of life." A third, " I am interring all that held me to the earth ; how I long to follow him !" And many, whom no one had previously recognized as children of God, then came forth from their secret corners, and said, " Oh if you knew how much the holy man was to us ! We hope God will reward him for it ; we never can !" Thus every heart was grieved, and every eye was moist. It was, indeed, an inconsiderable funeral procession ; but, at the same time, one so glorious, as seldom falls to the lot of the mighty of this world. Here, it was not " the dead burying their dead ;" but heirs of heaven plunging into the lap of earth, a seed of corn for an eternal harvest ; and angels of God walked mutely and invisibly in the procession, enjoined to watch the hillock, beneath which the body of the man beloved of God was to slumber, till the great morning of the resurrection. The dear remains, enveloped in white linen, were interred in the gloomy grave, and many a sorrowful, affectionate, and grateful adieu followed it. The mourners then retired, and a heavy stone closed the sepulchre. King Joash had provided an inscription over the tomb. It was as follows : " My father, my father, the chariot of Israel and the horsemen thereof !" We will add another from the word of the Lord to Daniel, chap. xii. 3 : " They that be wise shall shine as the brightness of the firmament ;

and they that turn many to righteousness as the stars forever and ever."

At the time of our entering the peaceful cemetery, near Jericho, Elisha, as already observed, had slept in his grave about a year, the dreamless sleep. Elisha? No, not he, but only his body, his earthly tenement. He himself is sitting at table with Abraham, Isaac, and Jacob. He no longer breathes the rude air of this world, but has shaken off the dust of this vale of tears from his feet, and mingles his exulting voice in the hallelujahs of the heavenly palm-bearers, where all sorrow and crying reaches its eternal termination in an endless acclamation of joy.

Elisha's corpse now lies in its sepulchre. Therefore, he was also obliged to go the way of all flesh. Yes, even he, who was Jehovah's favorite in a distinguished manner, and who, when viewed in the light, deserves the praise of having exhibited himself as more spiritually formed and sanctified than even his great master, the Tishbite. And yet no fiery chariot descended for him; on the contrary, he was obliged to submit to be unclothed, and leave his body behind him on the earth. By this, God designs to tell us, that Elisha lost nothing in consequence of so doing; for he would certainly not have permitted one, who was dear to him as the apple of his eye, to be the loser by it. Hence, it must be really no loss to lay aside the body; and therefore, what are called "the terrors of the tomb" are only specious and imaginary—phantoms, shadows, but nothing real. And such is actually the case. We suffer no shipwreck in the separation of body and soul, unless the bursting of the shell, from which a free and winged creature, a butterfly, rises up, can be called a shipwreck. And still less ought the dissolution of our bodies to bear such a name; for if the companion of our pilgrimage, the corruptible body, had become dear to us, we know that, though we lay it aside at death, we do not even lose it. We shall, in accordance with the Divine promise, receive it back in radiant glorification. The eye of God will watch it until that period as a valuable treasure. If it be difficult to believe, that a resurrection morn shall dawn, even upon the body, yet it will as surely ensue, as it once broke upon the grave of the Firstborn from the dead. Israel's Champion does not lie; the Almighty knows how to keep his word.

A year had already passed over the sepulchre of Elisha in the rock. It then happened, that troops of heathenish Moabites crossed over the borders with a view to plunder. They, of course, were no longer able to injure the departed man of God; but they give, very remarkably, the first occasion of his suddenly appearing again in Israel's history.

Let us imagine ourselves standing within the burial-ground. We behold a funeral procession approaching—one of those, which are every moment and uninterruptedly traversing the earth. An Israelite is being carried to his long home; probably one of the quiet in the land, who did not bow the knee to Baal. But he must have been a poor man, for there was no hewn sepulchre in readiness to receive him; on the contrary, the grave had still to be dug for him. But the moment the attendants are about to commence the work, spears and swords are seen glittering in the distance. A troop of Moabites is on the march towards them. What is now to be done? They cannot continue their work without imminent danger of their lives, or exposing themselves to the risk of a dreadful imprisonment. Close at hand is Elisha's tomb; and without reflecting long, they quickly roll away the stone from its mouth, and cast the corpse, for the time, on the bones of the prophet. But what is the result? Oh, what a miracle! No sooner does the corpse touch his remains, than the departed spirit returns to it. The man raises himself up, stands upon his feet, and, oh! the surprise and astonishment of the funeral attendants! he issues forth from the tomb alive!

But you ask, "Is he restored to life simply by touching Elisha's corpse?" Does this seem strange to you? What would you say, on being told that, on one occasion, the sick and possessed amongst the inhabitants of Jerusalem were carried on beds and biers along the streets, in order that, if the apostle Peter passed by, even his shadow might fall upon some of them; and those over whom it passed were made whole? And what would you say on hearing, that the believers at Ephesus held napkins and handkerchiefs, taken from the body of Paul, over the sick, and the disease departed from them, the evil spirits went out of them?

But you say, Does not the worshipping of relics in the Romish church find, in these facts, a certain degree of support and justification? God forbid!

For without taking into account—since it is of little or no moment with regard to the point in question—that the so-called relics are, for the most part, only pretended remains of saints—the Papists attribute to these relics, bones, vestments, and other objects, a species of magical power; and what else is this but superstition and heathenism? In the wonder at Jericho, as well as in the miracles of which we have just spoken, the miraculous power did not lie either in Elisha's bones, Paul's handkerchiefs, or Peter's shadow, but exclusively in the living God, who was pleased, for wise purposes, to make these objects, which, abstractedly considered, were entirely powerless, the vehicles of his miraculous power. Or else they ascribe the wonderful effects they promise, to human saints, whose skulls or garments they present to their devotees, to be touched, kissed, and adored; and what again is this deification of man but a specious idolatry? Or, finally, they come nearer the truth, and say, that God, or Christ, performs the miracles, through the medium of their sacred vestments, bones, or fragments of the cross, etc. But where can they point out any express word of promise, that God will really connect his aid with these objects? They have none, nor do they think they require them. They imagine that it follows of course, that in consequence of their *hocus pocus*, God must necessarily pour down his blessing. Because he once wrought miraculously by the mortal remains of Elisha, and the handkerchiefs of the apostle, he must also operate in a similar manner through every other holy man's relics. Thus they wish to dispose of God as they please; and without the slightest Divine assurance in their favor, by their own assumed authority, bind him and his wonder-working agency to their vile rags and broken bones. But this is daring and culpable impiety; and the more so, since, in their delusion, they not unfrequently desire, over and above, that the holy and true God should, by signs and wonders, confirm and establish their lies. After the miracle at the burial-ground near Jericho, probably many a Jew was tempted to believe that a kind of life-insurance place had disclosed itself in Elisha's grave; but they might have cast in thither many thousand corpses, and not one of them would have again awoke to life; for Elisha's bones could not give life.

In the reign of Hezekiah, it happened, that the Jews carried on a disgraceful idolatry with the brazen serpent, which Moses, centuries before, had been directed to make in the desert; and imagined that the copper figure must necessarily work miracles, because it had once done so, and healed the poisonous bite of the fiery serpents: just as if the figure had healed the wounded Israelites, and not the Almighty by its means; or, as if God had inclosed and left in perpetuity his miraculous power in the copper figure, and not much rather voluntarily attached it thereto for a temporary object. A holy indignation seized king Hezekiah, on perceiving the abuse that was made of the brazen serpent in the land. And what did he do? He took the brazen figure, which, in so far as it had become the object of such idolatry, he contemptuously called *Nehustan*, that is, "brazen dragon," pulverized the idol in the Lord's name, and strewed its ashes to the winds. Ah! how many fetishes there are in the world, with which we would gladly do the like.

But still we are told of wonders wrought, here and there, by these so-called relics. Alas! one lie begets another. But if, in the gloomy spheres of superstition, something of a miraculous nature really occurred, it would only fill me with surprise and horror; for in this case, the wonder-worker would assuredly not be God, but some other being: and I should be compelled to come to the melancholy conclusion, that God had given up these idolatrous people to the error of their ways. I could only regard the occurrence of such a miracle as a judgment of Divine wrath, but not as an act of Divine mercy.

II. But what was the reason, that God wrought this unheard-of miracle of restoring a man to life by the bones of Elisha? There was more than one sacred reason, which induced him to it. For, first, he was willing thereby to give to the people of Israel an additional tangible proof, that he, the God of Elisha, was the true, living, and omnipotent God, with whom it was a small thing to save, even from the dead, and whom it was therefore only requisite to have for a friend, in order no longer to be afraid of the Moabites. "Give this God the glory, fall at his feet, and confide in him," was the first sermon, which resounded from the miracle, with a voice of thunder, in the ears of the people.

The miracle next impressed a new and Divine seal of confirmation upon the whole of Elisha's acts upon earth; for the man, whom God thus honored and glorified, even in the grave, must have been a true prophet; his word, the unerring word of God; and his advice and intimations, infallible. This was now publicly manifested to the world, and king Joash might now as decidedly let go the last doubt of the certainty of the promises of victory, which had been given him by Elisha, as those must have condemned themselves, who had closed their ears to the words and instructions of this man of God.

Finally, God was willing, in this miraculous act, to hold up to view a mighty image of the future— of the emanating, regenerating, life-giving, miraculous power, which should eventually be shed abroad in the world, by the death of Elisha's great Master, Jesus Christ. By his death, Christ reconciled the world unto God; by it, he purchased and consecrated it to himself, as the scene of his renewing and wonder-working power; by it, he destroyed death, the child of the curse—the death of the body as well as that of the soul; and by it, he procured the sending of the life-begetting Spirit into the world, which, by his sprinkled blood, had been cleansed anew and rendered capable of receiving mercy. In his death, the great and priestly King laid the foundation of a new creation, in which no funeral banners would wave any more, no groaning of the creature, made subject to vanity, be any longer heard; but in which, the creature should be free from subjection to that which is transitory, and its anxious sighs and expectations terminate in the hallelujahs of an uninterrupted sabbatic festival. This new, spiritual, and vital principle has been increasingly penetrating, during the last eighteen hundred years, through the shell of the old accursed world, and the promise is hastening towards its accomplishment on every side.

Thou, also, my hearer, belongest to this new creation, so soon as thou hast entered, by a penitential belief, into the fellowship of Christ's victorious death. Thou then standest uncondemnable before God, freed from the curse, snatched from the powers of darkness, and diest no more; but being dead with Christ, art also raised up with him, and hast "passed from death unto life." Behold! thou who hast thus been transplanted into the element of Divine love, and even here in the body art already walking in heaven—thou child of the heavenly calling, already saved by hope, marked out for resurrection at the last great day, how thou art encouraged to look forward to thy resurrection, by the man who went forth reanimated from Elisha's sepulcre.

The miracle near Jericho reminds me of another, which I cannot refrain from mentioning to you. A friend, who is dear to the hearts of many of you, lost his wife. At their marriage, she had experienced something of Divine grace, but not a thorough regeneration; for the world, with its glittering tinsel, still acted powerfully upon her, and at her betrothment, she said jocosely, although with a serious meaning, being still very young, "You will not deprive me of my finery?" Here it must be observed, that, in our friend's native land, the women are wont to mark their abandonment of the world, by putting on an hereditary and a more simple dress, not subject to the changes of fashion. "I will leave you your trinkets and fine clothes," replied her intended, "until the Lord himself strips you of them." The marriage took place, and the young married woman lived for a while, though certainly with a degree of innocence, in the senseless gayeties of the blinded children of this world. But one day it happened, that whilst she was loitering in the garden, she was surprised by a heavy thunder-storm. The flashes of lightning rapidly succeeded each other, and every clap of thunder rendered it probable, that the lightning had struck somewhere in the immediate vicinity. The awful phenomena had raged for some time, when the poor woman, pale as a corpse, and trembling in every limb, rushed back into the house, and holding both her hands before her eyes, threw herself into a seat, and sobbed aloud. Her husband, who had never before seen her in such a state of excitement, hastened towards her with no small astonishment, and tenderly and soothingly asked his trembling consort the reason of her trepidation and her tears. "Oh, I feel," was her reply, "that if the lightning had struck me, I should have been lost, and have received sentence of condemnation at the bar of

God!" "Do you think so?" rejoined our friend, and was silent; but his soul secretly gave God thanks, and his hopes did not deceive him. The Lord soon arrayed the terrified woman in more splendid vestments, than the world can weave or offer.

Not long afterwards, she fell sick, and the sickness proved unto death. Her sick bed was a couch of triumph. She called upon every one to congratulate her on the prospect of so soon seeing her heavenly Bridegroom. A few days, however, before her departure, her rapture diminished, and at length she became entirely mute, and painful inward conflicts and a darkening of her faith took their place. She died exclaiming, "Lord Jesus, have mercy upon me!" Her heavily afflicted and deeply affected husband bedewed her corpse with a flood of tears.

The day fixed for the interment arrived. The coffin was about to be closed; the solitary mourner cast himself once more upon the dear remains, and exclaimed sobbing, "Ah, shall I ever see thee again?" for his mind was also obscured. He hoped, indeed, that she had received forgiveness before her departure; but he felt no joyful and triumphant confidence. His agitated spirit then broke out into loud supplication, and he exclaimed, "Lord, give me a sign that my wife is not dead, but liveth!" and scarcely conscious himself of what he was saying, he added, "Didst thou not confirm the prophet Elisha as thy servant, even after his decease, by the miracle wrought by his bones? how shouldest thou, therefore, not be able, in a similar way, to seal the adoption and glorification of my deceased wife!"

The coffin was closed, the funeral procession put itself in motion. The way to the church-yard was more painful to our friend than his own death would have been. The burial-ground was reached, and the corpse interred. The sorely afflicted husband, bathed in tears, then advanced to the edge of the opened grave, and with inexpressible emotion, began to address the assembled people. He brought forward those traits, from the life of the dear deceased, which assured his hope that she was not lost. He spoke of the nothingness of man; of the curse of sin; and with overflowing lips, praised Him who had overthrown death, the devil, and sin, and had brought immortality to light; yea, who was himself "the resurrection and the life"—Christ, the Saviour of sinners. Hereupon the grave was closed, and the funeral attendants, in solemn silence, commenced their return.

The next day, about the dusk of the evening, our friend sat plunged in sorrow in his chamber; the image of his departed wife hovering before his weeping soul. The question, whether she was really happy, still tormented him; at the same time, he resolved to plant a rose-tree on her grave, as an emblem of his love. One of his intimate friends now entered, and said to him, "Have you heard what has happened? By means of the address you gave at the grave of your wife, and especially by the traits you related of her last days, one of the bitterest opponents of the Gospel was suddenly awakened from his sleep of sin, brought to Christ, and born again to newness of life." The sorrowing widower, on hearing this, rose up, as if reanimated, from his profound melancholy, solemnly folded his hands, and said with joy beaming from his countenance, "Thou hast, therefore, O faithful God! thyself planted the rose on the grave of my beloved, and given me a more glorious sign than that, which was wrought by the bones of Elisha! Now I know the abode of my deceased wife." He spake, and no longer doubted.

The miracle of the prophet's grave is frequently repeated in the world, in spiritual antitypes. How often does God impress upon his servants the full credential seal only after their decease, either by removing the veil from the works of faith and love, which the spiritually fructified stem of their regenerate nature produced in deep concealment, or by permitting their words and example to operate the wonders of spiritual awakening and reanimation after their departure, for the manifestation of which, they vainly waited during the whole of their lives! Nor can a more beautiful memorial to a witness of the truth be erected, than the living one, which is built over his grave, in the spiritual children who are subsequently born from the quickened seed of his word and example. And when, ye fortunate inhabitants of this valley, was there ever a faithful pastor among you, carried to the grave, over whose remains a similar monument did not rise? and where is there a more beautiful attestation than that, which the Lord wrote with reference to him, who so very recently departed this life, and which he continues to write to this hour ?

But we must conclude, and bid our prophet farewell. When at length we shall walk with him under the palm-trees of Eden, he will explain the miracles and mysteries of his life to us, more fully and profoundly than we have been able to do, through the troubled vision of earthly manifestation. Till then, let his glorious image, surrounded by the fiery flame of love, continue to live in our hearts, as a radiant testimony what great things the Lord effects in the children of men ; and as a lovely star, pointing out to us the direction, which our course must take, if we wish to depart at length in peace.

The path of faith is a blissful path, which no one ever yet repented of having taken, however much it might have cost him.   Even though it may have been entered upon blindfold, yet it will be prosecuted with visions of the glory of God.   The inscription upon its boundary stone is, " Self-denial ;" but would a boatman call that too great a demand, if told to empty his vessel of its ballast, in order to load it with gold and precious stones ?   And truly, it is more than gold and jewels, which is promised us as a recompense for the loss of fancied blessings, which we have to suffer, in taking the first step on that holy path.   We exchange dead idols for the Living God, deception for truth, and darkness for light ; a church-yard tranquillity, pervaded by phantoms of horror, for a peace surpassing understanding ; the soiled garment of our own righteousness, for the white robe of the righteousness of God; the gloomy and afflictive world, for heaven itself. Incomparable exchange! Who would hesitate to make it? Come then, come all! We will follow in the steps of Elisha, that we may eventually land on the same shore with him.